An Ethnographic Approach to Peacebuilding

This book aims to outline and promote an ethnographic approach to evaluating international peacebuilding interventions in transitional states.

While the evaluation of peacebuilding and transitional justice efforts has been a growing concern in recent years, too often evaluations assess projects based on locally irrelevant measures, reinforce the status quo distribution of power in transitional situations, and uncritically accept the implicit conceptions of the funders, planners, and administrators of such projects. This book argues that evaluating the effects of peacebuilding interventions demands an understanding of the local and culturally variable context of intervention.

Throughout *An Ethnographic Approach to Peacebuilding*, the author draws on real-world examples from extensive fieldwork in Sierra Leone to argue that local experiences should be considered the primary measure of a peacebuilding project's success. An ethnographic approach recognizes diversity in conceptions of peace, justice, development, and reconciliation and takes local approaches and local critiques of the international agenda seriously. It can help to empower local actors, hold the international peacebuilding industry accountable to its supposed beneficiaries, and challenge the Western-centric ideas of what peace entails and how peacebuilding is achieved.

This book will be of great interest to students and scholars of peacebuilding, peace and conflict studies, transitional justice, African politics, ethnography, International Relations and security studies, as well as practitioners working in the field.

Gearoid Millar is Lecturer in Sociology at the Institute for Conflict, Transition, and Peace Research (ICTPR) at the University of Aberdeen, Scotland.

Series: Studies in Conflict, Development and Peacebuilding

Series Editors: Keith Krause, Thomas J. Biersteker and Riccardo Bocco, Graduate Institute of International and Development Studies, Geneva

This series publishes innovative research into the connections between insecurity and under-development in fragile states, and into situations of violence and insecurity more generally. It adopts a multidisciplinary approach to the study of a variety of issues, including the changing nature of contemporary armed violence (*conflict*), efforts to foster the conditions that prevent the outbreak or recurrence of such violence (*development*), and strategies to promote peaceful relations on the communal, societal and international level (*peacebuilding*).

The Political Economy of Peacemaking
Achim Wennmann

The Peace In Between
Post-war violence and peacebuilding
Edited by Mats Berdal and Astri Suhrke

Local and Global Dynamics of Peacebuilding
Postconflict reconstruction in Sierra Leone
Christine Cubitt

Peacebuilding, Memory and Reconciliation
Bridging top-down and bottom-up approaches
Bruno Charbonneau and Geneviève Parent

Peacebuilding and Local Ownership
Post-conflict consensus-building
Timothy Donais

Stabilization Operations, Security and Development
States of fragility
Edited by Robert Muggah

Controlling Small Arms
Consolidation, innovation and relevance in research and policy
Edited by Peter Batchelor and Kai Michael Kenkel

An Ethnographic Approach to Peacebuilding
Understanding local experiences in transitional states
Gearoid Millar

An Ethnographic Approach to Peacebuilding

Understanding local experiences in transitional states

Gearoid Millar

Routledge
Taylor & Francis Group
LONDON AND NEW YORK

First published 2014
by Routledge
2 Park Square, Milton Park, Abingdon, Oxfordshire OX14 4RN

and by Routledge
711 Third Avenue, New York, NY 10017

First issued in paperback 2015

Routledge is an imprint of the Taylor & Francis Group, an informa business

British Library Cataloguing in Publication Data
A catalogue record for this book is available from the British Library

Library of Congress Cataloging in Publication Data
Millar, Gearoid, author.
An ethnographic approach to peacebuilding : understanding local experiences in transitional states / Gearoid Millar.
pages cm. -- (Studies in conflict, development and peacebuilding)
1. Peace-building--Evaluation. 2. Peace-building--Social aspects. 3. Peace-building--International cooperation. 4. Peace-building--Sierra Leone--Evaluation. 5. Ethnology. I. Title. II. Series: Studies in conflict, development and peacebuilding.
JZ5538.M547 2014
303.66--dc23
2013045403

ISBN 13: 978-1-138-95306-2 (pbk)
ISBN 13: 978-0-415-87035-1 (hbk)

Typeset in Times
by Taylor & Francis Books

Contents

Acknowledgments

The ideas contained in this book have evolved over the past eight years during which I have lived in four different countries and worked with and learned from incredible colleagues and friends at a number of different institutions, all of whom deserve recognition. First, I thank former advisors and colleagues at American University's International Peace and Conflict Resolution (IPCR) program, Syracuse University's Program for the Advancement of Research in Conflict and Collaboration (PARCC), Radboud University Nijmegen's Centre for International Conflict Analysis and Management (CICAM), and the Institute for Conflict, Transition, and Peace Research (ICTPR) at the University of Aberdeen. Colleagues and friends at each have provided invaluable encouragement and advice throughout the early years of my career.

For financial and logistical support, I must thank the Maxwell School at Syracuse University for four years of teaching and research assistantships, with which I also funded my ten months of fieldwork in 2008/2009, the Faculty of Management at Radboud University Nijmegen for funding my six months of fieldwork in 2012, the University of Makeni in Sierra Leone for a great amount of assistance with in-country housing and logistics, and the Max Planck Institute for Social Anthropology in Halle, Germany, for a period as a guest researcher in May of 2013 during which I completed drafts of three chapters of the book in quiet academic isolation.

I also want to recognize all of the anonymous reviewers who have read and commented on my work in the past and made my ideas and my arguments stronger. Although they are more completely and forcefully articulated in these pages the ideas presented in this book have developed and been partially presented in previous articles in the *International Journal of Transitional Justice*, the *Journal of Peace Research*, *Conflict Resolution Quarterly*, *Human Rights Review*, *Peace and Conflict: The Journal of Peace Psychology*, *International Peacekeeping* and *Memory Studies*. As such, they owe much to the comments and suggestions of anonymous reviewers and the talented editors at these journals.

I thank my research assistants and interpreters – Bai Koroma, Edward Kanu, Emmanuel Conteh, and Mohamed Conteh – for their knowledge and insight, and various NGOs and organizations, that must remain de-identified, for their assistance and support. And, most importantly, I thank those who will never read these words. The individuals who have offered their thoughts and ideas in interviews conducted on hard wooden benches and low mud-brick walls, in the scorching heat or the mosquito riddled nights, and whose understanding, perception, and experience of international peacebuilding interventions form the very core of this book and of my own career. Without their contributions this book would never have come to be.

And, finally, I must thank those least involved in this research but to whom I am personally most indebted. Although they do not understand what I do for a living and have not read a word I have written, my parents have always encouraged me to follow my own course and never once implied that I might not achieve whatever I wanted in life. I thank them for their love and encouragement throughout my education and career. However, my wife and partner of 13 years deserves the most appreciation of all. She has supported me in Florida and in Washington, DC, in Syracuse and in Sierra Leone, in Nijmegen, and in Aberdeen. For your adventurous spirit and your willingness to take a risk, for your commitment, your caring, and most of all your patience; thank you.

Abbreviations

AFRC	Armed Forces Revolutionary Council
APC	All People's Congress
DDR	Disarmament, Demobilization and Rehabilitation
ECOWAS	Economic Community of West African States
EO	executive outcomes
EU	European Union
FDI	foreign direct investment
GIS	Geographical Information Systems
GSG	Gurkha Security Guards
HDI	Human Development Index
ICC	International Criminal Court
ICTR	International Criminal Tribunal for Rwanda
ICTY	International Criminal Tribunal for the Former Yugoslavia
IMF	International Monetary Fund
INGO	International non-governmental organization
M&E	monitoring and evaluation
NGO	non-governmental organization
NPRC	National Provisional Ruling Council
OECD	Organization for Economic Co-operation and Development
PPP	public-private partnership
RUF	Revolutionary United Front
SCSL	Special Court for Sierra Leone
SLPP	Sierra Leone People's Party
SSR	Security Sector Reform
TC	Truth Commission
TRC	Truth and Reconciliation Commission
UN	United Nations
US	United States

Introduction

The purpose of the public hearings, from the objectives of the Truth and Reconciliation Commission (TRC) for Sierra Leone was:

> To promote community and individual healing for victims, witnesses and perpetrators … To promote reconciliation through truth telling.
>
> (Truth and Reconciliation Commission for Sierra Leone 2004: 231–32)

Voices of local 'beneficiaries' of the TRC in Makeni, Sierra Leone, regarding their experience of the public hearings:

> The TRC only came to add wounds to people.
>
> (Hanna, 29, housewife)

> It seems as if it is only provocation to those that they seized advantage on during the war.
>
> (Alpha, 32, farmer)

Over the past two decades dozens of armed conflicts have undergone the transition from violence to relative peace and calm (Themnér and Wallensteen 2011). Over this same period, due to a number of factors, including the end of the Cold War, the consolidation of global interdependence, and the "global war on terror," the international community has taken on new responsibilities for securing the stability of such transitions. Today myriad projects, programs, and processes of reconstruction, reconciliation, and reform are being implemented in post-war and post-authoritarian settings; planned and funded by politicians and policy-makers in the powerful and wealthy institutions of the West and administered primarily by Western peacebuilding practitioners on the ground in transitional societies. These grand projects of transition – be they characterized as transitional justice, nation-building, peacebuilding, democratization, or international trusteeship – claim everywhere to provide for the future freedom and "emancipation" of those victimized by war (Richmond and Franks 2009). In short, "the overarching aim of outside engagement has been framed in largely identical terms, that is, 'to lay the foundation of lasting peace'" (Berdal and Keen 1997: 795).

But what do local people *experience* when the international community attempts to build peace? What do these many projects and programs do for their supposed beneficiaries? Do such projects provide – as their proponents claim – experiences of healing, reconciliation, peace, democracy, development, empowerment, and justice? Are they emancipatory? This book is motivated by the desire to see these questions answered and to understand how international projects are *experienced* by people on the ground. As the quotes at the beginning of this Introduction highlight, internationally planned, funded and administered projects often do not produce the expected results among local people. Instead, the actual social effects of peacebuilding interventions on the ground are commonly quite unpredictable and sometimes even conflict-promoting.

For example, in a recent article in *Memory Studies*, I describe the provocative effects of the truth-telling processes of the TRC among local people in the northern Sierra Leonean city of Makeni (Millar 2014). That article illustrates how the TRC's public sensitization campaign convinced the country as a whole to conceive of itself as victimized and to expect the truth-telling process to provide a healing experience. The entire country had been a victim of war, and the TRC was going to come and "help." Furthermore, the truth-telling process itself demanded that individuals perform the role of victim during the hearings; describing to their audience exactly how, when and where they were victimized. In this way the processes of the TRC (both the sensitization campaign and the public hearings) functioned to convince the population of Sierra Leone as a whole that it had been a victim, was in need of healing, and that the TRC itself would provide that healing experience.

However, within the local context, the role of victim was associated with that of a "client" and the role of the TRC was associated with that of a "patron." In such patron–client systems, as will be discussed further in later chapters, clients supplicate themselves to powerful "big men" and expect those big men to perform the reciprocal role of patron; to provide resources, services, and employment. Therefore, in Makeni, the truth-telling process was one in which individuals, having been primed to consider themselves clients, performed the social drama of "begging" and expected help in the form not of talk, but of resources. However, as the TRC had no budget to play that role, the vast majority of these clients found their pleas for help unanswered. No help was provided and most people presenting testimony and watching in the audience experienced the public hearings not as healing and justice, but as either a waste of their time or as an actively provocative event.

While this is only one simple example, in the past few years various authors have described similar dislocations between the practices of peacebuilders and the experiences of the "peace-kept" (Marten 2004). Isaacs (2009), Autesserre

(2010), and Robins (2011) provide three similar examples from completely disparate cases scattered over three continents. In each, the authors highlight the diverse problems encountered by international actors and how easily projects of intervention initiate experiences far removed from those predicted by the interveners. Similarly, a recent special issue of *International Peacekeeping* was devoted to the examination of the "*frictions*" that arise between "imported processes and indigenous practices" (Millar, van der Lijn, and Verkoren 2013) and earlier special issues of the journal, *Global Governance* (Jarstad and Belloni 2012) and the *Journal of Peacebuilding and Development* (Mac Ginty and Sanghera 2013) consider the concept of hybridity as a way to grapple with the clear separation between international plans and the eventual realities on the ground.

These diverse contributions are all wrestling with the same problem: when powerful international actors become engaged in transitional settings, they are always entering already complex and usually volatile social, cultural, political, and economic environments, about which they are regularly underinformed and sometimes quite ignorant. As a result, their interventions regularly have effects that were not, and perhaps cannot be, predicted. Most problematically, as in the example above, sometimes these effects are actively negative or potentially inflammatory but remain unrecognized because so few interveners have the tools to understand local experiences of peacebuilding interventions. Most people who set peacebuilding policy or who are active as peacebuilders take an *institutional* as opposed to an *experiential* approach to peacebuilding, assuming that institutions such as the TRC will automatically facilitate particular experiences in local contexts. They assume that elections provide accountability, local empowerment, and ownership over government, for example, and that a restructured military and police force will automatically make citizens feel more secure.

But the problem is that these assumed impacts of institutional solutions are social experiences and, as such, they are highly reliant on culturally variable concepts, ideas, and beliefs about the world. While institutional forms can be picked up and moved around from setting to setting – as the TRC has traversed across the globe over the past 20 years – individuals and communities will have varying experiences in response to those institutions and the processes or practices they demand. As a result, local experiences of institutions can be quite unpredictable and evaluating the impact of peacebuilding institutions demands evaluation of the experiences they facilitate. In the following chapters, therefore, I outline an approach to evaluating international peacebuilding through an ethnographic approach that sees peacebuilding not as institutional, but as experiential.

Further, I provide data from two such evaluations I have conducted in Sierra Leone over the past six years to illustrate the approach and highlight its particular strengths. I call this an *ethnographic approach* because it demands a willingness to study closely the local social and cultural context. In addition, while they do serve other valuable purposes, I will show that neither large-N quantitative nor national level qualitative case study methods of evaluation can bring to light the discrepancies between international expectations and local experiences of peacebuilding, nor usefully explore and explain those discrepancies if they are discovered. The ethnographic approach, on the other hand, allows the evaluator to understand local experiences of peacebuilding interventions within complex transitional states, and provides a more accurate evaluation of the local impacts of peacebuilding interventions.

A handful of caveats

Over the past six years I have conducted two evaluations of major international projects in post-war Sierra Leone. Over ten months in 2008 and 2009 I assessed the local experiences of the TRC in Makeni, the headquarter town of the northern Bombali district, and over six months in 2012 I began an evaluation of the local experiences of a large bio-energy Foreign Direct Investment (FDI) project covering some 40,000 hectares and approximately 90 villages in the rural north of the country. Both of these evaluations uncovered acute differences between the expectations of the international interveners and the experiences of the supposed beneficiaries of these projects. Indeed, in both cases the unexpected and unplanned negative experiences produced unpredictable and potentially dangerous effects, as will be discussed in greater detail in later chapters.

This book does not, however, seek to make claims about the effects of TRCs or FDI projects in all settings based on my research among local communities in Sierra Leone. While I do believe that these dynamics probably mirror those in other settings, the diversity of the "local" across the large number of transitional states that currently or may in the future host peacebuilding projects limits the generalizability of conclusions based on studies in any particular setting. Instead, the aim of this book is to describe and illustrate the particular approach I used in this research and to provide a framework to guide similar evaluations of local experiences in future cases. The aim is, in short, to present and defend *a particular approach to project evaluation* and show how this approach can assist in understanding local experiences of peacebuilding projects in any setting. It is important to note that some authors have made earlier contributions to this line of work.

In some ways, this book echoes Olivier de Sardan's *Anthropology and Development* (2005), which attempted both to describe the value of anthropology as an appropriate discipline for the study of international development and to propose a new "research program" for that purpose (ibid.: 14). My own work in this book attempts to outline an approach which can embody Olivier de Sardan's research program and easily be adopted by non-anthropologist academics and both evaluators and practitioners working in the field. Similarly, this book shares the spirit of work by authors such as Bichsel (2005, 2009), Denskus (2009, 2010), and Autesserre (2010, 2014), in their use of an ethnographic approach to study peacebuilding interventions, but differs from them in that these authors primarily use that approach to study the peacebuilders, as opposed to the experiences of such projects among the beneficiaries. On the other hand, while anthropologists such as Shaw (2007, 2010), Theidon (2006, 2013), and Honwana (2006) (to name just a few) have used ethnographic methods to study the impact of international interventions among "beneficiaries," they, like Olivier de Sardan, do not provide practical guidance for incorporating ethnographic methods into peacebuilding evaluations.

In short, while all of these authors would probably promote an ethnographic approach to peacebuilding evaluation, and Denskus has done so in one article (2012), no structured guidance has yet been provided for how to do this, and particularly for how to conduct ethnographic evaluations of "beneficiary" experiences of international peacebuilding. This book seeks to fill this void in the literature. To do so, I try to accomplish a number of tasks and, as a result, the book is a somewhat eclectic mix of genres. It is not primarily a monograph presenting data from the field, nor principally a work of theory, nor merely a methods guide. It is a combination of all of these. The book outlines a methodology for peacebuilding evaluation, incorporates data collected during two such evaluation projects for the purpose of illustration, includes a number of more theoretical considerations, and provides recommendations for a future research agenda. Finally, it also presents a number of reflections on my own research practice and contributes to ongoing debates regarding local ownership and empowerment in peacebuilding. Hopefully this combination of elements will be both interesting and convincing.

It is important to note that the approach to evaluation I propose evaluates peacebuilding interventions based only on the benefits vis-à-vis the intended beneficiaries claimed by those projects. I argue that such projects should not be evaluated based either on broadly but externally defined targets such as "social justice," "economic development," or "peace" writ large, nor on narrowly defined goals like the cessation of violence or the establishment of security. Instead each project should be evaluated based on the claims it makes about its benefits for local individuals and communities. Hence, I argue that evaluators following the ethnographic approach must understand the explicit claims of each project and assess its success accordingly. As all contemporary peacebuilding interventions claim to facilitate substantial experiences of some kind among local people – of reconciliation (TRCs), dignity (reparations programs), security (Security Sector Reform [SSR] programs), accountability (elections), transparency (Good Governance Programs), justice (criminal tribunals), etc. – understanding the local experiences of these projects should be a central element of any evaluation. Therefore, while the ethnographic approach can be used to evaluate the local experiences of a variety of peacebuilding interventions in any setting, the actual indicators of "success" will rely on the claimed or planned effects of each intervention; which experiences a project claims to create or facilitate.

And, finally, the ethnographic approach to evaluation should not be associated too closely with anthropology as a discipline. It is true that ethnography is often associated with anthropology, and it is also true that fieldwork requiring a fluent knowledge of the local language and a complete understanding of and participation in local ways of life remains a touchstone of that discipline, even as traditions of fieldwork and ethnography, and definitions of what constitutes "the field" (Madden 2010; Collins and Gallinat 2010) have changed and evolved (Clammer 1984; Coleman and Collins 2006). But the ethnographic approach I describe does not demand this particular conception of fieldwork, nor of the evaluator. Ethnographic evaluation demands recognition of the importance of culture in shaping how individuals see and experience their world and a willingness to try to understand alternative experiences of international interventions and processes, but this in itself falls short of the traditional conceptions of fieldwork within anthropology.

As such, while I do not believe that fluency in the local language or full participation in local life is required in order for non-anthropologists to adopt the form of evaluation I propose, the ethnographic approach does demand a healthy "anthropological imagination" (Dimen 1977; Parman 1998). Therefore, I argue that an ethnographic approach should be seen not as an extension of anthropology but as a tool for any discipline, or, as in my own case, any interdisciplinary scholar of peace, conflict, and post-conflict peacebuilding. While the laudable commitment of anthropologists to a more intense fieldwork experience can surely produce even more fine-grained and nuanced understanding of the local language, culture, and experience, I do believe that even non-anthropologists unwilling or unable to commit to this mode of ethnography can adopt and benefit from the evaluation process I describe. As a non-anthropologist, I therefore hope that this book will serve both to highlight the largely untapped potential of ethnography as an evaluative tool for scholars within international relations, peacebuilding, and transitional justice, and for practitioners in the field, and will encourage greater numbers of anthropologists to engage in the practical evaluation of international projects and processes. However, one does not have to be an anthropologist to use the ethnographic approach.

Outline of the book

This book is divided into three parts. Part I, comprising Chapters 1 and 2, provides necessary contextual information. In Chapter 1, I will review the recent literature on evaluation in peacebuilding and transitional justice and then provide an outline of the four pillars of my own ethnographic approach. Chapter 2 provides a background on the history and conflict in Sierra Leone, an introduction to the theories underlying the supposedly peacebuilding effects of TRCs and FDI projects, and a description of the setting of my studies, in the city of Makeni in the case of the TRC, and among the scores of villages spread over a 40,000-hectare land-lease area in the case of the FDI project.

No attempt is made in Chapter 2 to explore the local cultural context, as this will be explored fully in the later chapters.

In Part II, comprising Chapters 3–6, each chapter focuses on one of the four pillars of the ethnographic approach and then illustrates the importance of that pillar with data from the cases. These four chapters are cumulative, building on each other and showing the added nuance that the approach can provide when applied in a holistic manner. Chapter 3 will highlight the need for evaluators of peacebuilding interventions to see *peacebuilding as experiential*. This chapter argues that the experiences peacebuilding interventions are supposed to provide – of justice, healing, reconciliation, security, development, dignity, empowerment, etc. – cannot be evaluated by counting outputs or by national level measures, and will show that while new institutions and reforms will impact the contexts within which local people live their lives, the actual experiences of those infrastructures and reforms are far from predictable. While both of the projects I have evaluated in northern Sierra Leone were expected to be experienced by local people in particular and predictable ways, this chapter will show how the assumptions of the interveners proved to be inaccurate in relation to actual local experiences. The chapter illustrates, therefore, the great potential of the ethnographic approach to evaluate exactly *how* local people experience peacebuilding interventions.

Chapter 4 will describe the importance of *ethnographic preparation*, or the value of existing ethnographic analyses as the context for evaluation of local experiences of peacebuilding interventions. While such preparation seems like a very simple and practical first step for research in a foreign country – conducting a thorough literature review of the prior ethnographic studies of the context – it is regularly omitted from both preparations for and evaluations of peacebuilding interventions. This chapter will show how important ethnographic preparation is to evaluations in complex and culturally dissimilar settings and how local experiences of peacebuilding interventions must be understood as nested within culturally defined systems of meaning. This chapter focuses specifically on the impact of the "patron–client" system (Nyerges 1992) on local experiences of both the TRC and the FDI project and illustrates the power of this pillar of the ethnographic approach to evaluate *why* peacebuilding interventions are experienced as they are.

Chapter 5 will discuss the need for *local engagement* in peacebuilding evaluation. It will first provide a definition of the "local" as specific to the beneficiary population claimed by the peacebuilding project being evaluated, and then proceed to highlight the dangers of relying on particular sub-groups of that local population in evaluations of peacebuilding effects. I will highlight in particular the dangers of relying on the educated, professional, and political classes when evaluating the experience of peacebuilding interventions designed to benefit either the nation as a whole or marginalized groups such as women, displaced persons, refugees, war-wounded, former soldiers, etc. This chapter will describe both the challenges and the benefits of interviewing non-elites in transitional states and show that, while pillar one is focused on uncovering *how* peacebuilding is experienced and pillar two tries to discover *why* this is so, local engagement is necessary to uncover and then understand the *diversity* of experiences that will be evident on the ground. To highlight the value of local engagement, therefore, this chapter will describe the significant difference between how elites of various stripes and local non-elites have experienced the TRC and the FDI project.

And finally, concluding Part II, Chapter 6 will argue that to accomplish the goals of the first three pillars, evaluators of peacebuilding interventions must be able to question their own conceptions of social experiences; that they must commit to an *appraisal of their own implicit assumptions*. Specifically, an evaluator must have the ability to question his or her own concepts of the social goods that peacebuilding interventions claim to provide; of justice, healing, reconciliation, development, empowerment, security, dignity, etc. This chapter will show that an uncritical reliance on one's own implicit assumptions will lead to inaccurate evaluations of local experiences because the evaluator inherently assumes that the experiences will mirror what he or she believes happens in their own society. This chapter endeavors to illustrate clearly, therefore, how secondary concepts such as justice or empowerment are founded on implicitly accepted but nonetheless culturally variable foundational conceptions of self and sociality. This demands, therefore, that evaluators question their own norms and see the world from another's perspective, in order to evaluate the other's experiences. In short, evaluators must be able to imagine other ways of living within the world, and understand the world, in order to evaluate how beneficiaries experience peacebuilding interventions.

After describing the strengths of the ethnographic approach and the quality of the data that can be captured through illustrations from the projects I have evaluated in Sierra Leone throughout Part II, the chapters in Part III will explore in additional detail, and with reflections from my own fieldwork, some of the challenges and strengths of the approach. Chapter 7 will note the challenges of the ethnographic approach and provide practical suggestions for overcoming them. It is divided into two main sections. The first section will describe the practicalities of dealing with physical, medical, and psychological security in transitional settings and the difficulty of working in the field with local people suffering from disease, poverty, isolation, and hardship. The second section will discuss issues regarding funding, ethics, and the evaluator's responsibility to the populations within which research is conducted, highlighting the difficult role played by evaluators when they are seen by marginalized local people as potentially influential international actors while they themselves attempt to maintain neutrality in the field.

Chapter 8 addresses the differences between and the potential complementarity of the ethnographic and quantitative approaches to evaluation. This chapter also is divided into two sections. The first section will describe my experiences with two separate quantitative surveys conducted in rural Sierra Leone and the debilitating limitations posed on the quantitative approach in often impoverished transitional states. This section of the chapter will, therefore, serve to underline the various limitations of the quantitative approach to evaluation in transitional states often characterized by a weak infrastructure and little human capacity. However, the second section of this chapter will then describe the potential to overcome these challenges through the possible combination of the quantitative and ethnographic approaches. I will describe here how a multi-methodological approach to the evaluation of peacebuilding interventions could combine the strengths and avoid the weaknesses of both and provide a potential future research agenda.

The final chapter of the book (Chapter 9) will provide a synopsis of the argument presented and then describe the various practical and political problems limiting the use of ethnographic data and long-term fieldwork in project evaluation. The chapter will progress, however, to present my argument for why the benefits of this approach outweigh any of those limitations. Indeed, this chapter will conclude the book with an argument in support of incorporating trained ethnographers and capable qualitative fieldworkers into the life cycle of peacebuilding interventions so as to ensure more predictable and positive experiences for local beneficiaries and, indeed, the full inclusion of local people themselves so as to empower instead of marginalize those who are supposedly benefiting from intervention. At the very least, such changes can avoid the potentially combustible or conflict-promoting experiences that interventions often unwittingly inspire.

Part I

Introduction to the ethnographic approach

1 Peacebuilding, empowerment, and evaluation

Over the past 20 years, and particularly since the publication of the United Nation's (UN) *Agenda for Peace* in 1992 (Boutros-Ghali 1992), the international community has come to see the building of peace as one of its core responsibilities. In the aftermath of violent conflict today a host of international actors pursue projects designed to provide transitional justice, economic development, intergroup reconciliation and dialogue, and various forms of political, judicial, economic, social, and security sector reform. Each of these projects can be seen as one element of the broader peacebuilding agenda and the actors involved and the projects embarked upon can be seen as extensions of a broad and powerful shift towards intervention, first, in the post-Cold War period and now in the post-9/11, post-Arab Spring context. However, as this broad peacebuilding agenda has expanded, a number of closely related dynamics have developed that greatly complicate the relationship between the international practices and the local experience of such interventions.

First, as the practice of peacebuilding has expanded, particular forms of intervention have become recognized as acceptable solutions to post-war problems – as tools in the post-war "tool-kit" (Shaw 2005; Donais 2009: 23; United Nations 2012) – and the notion that "peace can be achieved by bureaucratic means" has come to prevail (Goetschel and Hagmann 2009: 66). Included here are all the "best practice" mechanisms which Pugh regards as "problem-solving" approaches (2011: 308) and Mac Ginty has described as "technocratic ministrations" (2010a: 408). Second, this standardization of peacebuilding has contributed to a sense within much of the field that the end-goals are set – democracy, free markets, rule of law – and the only significant questions that remain are about how to reach those ends. Paris has called this approach "Wilsonianism" (2004: 6), though it is widely known today as the "liberal peace." Much of the field has, in essence, become fixated on particular outcomes and considers substantive reflection on what kind of peace is being built to be more of a distraction than a valid point of debate (Richmond and Franks 2009: 4; Mac Ginty 2012).

Therefore, while critical responses to this liberal peace have been quite a vocal minority in peacebuilding scholarship over the past ten years, responses to this critique in the form of policy and practice have been limited (Mac Ginty and Richmond 2013: 775–76). As much as the liberal peace approach has come under fire from scholars, the practice of peacebuilding as a liberal project of social engineering has continued unabated. Indeed, even the concepts deployed by critical scholars as tools of critique have been subsumed by the liberal peace approach. As Richmond describes the idea of "local ownership", for example, while the concept itself is accepted and inserted into policy debates, "it is little more than rhetoric, used to legitimize externality" (2012: 372; see also Donais 2012: 6). As such, the technocratic ministrations – the tool-kits and cookie-cutter responses – carry on even as scholars note their failure and, in many cases, their actual negative impacts on peacebuilding.

Third, these technocratic and professional approaches to peacebuilding have become ever more internationally controlled processes. In short, the significant actors in peacebuilding contexts today are the interveners, while those who experienced violence as victims, witnesses, and survivors are considered recipients or "beneficiaries" of international largesse (Autesserre 2010: 25–26). We see this transfer of influence most clearly in bodies such the UN's peacebuilding Commission, the International Criminal Court (ICC), or contemporary peacekeeping missions empowered by enforcement measures such as the current mission in the Democratic Republic of Congo which clearly distributes power not to local actors, but among international technocrats, professionals, and practitioners (Clark 2011; Teethling 2011). For these reasons Richmond has described peacebuilding practice as a colonizing process dominated by international actors and failing to provide an "emancipatory version of peace" (Richmond 2006: 389), while others have noted the clearly illiberal tendencies of this "liberal peace" which sees international expertise and knowledge as superior to the local (Ignatieff 2003; Chandler 2006; Pugh 2011; Laffey and Nadarajah 2012).

Fourth, as these processes have become standardized and internationalized, there have arisen increasing calls for the professionalization of the field (see Kritz 2009: 14; Sending 2009: 3; Mac Ginty 2012: 289). In essence, the increasing amount of funding spent on intervention has attracted ever more organizations to enter the peacebuilding business and increasing numbers of young professionals to consider peacebuilding as a career path. In response there have emerged: (1) professional training courses and graduate-level university programs focusing on producing future peacebuilders to design and administer projects in transitional settings; (2) large numbers of academics studying peacebuilding theory and practice and publishing hundreds of books and thousands of scholarly articles on the subject; and (3) a massive collection of non-governmental organizations (NGOs) at both international and national levels which claim to contribute to peacebuilding in war-torn states. Each of these dynamics has contributed to the development of what some have come to call the "peace industry" (Mac Ginty 2012: 289; Denskus 2012: 151).

And, finally, all of this has led to increasing demand for evaluation of the many projects claiming to contribute to peacebuilding (Paffenholz and Spurk

2006: 19; Blum 2011: 1; Bush and Duggan 2013b: 5). While just a decade ago there had been little in the way of peacebuilding evaluation and many individual mechanisms were promoted with little critical assessment or understanding of local effects (Mendeloff 2004; Brahm 2007), over the past ten years a number of evaluation processes have been promoted and deployed. Recent special issues of the *International Journal of Transitional Justice* (Duggan 2010) and the *Journal of Peacebuilding and Development* (Paffenholz, Abu-Nimer, and McCandless 2005; Bush and Duggan 2013a) have focused on this topic, for example. In addition, as will be described below, a series of academic publications and institutional guidelines have been published which either report on new evaluation results or instruct peacebuilding professionals on how to carry out evaluations of their own projects. It has, in essence, been made clear to the peace industry that it is insufficient to administer peacebuilding projects without *proof* that those projects are effective (Paffenholz and Spurk 2006: 19).

However, the majority of this new literature on evaluation fails to seriously engage with local concerns, needs, and concepts and so "avoid[s] fundamentally challenging debates about the *telos* of peacebuilding" (Denskus 2012: 151). It focuses instead on increasingly technocratic and professionalized processes of coding, cataloging, and counting, or what Mac Ginty and Richmond describe as "tick-box" evaluations seeking "standardized information" (2013: 778), and which fail to understand the importance of local experiences. In short, the peacebuilding field has been led – inexorably over the past 20 years – to increasing standardization, professionalization, and evaluation but with little focus on how any of this is experienced by local people on the ground in transitional states.

Therefore, while this period has seen both the development of a vast array of peacebuilding practices and the consolidation of peacebuilding as a subfield within academia, the growing interest has not resulted in emancipatory experiences among local people in post-war settings (Richmond and Franks 2009). Further, while critical scholars such as Ignatieff, Chandler, Richmond, Mac Ginty, and Pugh have highlighted the illiberal nature of the "liberal peace" agenda, nobody has yet provided clear guidance on how to promote or encourage an emancipatory peace. Indeed, the approach of critical scholarship seems to be restricted to critique and provides little in the way of practical solutions. While many scholars hope for a peace grounded in local agency (Pugh 2011), in local resistance to international impositions (Richmond 2009a), and in local ownership (Donais 2009, 2012), clear descriptions of how exactly this can be encouraged have not been forthcoming. Quite to the contrary, critical scholars seem unable to propose steps towards such a peace for fear once again of imposing technocratic solutions. How can scholars and practitioners avoid subverting local voice, ownership, and agency, even if consciously attempting to establish exactly that?

I argue here that the first step is not to attempt to create anything – not to start by planning, designing, or doing – but to start by *understanding*;

understanding what is already happening from the perspective of local people. I argue that we must consider local people's perceptions and experiences of conflict, justice, security, development, empowerment, dignity, opportunity, and peace itself, as the starting point for any further theory and certainly as the foundation of any further international action that might hope to facilitate local voice, agency or an emancipatory peace. Understanding, however, demands a grounded, ethnographic approach to evaluating *local experiences* of international processes. Ethnographic evaluation is therefore key not only to understanding what has been done, but to considering what to do in the future.

Evaluation, understanding, and emancipation

This book responds to a number of issues within the literature regarding peacebuilding evaluation. First, it directly addresses the divergence between theory within the peacebuilding literature and the experiences of peacebuilding practice on the ground in transitional states. While conducting research on peacebuilding, I have always been struck by the discord between ideas of how peacebuilding projects should work and the evaluations of anthropologists and critical theorists. The massive divergence, for example, between the expected positive effects of truth commissions (Tutu 1999; Hayner 2002) and the critical evaluations of those processes by anthropologists working in the field (Wilson 2001; Ross 2002; Kelsall 2005; Shaw 2005; Colvin 2006; Castillejo Cuellar 2007; Theidon 2013), and that between the supposed stabilizing and peace-promoting effects of economic development, free markets, and democratic "good governance" (Collier and Hoeffler 1998; Doyle and Sambanis 2000; Paris 2004) and the many critics of this liberal peace (Ignatieff 2003; Chandler 2006; Richmond 2006; Duffield 2007; Mac Ginty 2010b; Cubitt 2012) have inspired my own approach to evaluation which seeks to understand such divergence.

While each of these critical studies highlights the discord between the assumptions implicit within peacebuilding theory and the primary effects of those interventions in transitional states, these authors do not provide a framework to guide evaluation of those impacts or of local experiences of peacebuilding interventions. Further, they do not describe either a process of evaluation other scholars can use to replicate their work or many practical ways for peacebuilding as a field to overcome the problems they identify. This book attempts to fill this void both by describing and illustrating a framework for an ethnographic approach to evaluating peacebuilding experiences, and by showing, in the concluding chapter, how this approach itself can be incorporated into the life cycle of peacebuilding interventions to overcome some of the problems identified by these scholars.

Second, this book responds directly to the emergence of evaluation literature adhering to a formal quantitative approach which largely sidelines local conceptions or experiences of the complex and culturally variable phenomena under study. For example, quantitative work emerging over the past few years has attempted to measure the impact of transitional justice processes by quantitative means (Sikkink and Booth Walling 2007; Olsen, Payne, and Reiter 2010; Wiebelhaus-Brahm 2010; Dancy and Wiebelhaus-Brahm 2011). These evaluations seek to measure the impact of transitional justice processes on state-level variables such as respect for human rights or democratization. However, out of necessity, they use proxies for the independent variable such as a *count* of "trial-years" as a measure of the level of justice provided by criminal tribunals. This is similar to how peace and conflict scholars have measured the success of peace agreements by the *number* of years the peace holds after the agreement is signed (Hartzell, Hoddie, and Rothchild 2001; Fortna 2004), or how practitioners of economic development have often considered the *amount* of aid disbursed to be a valid measurement of project success (Boyce 2002: 66).

However, measuring "justice" by counting "trial years", or the impact of transitional justice processes based on a national-level score of democratization or human rights does not provide an understanding of local experiences of justice, democratization, or human rights. Similarly, measuring the success of peace agreements by the number of years of peace ignores how peace is experienced by people on the ground and fails to distinguish between peace that is inclusive and progressive – or what Galtung considered "positive peace" (1969) – and peace that is more akin to security or even repression. As William Easterly forcefully states, even development cannot be evaluated at the national level, but must consist of "truly independent scientific evaluations of specific aid efforts; not overall sweeping evaluations of a whole nationwide development program" (2006: 194; see also Jackson 2005: 160). In short, while such large-N studies are admirable attempts to evaluate the impact of transitional justice mechanisms, peace agreements, or development projects, they fail to understand or even consider justice, peace, or development as complex processes that demand, at their core, *culturally variable social experiences.* This is true also of evaluative efforts based primarily on qualitative case study analysis such as that of Paris (2004), or Wiebelhaus-Brahm (2010), which, though utilizing qualitative data, still rely primarily on national-level measures with little consideration for local experiences. This book provides an alternative, or more appropriately, a complement, to these two traditions of peacebuilding evaluation.

Third, this book responds to and contributes directly to the literature that has emerged prescribing appropriate processes of evaluation for peacebuilding practitioners in the field, produced by both scholars (Bush 1998; Anderson 1999; Paffenholz and Reychler 2007), and international organizations (Catholic Relief Services 2010; OECD 2012; United Nations 2012). This literature has become influential among practitioners in the fields of humanitarian aid, international development, and post-conflict peacebuilding, but again, fails to significantly address the culturally variable nature of the phenomena under study – along with a number of other failings (see Blum 2011; Denskus 2012) – and considers only perfunctorily any fieldwork requirement or ethnographic knowledge of the local context. A recent meta-review of evaluation processes by Abu-Nimer *et al.* (2013), for example, highlights both the strengths and weaknesses of evaluation "best-practices" in the field but illustrates clearly, by its complete omission, the marginality of any fieldwork component in evaluation processes (ibid.: 34).

Similarly, a summary of "selected conflict analysis tools" included in the OECD "Guidelines" for evaluation shows that *none* suggest more than brief in-country workshops or a three to five day "field mission" (2012: 79). Therefore, while this evaluation literature too represents an admirable step towards better understanding of peacebuilding impacts in transitional settings, the provision of do's, don'ts, and checklists that comprise its primary contribution, while streamlined and simplified enough to provide guidance for project administrators, are not enough to result in substantive understanding of the local experiences of intervention. They provide a largely technocratic response to evaluation that further feeds the general standardization and "problem-solving" focus that characterize the field as a whole. Again, this book provides an alternative or complementary ethnographic approach to the evaluation of peacebuilding interventions and their potential conflict-inhibiting or conflict-promoting effects.

In summary, while both the academic literature evaluating peacebuilding interventions and that providing guidelines for evaluation to practitioners have grown over the past 15 years, neither has articulated and defended to either the policy community or peacebuilding practitioners a process by which to understand and evaluate local experiences of peacebuilding among the supposed beneficiaries in local settings. Further, while recent literature is replete with references to local ownership and engagement (Pouligny 2005; Donais 2009, 2012; Richmond 2009b), these debates have failed to result in peacebuilding projects that local people actually design and apply to meet their own ideas of what is needed in the post-war setting (see Cubitt 2012). Much as Duffield (2007: 215) claims regarding the development field, peacebuilding has become expert at repackaging itself as a reformed enterprise without actually making significant changes to its programmatic policies and approaches which sideline and ignore local experience, or as Easterly argues, also concerning development, no matter how much we talk about "local ownership," we cannot seem to figure out how to actually allow it to emerge (2006: 196). Therefore, while this book admittedly presents yet another method of peacebuilding evaluation, it fills a significant gap in the literature by providing clear guidance for an ethnographic approach to evaluation that can also act as a step towards international accountability to the beneficiaries of intervention; accountability which can, in turn, be the first step towards local ownership, empowerment, and emancipation.

The four pillars of the ethnographic approach

The ethnographic approach presented in this book will be divided into four pillars, each of which will be described and illustrated in one chapter.

However, before proceeding, I will describe each pillar in brief. The first pillar of the ethnographic approach is a commitment to see *peacebuilding as experiential*. As already argued, it is my contention that one of the primary goals of all peacebuilding interventions is the provision of particular experiences to a beneficiary community. It is of course true that peacebuilding also serves the needs of the actors who fund and practice it; those who plan, fund, and administer peacebuilding projects clearly have their own agendas, and in supporting peacebuilding projects they also meet their own needs to some extent (Boyce 2002: 61; Paris 2002: 652–53). But few would argue against the claim that one of the primary goals of peacebuilding is to develop the potential for sustainable peace by *providing experiences* that will lead local people to accept and support the transition to peace. International criminal tribunals, for example, claim to provide an experience of justice to those who have experienced injustice, so that they will not resort to vigilantism and violence. Intergroup dialogue processes claim to provide an experience of reconciliation so that individuals will live side-by-side with their former foes. Post-conflict development projects claim to provide an experience of development, to ensure experiences of opportunity and to decrease experiences of deprivation, hunger, and economic insecurity.

This book argues that the experiences local people have of transition and of the peace that is being built should be considered the prime outcome of peacebuilding processes. If, in the aftermath of war and violence, the experiences beneficiary communities have of peacebuilding interventions are not what is expected by the planners and administrators of those interventions, then the various projects of peacebuilding will have unexpected, unpredictable, and potentially negative results. If we accept that individuals – victims, survivors, or witnesses of atrocities, for example – have a need for justice after violence, but the international interventions planned and administered to provide justice are instead experienced as unjust or as a provocation, then the social effects of that intervention may not support peace. If projects administered for the provision of employment, opportunity, and local empowerment are instead experienced as disempowering, alienating, and disruptive, then those projects will potentially have negative and destabilizing effects. In short, *understanding local experiences* of international peacebuilding interventions must be the prime concern of those who intervene and, by extension, those who evaluate intervention.

However, the technocratic approach to evaluation described above tends to ignore local experiences of intervention. The recent attempts to evaluate the effects of transitional justice processes, for example, which use national-level measures of democratization and human rights protections as their dependent variable, fail to take into account local conceptions of democracy, rights, or justice. They fail to ask local people how they define justice, or what legitimate government would look like to them. Those who plan, fund, and administer such projects seem to assume a direct – and predictable – relationship between the administration of an institution and the provision of an experience. But such assumptions remain unstated, and perhaps even unrecognized. Counter to this, the ethnographic approach demands that such theories be explored and interrogated and that concepts such as justice, reconciliation, healing, development, or empowerment, be seen as culturally variable.

The noted problems with the recent evaluation efforts highlight how difficult it is to operationalize most of the outcomes we hope to measure in our evaluations of peacebuilding intervention. These quantitative projects are attempting to prove peacebuilding impacts across cases, but this approach inherently demands some proxy measure such as elections and successful transfers of power, amount of foreign direct investment, or years of criminal tribunal proceedings, which can be measured and compared across a number of cases. Such approaches assume that the observed proxy will accurately reflect an experience – of legitimate government, of development and empowerment, or of justice in these examples – but there is little reason to assume that such events automatically correlate with such complex experiences across societies. By conceiving of concepts such as justice, reconciliation or development as experiential, the ethnographic approach demands that the evaluator allow local people to define such concepts for themselves and then evaluate if the intervention was able to provide such an experience. As such, this approach does not require the evaluator to independently operationalize complex and culturally variable concepts. Instead, it demands that those concepts be defined by the beneficiaries.

Following on from this need to understand local experiences, the second pillar of the ethnographic approach is very practical, it is *ethnographic preparation*. Over the six years I have been studying peacebuilding in Sierra Leone I have been constantly shocked by how little anthropological literature is read by individuals who are planning, administering, and evaluating projects in Sierra Leone. On my first extended stay in Makeni, in 2008/2009, I ran into a fellow Irishman while at the Ministry of Education office in Makeni. As one did back in the days when there were only a handful of expatriates in town, I asked if he would like to meet for dinner that night and we went to one of the small local restaurants near the center of town for some rice and *plasas* (the local stews that are served with white rice). He told me that he was a PhD student and that he was interviewing each of the ministers of education in each of the districts in order to understand the effects of Sierra Leone's ongoing post-war decentralization process on education policy. He would be in the country for a few weeks.

But if he had read a sampling of anthropological literature about Sierra Leone, or spent more than a few weeks in country, he would have been aware of the futility of this kind of "parachute research" (Bastida *et al.* 2010) in a country where knowledge is managed, massaged, and controlled to ensure optimal outcomes for the speaker. If he had read literature by Ferme (2001), Shaw (1996, 2002), Murphy (1990, 1998), or other anthropologists who have worked in the country for decades, he would have realized that collecting data on such a short visit and relying on elite interviews would be filled with problems, both methodological and ethical; data which can only be a poor reflection of the actual, on-the-ground phenomena he was hoping to study, and which are quite likely to misrepresent the facts on the ground. Unfortunately, he appeared to have read none of these ethnographic studies.

Similarly, during my six-month stay in 2012, I was contacted by a staff member of a large and well-meaning NGO from the UK regarding my work evaluating the FDI project. She was coming to the area for four days, with a research consultant, to evaluate the same project I was studying as an example of a public-private partnership (PPP), but neither she nor the consultant had ever been to Sierra Leone before. On meeting them a few weeks later, they proved to have very little knowledge of the country and almost no knowledge at all about the culture or life in a rural Sierra Leonean village. Both were able to talk about other situations in other African countries, but neither seemed to have read any of the existing literature about the culture or the people in this particular setting; information, I would argue, that is clearly necessary if the goal is to understand *local experiences* of any large international project and how it is impacting local communities.

Time and again, this has been my experience of evaluation processes in Sierra Leone – evaluators conduct little to no ethnographic preparation before coming to the country. This would be excusable, even understandable, if local knowledge, worldviews, lifeways, or concepts were considered unimportant and to have no effect on how interventions are experienced. If we know that interventions will be experienced everywhere, at all times, and by all people in the same way, then we need not bother to understand local cultures, concepts, or beliefs; we can accept technocratic, top-down, and institutional approaches as universally applicable. But rarely do you read or hear such a denial of cultural variability. Quite to the contrary, academics and practitioners are quite vocal about the importance of cultural diversity, local ownership, and grassroots approaches. But yet few evaluators, never mind those who fund, plan, and administer international interventions, take the time to learn about the local culture prior to conducting or evaluating their projects.

This second pillar, therefore, demands that existing literature on the place, and the people on whom the intervention has been imposed, be reviewed by evaluators and incorporated into, and acknowledged as important contextual information for, the process of evaluation. Of course, an expert in truth commissions, intergroup dialogue, micro-finance, or judicial reform will never have a complete knowledge of the past ethnographic studies of a particular case or a fluent grasp of local culture, but neither is necessary in order to know enough to avoid misconstruing information and eventually writing misinformed and uninformative reports. Ideally, NGOs and other organizations who conduct evaluations of peacebuilding interventions would hire both staff and consultants not only for their technical knowledge, but also for their knowledge of the case and the culture, though this is not currently the norm (Autesserre 2014). It would also be useful if NGOs would take advantage of other sources of country-specific knowledge, such as long-term expatriates, clergy, academics, or local people themselves in order to prepare for evaluation projects. Indeed, as I will show in Chapter 8, ethnographic preparation is necessary not only for qualitative evaluations but also for quantitative evaluation, as designing surveys and interpreting answers in culturally diverse settings demands significant ethnographic knowledge.

The third pillar of the ethnographic approach is *local engagement*. Having accepted that peacebuilding should be seen as experiential, and then completing ethnographic preparation, the evaluator must spend time in the setting and engage substantively with the supposed beneficiaries of the peacebuilding intervention. While other approaches to peacebuilding evaluation call for field missions, even in the best of such approaches work in the field is only a small element of a wider and far more checklist-laden evaluation process (Paffenholz and Reychler 2007: 46). By contrast, the field component is the central event in the ethnographic approach to evaluation and includes the core data collection, analysis and theory formation elements of the evaluation process. In the ethnographic approach, the fieldwork must be long enough to allow the evaluator to come to understand the setting, the lives of the people who live there, and the impacts of the ongoing processes of peacebuilding. While I do not believe it is necessary to spend years in one town, learn the local language fluently, and adopt local ways of living, it is necessary to spend enough time with and among local people to gain some understanding of how they define the social goods that a peacebuilding intervention was or is supposed to be providing. It is this understanding, supplemented by prior ethnographic preparation, which will give context and meaning to data collected through surveys and interviews. Indeed, I will argue that without this contextual understanding, the data collected will easily be misinterpreted and the eventual evaluation will be misinformed.

Throughout the process of fieldwork, therefore, it is of paramount importance that the evaluator engages with an array of actors in the local setting, actively attempting to understand the lives, experiences, and worldviews of those unlike themselves; including the illiterate, impoverished, rural, young, old, women, and unemployed. The practical problems that often limit local lives, such as poverty, illiteracy, isolation, and marginalization, hinder the collection of data among non-elite populations during evaluation, in that many evaluators focus only on those who are, for various reasons, easily accessible. Too often, therefore, evaluation is conducted only among those who completed formal education, have access to structures of knowledge and power, and speak the language of the evaluator. But even if they are nationals of the state within which the peacebuilding intervention occurs, such people do not share the experiences of their less privileged countrymen. As a result, problems of accessibility must be overcome and local voices must be uncovered during evaluation.

In short, the evaluator must go out of their way to work around prevailing social structures and invest time and effort to understand the intervention from the perspective of all the intended beneficiaries. In this sense, the "local" are the population claimed as "beneficiaries" by the intervener and "local engagement" is best described as a good faith attempt to evaluate the experience of the project among representative samples of that population. For almost all contemporary peacebuilding interventions, any representative sample of beneficiaries will overwhelmingly consist not of elites, but of the marginalized, illiterate, displaced, and victimized; unfortunately also those most difficult for international interveners to contact and interview. It is for this reason, however, that problems of accessibility must be tackled and overcome in the ethnographic approach to evaluation. As I will show in Chapter 5, failing to accomplish this task can have disastrous effects for any project hoping to evaluate intervention effects among beneficiaries as local elites have a substantively different experience of intervention than do the "local-locals" (Richmond 2009a: 334).

The fourth and final pillar of the ethnographic approach is the *appraisal of one's own implicit assumptions*. One of the most troubling aspects of the peacebuilding field, and perhaps that which most limits our ability to understand local experience, is that most peacebuilding "experts," both academic and practitioner, seem unable to question the implicit assumptions of their own culture. I remember an early presentation of my dissertation material in which a senior academic – not active in peacebuilding research – responded heatedly to the idea that I would consider justice to be culturally variable. We all know what justice is, seemed to be his argument, the Greek philosophers defined it for us a long time ago. Similarly, much of the literature in conflict resolution, peacebuilding, transitional justice, and development studies is wedded to its own culturally defined ideas of peace, conflict, reconciliation, justice, development, and empowerment. We can see this in transitional justice literature, where there is often an assumed "fundamental conception of universal justice" (Akhavan 2009: 625), and in psychosocial literature within conflict resolution where it is assumed that all conflicts everywhere have psychological effects, such as humiliation (Lindner 2002), victimization (Montville 2001), disempowerment (Abu-Nimer 2001), trauma (Roht-Arriaza 2006: 4), resentment (Murphy 1988), or shame (Retzinger and Scheff 2000), and, therefore, must have psychological solutions (Rothstein 1999: 239). It is also evident in religious approaches to reconciliation (Millar 2012a), and even in some critical appraisals of post-Cold War peacebuilding which fail to question fundamental ideas about the inherent and assumed benefits of liberalism (see, for example, Paris 2004).

The primary problem with this is twofold. First, accepting uncritically the Western definition of a concept such as reconciliation, justice, or development means that we accept an image of what the worldly expression of that concept will look like. Reconciliation, if conceived as a political reconciliation, will simply require the acceptance of an agreement to form a unity government or a public expression of apology for past wrongs by a political leader. But if reconciliation is conceived as more in line with Galtung's (1969) "positive peace," it will require intergroup cooperation, trust, and shared community. The definition we accept of the concept "reconciliation" will determine what we expect to see in the world as an expression of that concept. Similarly, if we accept a definition of development as "sustainable development," then, as articulated recently by Mark Duffield (2007: 56), perhaps all that is necessary is local self-sufficiency, and not state-ensured social services, as have been provided in the Global North. Accepting a definition of development as the provision of social services, functioning infrastructure, accountable governance, transparent bureaucracy, etc. will demand a very different and much more comprehensive worldly expression than mere sustainability. So, the first problem with an uncritical acceptance of the concepts provided by one's own culture or discipline is that those definitions form the foundation of what we will then expect to see in the world.

The second problem is that, for potential interveners, the concepts accepted of justice, peace, reconciliation, development, etc. and, therefore, the expected worldly expression of those concepts, will *govern the action taken* in intervention. For the powerful international actors who fund, plan, and administer peacebuilding interventions, concepts lead to visions of what should be, which, in turn, lead to the design of interventions. This is not a new insight, as many scholars have noted that perceptions of a problem determine one's approach to a solution (Kaufman, 2006: 204; Talentino, 2007: 153; Autesserre 2010: 11), but it is the reason why this fourth pillar is so central to the ethnographic approach to evaluation. If evaluators are unable to step outside of their own view of the world and acknowledge that their own concepts of justice, peace, reconciliation, development or empowerment are culturally defined, they will have no reason to commit to Pillars I–III. Indeed, the entire ethnographic approach to evaluation relies on the evaluator's ability to recognize the nature of their own implicit assumptions and be able to step outside the comfort of culture and discipline. Only through this process will evaluators be open to truly hearing the voices and understanding the experiences of those among whom they work in the field.

Conclusion

Together, these four pillars form the structure of the ethnographic approach to evaluating local experiences of peacebuilding interventions in transitional societies. They are interdependent and it is therefore unlikely that using one pillar without the others will allow an evaluator to accurately assess local experiences. However, as this book will illustrate, when they are used together, they give structure to an evaluative process that both reveals local experiences and provides a pathway towards local empowerment. I argue explicitly that the ethnographic approach to evaluation provides a uniquely substantive form of data and an in-depth understanding of peacebuilding processes and experiences, both of which are needed to address some of the most central concerns within the peacebuilding literature today. The ongoing debates regarding the liberal and hybrid peace models (Richmond 2006; Richmond and Franks 2009; Mac Ginty 2010a), for example, can be constructively approached from this perspective, as can debates regarding local ownership (Chesterman 2007; Donais 2009, 2012), accountability (Murray 2002; Pouligny 2005; Pugh 2010) and engagement (Paffenholz and Spurk 2006). This is true also of the literature debating the trade-offs between justice and peace (Popkin 2000; Bloomfield 2006; Sriram and Pillay 2009) and experiences of globalization and international peace more generally (Keen 2006; Duffield 2007).

All of these debates center on sites of interaction between internationally conceived and applied processes of international intervention and the choices, decisions, or reactions of actors within the local setting. Their central subjects of interest are the "frictions" that exist between externally derived plans and how they come to pass on the ground (Tsing 2005). I argue that justice, healing, reconciliation, development, empowerment, security, dignity, and even peace itself, are by their very nature experiential and culturally variable and, therefore, that debates surrounding the interaction of the international and the local can be greatly informed by applying the ethnographic approach. Without exploring local conceptions of these concepts, scholars cannot fully explore local experiences of international intervention and can, therefore, never understand such frictions. This is what is missing from both small-N qualitative case study analyses and large-N quantitative analyses which fail to engage with local conceptions and experiences. Because the ethnographic approach takes as its central premise the belief that these concepts are culturally variable and demands that scholars center their evaluations on grounded knowledge of how local people conceive of these concepts, it can provide the necessary understanding to engage constructively in these ongoing debates.

It is for all of these reasons that I ask the reader to proceed and, if a critic of qualitative evaluation or if concerned about a move towards cultural relativism, to attempt at least for a while to imagine the possibility that the international community is not as international as some would like to believe and that "international norms" are, perhaps surprisingly to some, not so normal. What the material in this book demands is that the reader reflect on what is largely taken as given within the community of planners, funders, administrators, and evaluators – those who wield the power – and recognize that among those for whom all of this activity occurs those norms are at best contested, and at worst, alien or imposed. What I ask is that the reader consider the possibility that evaluating the impact of international projects with clearly social and experiential aims, demands an understanding of the experiences of those projects among the beneficiaries, and that understanding those experiences requires significant engagement with an ethnographic approach.

2 Historical, political, and social context

Over the course of its history the land and people of Sierra Leone have experienced long periods of disruption. Most recently the country experienced an 11-year civil war that witnessed some of the most horrific forms of violence; including rape, amputation, and the abduction and indoctrination of child soldiers. However, though this small country is home to 17 different ethnic identities, is shared between Muslims and Christians, and is dominated by two large ethno-linguistic groups (together comprising 66 percent of the country), this conflict was not spurred by ancient tribal hatreds or characterized by ethnically or religiously targeted violence. On the contrary, the war was a product of complicated historical patterns of patron–client governance, elite corruption, and individual decisions of survival. Indeed, the war has been seen as a paradigmatic case of "post-modern war" (Humphreys and Weinstein, 2008: 439) or of "greed-driven rebellion" (Ballentine and Sherman 2003: 10) and is, therefore, of great interest as an example of contemporary conflict (Millar 2012b), as will be discussed below.

As the war came to an end, in fits and starts, culminating with a lasting peace in the Spring of 2002, the international community, spearheaded by the UN, began a process of comprehensive peacebuilding. Over the decade that followed, hundreds of different organizations and agencies planned, funded, and administered peacebuilding interventions in Sierra Leone, covering the entire range of available options – from truth-telling processes to economic reforms, democratization to legal services, Disarmament, Demobilization and Rehabilitation (DDR) programs to the Special Court for Sierra Leone (SCSL). As such, this case is also of great interest to peacebuilding scholars as it "benefited," along with Cambodia, East Timor, Kosovo, and a handful of other cases, from a "comprehensive" approach to international peacebuilding and served as a kind of laboratory or test-case for the liberal peace experiment.

This book focuses on only two of the large international projects that have been implemented in post-conflict Sierra Leone. But given the complexity of the case, this chapter attempts to provide the reader with a general understanding of the context within which these projects were administered. The first section, therefore, provides a brief background of the most important historical periods and events that defined the context of the war and modern

Sierra Leone. The second section provides information regarding the key events and actors of the war itself and describes the challenges of the post-war period. The third section describes the settings of my research projects; the city of Makeni and the villages within the FDI project's land-lease area in the rural north of the country. The final section provides a brief description of the two interventions evaluated and used as illustrations throughout the book. As the central argument of this book is that local experiences must be understood within the specifics of local contexts, it is clearly important that the reader have some knowledge of the context of my own studies. This chapter will accomplish that goal.

Background to war

The land that forms modern-day Sierra Leone has long been the site of political, social, and cultural turmoil. Historians have described even the decades prior to European arrival in the region in the fifteenth century as characterized by successive waves of in-migration and "political and social upheaval" (Siddle 1968: 50). This upheaval was spurred by the rise and fall of the centralized kingdoms of the Sahel region in modern-day Mali and Niger and the waves of migrants and refugees spilling eastward along the Niger river, south into modern-day Nigeria and back westward along the Atlantic coast towards modern-day Sierra Leone (Rodney 1967; Fulton 1972). Following European contact, but prior to the period of colonialization, came a further "destabilizing force" in the form of the slave trade (Fanthorpe 2001: 374), during which as many as 20 million West Africans were ripped from their homes and sent either to the New World or to Europe (Inikori 2003: 171).

Subsequently, after the slave trade was made illegal in Britain in the early nineteenth century, the anti-slavery movement itself brought yet further social disruptions in the form of repatriated slaves. There came first three small groups from London, Nova Scotia, and Jamaica (Isichei 1977: 128), which would together form the nucleus of the tiny peninsular settlement that would later become the English colony of Freetown (Webster and Boahen 1970: 131). After this, with the creation of an English naval squadron and a "Court of Vice-Admiralty" to try slaving crews in Freetown (Porter 1963: 11), there came an even larger group of freed slaves known as the "recaptives." This group was composed of the many different West African peoples freed from slave ships off the Atlantic coast. Together these two groups, over time and with much mingling and cultural interaction, multiplied the size of the Freetown colony (Isichei 1977: 129) and formed a new society on the West Coast of Africa.

The Creole society that emerged – a mixture of English culture and those of the many West African societies from which the freed slaves had been taken – flourished in the small colony and produced "many of the 'firsts' of the professional class of West Africa," doctors, lawyers, clergy and businessmen (Webster and Boahen 1970: 136). As such, the Creoles felt themselves a civilized and capable extension of European society, equipped to work alongside the English in governance and trade, and for some years they were considered so by the English and served in many high posts within the colonial administration. However, in 1886, the British decided to extend their rule from the colony on the peninsula to the Sierra Leonean hinterland; the upland regions previously excluded from the colony and largely untouched by British administration. With this decision the peoples of the new "protectorate" came to threaten the Creole place in the colony's hierarchy. The Creoles were greatly outnumbered and saw themselves as under threat from the population of the protectorate, who shared little culturally or linguistically with the colony. This conflict was only further aggravated by the "Mende Rising" in the south of the country (Keen 2005: 9), during which the Mende tribe that dominates the south and east of Sierra Leone even today "attacked all the Europeans and Creoles, missionaries and traders, in their midst" (Isichei 1977: 198). This clash, together with the threat posed to their political and economic dominance by the protectorate, led to a historically significant divide between the Creoles and the protectorate peoples (Kandeh 1992: 83); a divide that echoes even today in the ongoing rift between Freetown and the districts.

However, even more important has been the divide between the Mende and Temne within the protectorate itself. It was this divide within the protectorate, between the Mende in the South and East and the Temne in the North and West (each comprising about one-third of the country's total population) which, when sparked by political competition at the very birth of the nation in 1961, provided fuel for much of the political and military conflicts in later years. As independence approached, and it became clear that the protectorate would wield power in an independent Sierra Leone due to its numerical advantage over the Creoles on the peninsula, the two main rivals for power in the protectorate, Milton Margai and Siaka Stevens, consolidated organizations centered on tribal identifications. The Temne and smaller groups in the north broadly supported Stevens' All Peoples Congress (APC) Party, while the Mende and associated groups in the south overwhelmingly supported Margai's Sierra Leone People's Party (SLPP) (Pedler 1979: 41).

In the run-up to independence, animosity between these two groups was so strong that Margai had Stevens imprisoned even before independence was granted on April 27, 1961, while he proceeded to take power and became the country's first prime-minister. By 1967, the rivalry between the two parties had become so toxic that the army attempted a coup in order to maintain order (ibid.: 246). Shortly after, a national election was so closely contested that the governor-general had to call it in favor of Stevens' APC. However, this victory was quickly overturned when the return to democracy was aborted by yet another coup and a short period of military governance. Perhaps not surprisingly, when civilian government eventually returned in 1968 and Stevens finally held power for the first time under APC rule, he quickly proceeded to consolidate power, unseat SLPP parliamentarians, and place restrictions on the military. Over the next decade Stevens built his APC Party into the central organ of the state and eventually orchestrated what Pham has called the "farcical referendum" of 1978, which allowed the creation of a one-party state (2007: 36). It was this party that ruled the country up until the outbreak of war in 1991.

And so we see that, from the waves of in-migration and tribal instability before European contact to the slavery and colonialism after contact, and on to the pre-independence domination of the Creoles and the post-independence rift between the Temne and Mende, Sierra Leone has been a land of regular disruptions. Relative to these periods of economic, social, and political upheaval the 23-year APC rule that followed Stevens' rise to power could almost be seen as a period of stability, if it were not for the progressive decline in the nation's fortunes over that time. Indeed, by the late 1980s, after two decades of APC rule, the complete retraction of the state's administrative capacity, the collapse of the social welfare system, the suppression of any political alternatives to the APC, and the rise in poverty and unemployment throughout the country, had led to a tense and combustible situation. One that was ripe for war and the invasion of the Revolutionary United Front (RUF).

War in Sierra Leone

Analysts have identified a number of potential reasons for the war in Sierra Leone. These include the scale of impoverishment (Pham 2007: 36), the conflict in neighboring Liberia (Bøås 2001: 714), and the presence of large amounts of alluvial diamonds in the country (Gberie 2005). Others point to the system of patrimonial government operative prior to the war and the crisis of patrimonialism that ensued when resources became scarce and patrons could no longer provide for their clients (Reno 1997: 203; Kpundeh 2004), which Richards argues led to a "sectarian intellectual response to the perceived corruption of a metropolitan patrimonial elite" (1996: xviii). Other analysts, such as Muana (1997), Abdullah (1998), Kandeh (1999), and Fanthorpe (2006), argue that the war is best explained as a lumpen-proletarian response to violence, where the unemployed and uneducated masses (primarily youth) took their opportunities where they found them and violence became as much about survival as about ideology. Such scholars highlight the often very individual and local motivations for violence within contexts characterized by deprivation and lack of opportunity (see particularly Archibald and Richards 2002). However, in the final analysis, it seems that no one cause provides a full explanation of the war; that "[v]iolence does not have only one logic, but several" (Bangura 1997: 130).

An additional scholarly debate has ensued regarding not why the war started, but why it went on for so long and why it became so violent. In this regard Arthur Abraham has noted that the war lasted so long not because of the "strength and power of the RUF," but because of the "debased responses" of the various governing bodies that came to power throughout the period (2004: 120). Indeed, an impressive succession of governments either failed to counter or became actively involved in this progression of violence. For example, according to its leader, Foday Sankoh, the RUF began the "revolution" in 1991 to unseat the APC government of Joseph Saidu Momoh – the hand-picked successor to Siaka Stevens. However, when in little over a year of fighting Momoh was overthrown by the National Provisional Ruling Council (NPRC), the war did not end. Although the RUF called a ceasefire, Valentine Strasser, the leader of the NPRC and the youngest head of state in the world at the time, dismissed the rebels as "bandits sent by Charles Taylor to wreak havoc on the country." Instead of planning for a peaceful post-APC Sierra Leone, Strasser demanded a complete surrender and turned his guns on the RUF (Gberie 2005: 74). A massive NPRC offensive on RUF positions quickly led to the RUF being scattered and disorganized but they were not defeated. In fact, shortly before Christmas 1994, "the RUF launched a major offensive" throughout the country and was quickly within a few miles of Freetown (Bøås 2001: 714).

Over time, the NPRC proved itself not only incapable of defeating the RUF, but just as corrupt and incapable of governance as Momoh's APC had been. As a result, defections from the army began to become prominent at the same time that the RUF was launching its 1994 offensive, leaving holes in the army's defenses and adding trained soldiers to the RUF forces (Gberie 2005: 80–81). Strasser's government was coming under increasing pressure and his army was unable to repel the RUF advance on Freetown. His response was to announce a speedy return to democracy (Bøås 2001: 715), and again, this seems to have been a point when the RUF could have laid down its weapons and accepted democratic governance, as Sankoh had claimed was their goal. Instead they pressed their military advantage and drove the NPRC to hire two mercenary groups – first, the Gurkha Security Guards (GSG) and then the South African Executive Outcomes (EO) – in an effort to keep the RUF out of Freetown. In this volatile climate, Strasser was ousted by his own deputy, Brigadier Julius Maada Bio, just two months before the elections planned for January of 1996. Luckily, Bio did allow the elections to go forward and, in 1996, Ahmed Tejan Kabbah of the SLPP, a former UN bureaucrat, was elected president of Sierra Leone (Kandeh 2004: 129). At this point the near defeated RUF, outmatched by EO, finally did agree to end the conflict and many thought the war was over.

However, a year later, Kabbah too proved incapable of maintaining the peace when he was overthrown by a combined group of former army soldiers, convicts, and RUF rebels calling themselves the Armed Forces Revolutionary Council (AFRC) (Gberie 2005: 94–96). The AFRC came to power "[a]ccusing Kabbah of failing to consolidate the peace with the RUF" and "immediately invited the rural-based rebels to the capital and announced that they were part of the government," describing the united forces as the "People's Army" and declaring the war over (Gberie 2004: 145). What followed was, predictably, "[l]ooting and apparently aimless destruction of property, raping of women and general vandalism" throughout Freetown (ibid.: 147). There was an "unprecedented level of carnage upon the city" and about 90 percent of eastern Freetown was destroyed while the AFRC forces killed "an estimated 5,000–6,000 people and injured, maimed, raped, and abducted thousands more" (Williams 2001: 156–57).

Peace was not restored until troops from the Economic Community of West African States (ECOWAS) forced the AFRC out of Freetown and restored Kabbah to power in 1999. The peace accord signed in Lomé, Togo, on July 7, 1999, officially ended the conflict, provided a blanket amnesty to the rebel forces, and appointed Foday Sankoh the "director of the National Resources Commission" (Williams 2001: 140). However, unsurprisingly, the Lomé Accord did not actually end the violence, Kabbah proved again incapable of maintaining order while the RUF increasingly and flagrantly breached the accords. Eventually this stimulated a military reaction from the British government who deployed 1300 troops tasked with "equipping the Sierra Leone government with an effective and accountable military … restor[ing] momentum to the peace process … and reduc[ing] the incentive that the illicit trade in diamonds had provided for the violence" (ibid.: 140). These operations were successful, control was restored, and the violence largely stopped, finally. Formal fighting was eventually ended in the Spring of 2002, after 11 years of sporadic warfare.

Today, over a decade since the violence of the war ended, Sierra Leone is a country wrestling with the combined effects of two decades of failed government, followed by more than a decade of civil war and another of plodding reconstruction. The country is in a sad state by any world standards and, though there is now peace, it is no less afflicted with the ills of deprivation and poverty than it was more than two decades ago when the war began. According to the United Nations Human Development Index (HDI), in 2013, Sierra Leone had the lowest life expectancy in the world, at 48.1 years (UNDP 2013: 24), 77 percent of the population was living in poverty (ibid.: 27), and the country as a whole was ranked 177th out of the 186 countries included in the Index (ibid.: 146). The poverty that pervades the country only compounds the legacy of wartime violence and destruction (Shaw 2010). Progress is being made, but only slowly and largely in areas where progress is a straightforward matter. Much attention, for example, is paid to the rebuilding of roads, the reconnection of the railway line and ports for the export of iron and other mining products, and the completion of the new hydroelectric plant at Bumbuna; all easily measurable achievements touted by the elites of the country and the international development organizations. However, less attention is paid to the amputees, the polio victims, the aged and the unemployed; those who are easily ignored and made invisible to those who evaluate.

The scars of the war can be seen in the tensions that exist within the country. It is etched in many ongoing national debates. Post-war politics, for example, is dominated by the rift between the APC (northern and Temne-dominated) and the SLPP (southern and Mende-dominated), as it was prior to Stevens taking power in 1968. In the still fragile democracy, debates about the causes of the war are weapons waged in a struggle for national political dominance among elites, wherein each side identifies itself as the victimized group and the other as in some measure guilty. Similarly, the ongoing failures to reignite investment and development, provide jobs, combat unemployment, or rebuild schools, hospitals, and utilities, are constantly on the national agenda. While development was sidelined and subjugated to the elite's personal enrichment in the decade before the war, today development and national progress are chips to be dealt in political games. Nowhere is this more important that in the rural north of the country, long underprivileged even within Sierra Leone (Bolton 2012).

The research setting

Makeni

Makeni is the largest town in the north of Sierra Leone and the capital of the northern district of Bombali. From the eastern reaches of Freetown, Makeni is only a 2-hour drive east on a relatively serviceable two-lane highway that passes through lowland bush and dozens of small villages. Only a handful of towns along the way house more than a few hundred people and these are located primarily at intersections where the other main roads branch off towards Bo, Kenema, and Port Loko. Makeni lies where the lowlands, which stretch east from the coast, meet the hills that progressively rise towards the Guinea border. Just a few miles before you arrive in Makeni, you rise up a hill into the village of Makeri and in your rearview mirror you can see the broad flat plain of the lowlands stretching back towards the coast. As you speed on towards Makeni, through a few more small villages now pock-marked with boulders, you meet the twin bulks of the Wusum and Mena hills which overlook the city and form the first significant break from the lowlands since the Peninsular hills around Freetown itself.

The highway runs directly between these two hills as it passes through Makeni, and when in the town you are rarely out of sight of one of these rocky sentinels, named for the husband and wife devils, Wusum and Mena, who live on them. From the top of Mena hill you can see across the entire town, stretching out before you to the foot of Wusum and off to the north where, in the distance, the higher peaks stretch between Makeni and Kabala, in the northeast. From this height, it is hard to make out much detail on the ground as many of the roads themselves are obscured by tree cover, but looking towards the center of town you can see the weathered minarets of the Central Mosque and throughout the town you can see hundreds of zinc roofs peeking out from behind green palms, some brown and rusted and others shining and new. As Makeni is the fourth largest town in the country and has a sizable population of some 300,000 (Bolton 2012: 243), it also boasts the largest market in the north, the Regional Hospital, the Catholic University of Makeni, the Northern Polytechnic, a stadium with a professional football team (the Wusum Stars), and a diverse population of rich and poor, Christians and Muslims, Temne and non-Temne.

Makeni enjoys a series of paved roads, which multiplied from just four during my first extended stay in 2008/2009 to more than ten in 2012, and a rudimentary water delivery system that provides some neighborhoods with communal taps. There are dozens of "entertainment centers" where locals can see Nigerian, Bollywood or Asian martial arts films as well as European football games for 1000 Le (about $0.25 in 2012), and many small bars and shops. Makeni hosts the regional offices of many large international non-governmental organizations (INGOs) such as PLAN and CARE, and even has a thriving handful of dance clubs. In 2008, a very expensive hotel called the Wusum Hotel opened – apparently charging $150 per night in 2012 – while two Lebanese-owned supermarkets appeared between my leaving in 2009 and returning in 2012. More recently, in 2011, a European-style restaurant was established (primarily frequented by the large number of expatriate mining company employees who now live in and around the town), with another opening in 2013. In short, though it has always lagged behind Freetown, Bo, and Kenema in many ways, Makeni is itself an urban center.

However, in other ways, and primarily for non-elites, Makeni retains the characteristics of a rural town. Makeni's market, for example, located near the center of the city and primarily comprised of two main streets in the shape of a "T" and two large gloomy concrete pavilions with zinc roofs and scores of tightly packed concrete slab tables, is a dimly lit hubbub of humanity that has changed little with time. Here young girls and boys work alongside a few men and hundreds of women to sell scores of local staples, from groundnut paste and cassava leaves to rice and beans, locally made shampoo and soap to salt and sugar. At the market some women sit slumped on a half-empty sack of rice or an upturned crate, no longer bothering to try to attract customers, while others cry out their wares and their prices over the din of competing cries and the noise of children playing among the stalls or babies sitting on top of a table here, under a table there. Sites like the market remind visitors to Makeni of the flip side of the development coin.

These are sites where nothing much has changed in the years since the end of the war and struggles go on. In the market, young children – sometimes just 5 or 6 years old – proceed from person to person trying to sell dried fish, pieces of hotdog on toothpicks, hard candies, plastic bags, or any number of other cheap provisions. Here you can often see women barely able to remain awake, exhausted perhaps by the heat, the noise, typhoid, malaria, or some combination of them all. At the lower end of the market in 2012, where the two main market streets come together, you could find a massive pile of waste, swarming with flies and stinking of decay, around which yet more women sat selling their wares, often edible provisions such as beans, rice, fish, cassava and eggs, around and on which the flies swirled. In this way, while the market is a site of commerce and activity, it is also one place where a visitor can see those left behind by progress and "development." While for some the increasing numbers of paved roads, motorcycle taxis, entertainment centers and bars seem to indicate rising standards of living, those working in the market seem to have benefited little from such developments. Indeed, "development" things are located not in or near the market, but on the main road going through town, when the NGO- and corporate-owned trucks can easily stop, avoiding the traditional commercial center of the town.

Other sites that remind us of these distinctions are the lorry parks, where travelers and traders try to arrange passage to other towns and villages. There are two sites in Makeni that serve this function. The larger is on Rogbanai road just north of the city center, near the stadium of the Wusum Stars, and the smaller is at NP junction, at the entrance to the University of Makeni and directly between the Mena and Wusum hills where the Freetown Highway enters town. At both of these lorry parks the press of humanity attempting to cram into taxis, *poda podas* (minibuses), and onto the back or even the roofs of trucks and cars, reminds visitors again that even in this new "developed" Makeni, most people are not enjoying the benefits of progress but are continuing to struggle through life, day by day. At both of these sites young men and women run eagerly to every window of every vehicle begging for someone to buy their cassava, roasted meat, bread, boiled eggs, or whatever else they carry on their heads all day, hoping desperately to earn their day's *chop* (food). It is here too that a visitor can witness interaction between the elite Sierra Leoneans and expatriates in late-model Land-Rovers and the average Sierra Leonean; that of a quick unequal economic exchange; of unquestioned superiority and obsequies deference.

Similarly, while the houses in Makeni are of a regular, relatively simple style, they vary greatly in their quality and state of repair. Regularly a bare unpainted block house, with wooden shutters instead of glass windows, sheets for curtains instead of doors, and patched, leaking zinc (corrugated steel) roof, will stand next to or across the street from a newly refurbished house with glass windows, solid wood or metal doors, whole or even new zinc, and level, solid concrete floors and walls. These are the inequalities of any town, but they are made more evident by the extreme poverty of many lives in Makeni. These sites of interaction and examples of inequality are where the different experiences of peacebuilding and development become most clear. While there are sites of dynamism and "progress" in Makeni today, the majority of the town has not experienced these benefits; many local people are left behind.

In short, while development in Makeni has meant great wealth for some, for others it has simply meant increasing costs for food and housing and a further marginalization from power (prices of some commodities – including rice and housing – doubled between 2008 and 2012). Where most Makeni residents live their lives; on the red rutted dirt roads and compound courtyards that sprawl between the paved spokes of Makeni's commercial streets, life has not much changed. It is here that children roam around in their underwear or take their baths in buckets of water in the front of the house, boys congregate and play football barefoot or in much patched plastic sandals, tired men sit drinking *attire* (Chinese tea) and *poyo* (palm wine) and discus the issues of the day, and women young and old talk, prepare dinner, and keep children in line. These are the voices heard in the evaluation of the TRC in the coming chapters; those who are disconnected from the elite networks of NGO workers, civil society, and international projects; those whom Richmond has called the "local-locals" (2009a).

The villages

The villages within the land-lease area of the 40,000-hectare FDI project, most of which are relatively small, isolated, and impoverished, do not, by any stretch of the imagination, exhibit the wide diversity found in Makeni. While contrasts of fortune and wealth are a hallmark of "developing" Makeni, the villages within the land-lease area of the FDI project simply do not have enough wealth to allow for the same level of diversity. None of these villages can boast even one paved road, none have access to electricity apart from the rare small generator, and in 2012 none enjoy entertainment centers, restaurants, or bars. In addition, while Makeni has been the site of intense expatriate interaction since the end of the war, before the arrival of the FDI project, these villages were rarely the sites of interaction between expatriates, national elites, and the average citizen. Unlike in Makeni where you find many different ethnic groups, Muslims and Christians, and a diverse array of professions and education levels, in the villages the overwhelming majority of people identify themselves as Muslim Temne farmers and petty traders with little or no education. These are people who are generally illiterate, live off the land as farmers practicing subsistence agriculture, have no formal legal title to the land they occupy, and speak only Temne (very few speak even Krio, the lingua franca in Sierra Leone).

During my fieldwork in 2012, I had the enviable opportunity of visiting many of the 90 or so small communities affected by the land-lease project; traveling around the area on the back of a small *okada* (small motorcycles used primarily as taxis) driven by my research assistant. Although no village is quite like another – I visited villages that were as small as four buildings and as large as a few hundred – I believe it is possible to paint a picture of the project area communities as a whole. For example, unlike Makeni, there are few signs that development has arrived in these villages and any inequalities in wealth are *relatively* small. The villages are usually clusters of houses arrayed along a road, or, in the case of villages with no road access, they are clusters of houses centered around the village mosque – an oval of thigh-high wooden posts hammered into the ground and within which prayers are conducted. The vast majority of village houses are of mud-brick construction and thatched roof, with the number of plastered walls and zinc roofs being proportional to the size and relative wealth of the village – a couple of the villages I visited had, in 2012, not one piece of zinc or a single plastered wall. Each household has a "kitchen" in the back of the main house; a round thatched roof constructed on top of a series of vertical poles set into the ground in a circle. Inside the small area of each kitchen sit a number of fire pits and an array of cooking utensils, pots, and pans. Often during the day, while my research assistant and I conducted interviews on a bench or sitting on a wall nearby, women and young girls worked preparing the evening meal in their kitchen; chopping potato leaves, pounding pepper, preparing rice and, I'm relatively sure, making fun of the white man.

Very few of these villages have any access to improved water sources or sanitary toilet facilities. Those located along the river use river water for their drinking as well as washing and laundry and, as most of the villages have no latrines, any human waste also flows eventually into this water source. Those villages located some distance from the river often have hand-dug wells, but these usually go dry during the worst of the dry season – sometimes from February to early June – and alternative sources of water must be sought. Similarly, none of these villages have any access to electric power so there are no sources of light after sunset and none of the entertainment centers, bars and internet cafés that provide entertainment for people in Makeni. Indeed, many of these villages do not even have elementary schools, and those that do are usually community schools where volunteer teachers with very little training work without salaries. In villages that do not have even elementary schools, young students have to walk to another village each morning, and in order to attend secondary school many children must move to a larger town; outside the land-lease area of the project and far away from their home villages.

The larger villages, therefore, might have an elementary school, an open-sided community center where elders hold town meetings and the young hold parties, a communal latrine, a well, and one or more "dry-floors" (concrete slabs on which rice, beans, peppers, or any number of agricultural products are spread to dry in the sun), while the smaller villages, in contrast, are often composed of only a small number of houses, with no community buildings. It was common, indeed, for my interviewees in smaller villages to lament the lack of such "development things" in their villages. On the whole, however, while there are these basic differences between the larger and the smaller villages, and between families within these villages, the differences were minor compared to those in Makeni. Historically there has simply not been enough wealth in the villages within the project area to allow the very large inequalities that exist in Makeni to hold between the families living in these villages. At least until the coming of the FDI project there were few distinctions in actual income and lifestyle; everyone working the land in a similar fashion and living in relatively comparable housing.

It is important also to describe the lands of these villages, as indeed, the social and economic life of a village is primarily rooted in the land and productive capacity it provides. Around all Sierra Leonean villages are the farms and gardens where all village residents have, often for generations, grown their food and earned their living. Gardens are areas planted with long-term crops – usually oil palms – which are harvested and primarily sold for the cash necessary to buy provisions, clothe the family, send children to school, deal with medical or other emergencies, or make improvements to housing and infrastructure. Farms, on the other hand, are areas where the land is cleared and made into *heaps* (round raised beds around which the water can flow), sown with seed, weeded, and harvested. It is here that village residents grow the staples that provide the bulk of their food; rice, cassava, potato leaf, ground-nut, etc. Sierra Leonean farmers rotate their crops and at any given time much farmland is fallow. However, throughout the land other resources are extracted by local people, such as firewood, bush-meat, wild fruits, saplings for construction, and thatch for roofs, and so even land that is not currently under cultivation or part of a long-term garden has value to local villages.

This land, technically still the legal property of the government, is "owned" by the families descending from the original settlers of each village and is parceled out for use to non-descendant or "stranger" families who "beg" for land and often pay a small use fee in cash or in kind to the "land-owning" family, but this fee has traditionally often been marginal and sometimes only a symbolic contribution. The governance of this land is left to these descendant families but is under the eventual control of the local paramount chief who acts as the "custodian" of the land, the repository of the collective memory of the area. It is the paramount chief who is responsible for remembering the history of the families and the land, thus ensuring that there is one final arbiter to decide which families "own" which farm or garden, which families have access to which land, and the specific details of the deals that have been struck and the bargains that have been made. It is true, therefore, that land-owning or "settler" families have traditionally had more control of the land and may have had a marginally better economic position as a result. However, the dictates of the customary patron–client system, as will be discussed in Chapter 6, have placed extreme restrictions on economic exploitation and inequality in such settings. As a result, mutually reciprocal relationships and interdependence have been the norm and, unlike Makeni, large inequalities have been socially stigmatized. It is into these two settings that the TRC and the FDI project, respectively, attempted to intervene as embodiments of specific elements of the liberal peace agenda.

Peacebuilding interventions

The TRC

The first of these, the TRC, is one example of a broader class of institutions – Truth Commissions (TCs) – that have become increasingly popular as mechanisms of transitional justice over the past 30 years. Initially concerned largely with investigating wartime violence committed by the state during civil war and authoritarian rule, the first of these mechanisms were considered alternatives to criminal prosecution in that acknowledgment of past wrongs on the part of the state was itself considered a form of justice for victims and survivors of atrocity (Landsman 1996; Minow 1998: 55; Popkin and Bhuta 1999; Opotow 2001: 154). With the passing of time, however, and with the paradigm-shifting example of the South African TRC in the mid-1990s (Freeman 2006: 26), the TC has evolved into something quite different. More recent versions, following South Africa, have placed significant attention on the *public presentation* of truth in the form of victim, witness, and perpetrator testimonies. Such testimonies are thought to create a "common narrative" and a shared understanding of past events in order to "start rebuilding a new social solidarity" (Sooka 2006: 319).

It is argued by many that these testimonies, presented in public forums and then broadcast to a national audience through the television and radio media, also provide experiences of justice and reconciliation that extend beyond the individuals directly involved in the process. In the case of the TRC for Sierra Leone, this was clearly the goal. The commission attempted this work through a process of sensitization, statement taking, thematic, institutional, and event-specific hearings in Freetown, and four days of public hearings – and one day of closed hearings for women and children – in each of the 12 headquarter towns throughout the country. During these hearings witnesses, victims, survivors, and perpetrators told their stories to live audiences in many town halls and community centers throughout the country and the TRC itself argued in its 2004 report that the public hearings:

> provided the people of Sierra Leone with a forum for private and public acts of reconciliation. These included public confrontations between victim and perpetrator that led to various expressions of contrition and a desire on both sides to put the past behind them.
>
> (Truth and Reconciliation Commission for Sierra Leone 2004: 45)

This claim echoes the assumption that such processes will lead to both individual and collective psychological healing. Robert Rothstein, for example, has argued that "there is obviously an important psychological or emotional component of protracted conflicts," and concludes, therefore, that the "victimized individual and the victimized group need to have their losses recognized by the enemy so that their 'grief is validated' and their self-esteem is raised" (1999: 239–40). Johan Galtung defines reconciliation itself as "the process of healing the traumas of both victims and perpetrators after violence, providing a closure of the bad relation" (2001: 3), and Archbishop Desmond Tutu, the Chairman of South Africa's TRC, had a "tendency to understand the task of the [South African] TRC in terms of the metaphor of 'healing the body' of the nation" (Lund 2003: 113) and the first step towards reconciliation was, therefore, the investigation of the past conceived as analogous to a wound or infection that needs to be cleaned out. Again, the TRC for Sierra Leone itself claimed that its public hearings would "cater to the needs of the victims" and promote "social harmony and reconciliation" (Truth and Reconciliation Commission for Sierra Leone 2004: 231).

It was to explore these claims that I conducted my initial fieldwork in Makeni in 2008/2009. As Makeni is the headquarter town of Bombali district, it played host to five days of hearings between May 26th and 30th of 2003. Over this time a total of 26 individuals presented their stories to the commission, at the old town hall on station road (a new town hall has since been built), and in front of large live audiences and whoever chose to listen on the radio. From all accounts, the first day of the hearings in Makeni was heavily attended, as the commission's sensitization campaign had successfully communicated to the residents of Makeni that the TRC was coming to *help* the victims and survivors of the war. My interviewees described the hall as being filled with young and old, the *big men* (elites) and the poor, market women and school children, polio victims and amputees; a cross-section of Makeni's population. However, as I will describe in later chapters, this early enthusiasm for the process was not sustained over the course of the week, and the process was not, in the end, considered a success by most local "beneficiaries" to whom I spoke. The chapters that follow will explore many of the problems emerging from this process and illustrate the strengths of the ethnographic approach for understanding the nuances of local experiences of such interventions.

The FDI project

While the theorized peacebuilding effects of TCs are thought to be justice, reconciliation, and psychological healing, the FDI project currently being administered over a 40,000-hectare plot of land encompassing over 90 villages and somewhere between 25,000 and 30,000 individuals, represents a very different element of the peacebuilding industry. The hoped-for beneficial impacts of such FDI projects on sustainable peace are rooted in a literature that theorizes a connection between economics and armed conflict and assumes that, as a lack of opportunity and security drive participation in or even the outbreak of violence, economic development and employment opportunities are necessary for peace. Whereas a decade ago Berdal and Malone claimed that "comparatively little systematic attention has been given" to the role of economic motivation in civil war (2000: 1), today this is far from the case and economics and conflict – and thus post-conflict peacebuilding – are today seen as integrally related.

Over the past 15 years significant scholarship has investigated this intricate connection spurred by reaction to the work of Paul Collier and his World Bank colleagues who questioned the long-held theory of "grievance-based" civil war and argued instead that many intra-state conflicts are economically motivated (Collier 1999, 2000; Collier and Hoeffler 1998; Collier, Hoeffler, and Soderbom 2004). Some of this literature argues that if a country gains much of its wealth from extractive industries such as oil, gas, or mining, then those commodities are easily "lootable" by armed groups and can be used to fund insurgency for economic and/or political motives (Ross 2004; Fearon 2005; Lujala, Gleditsch, and Gilmore 2005). While this stream of literature has developed and become greatly more nuanced over time – particularly in a series of enlightening publications organized by the International Peace Academy (Berdal and Malone 2000; Ballentine and Sherman 2003; Pugh, Cooper, and Goodhand 2004; Ballentine and Nitzschke 2005) – it continues to highlight the economic dimensions of civil war and propose economic, financial, and investment-related policies designed to disincentivize conflict.

At the same time, this work has been complemented by the work of scholars such as Kaldor (1999), Duffield (2001), Keen (1998, 2005) and Reno (1997, 2002), who each highlight, in different ways, the manner in which new sources of wealth and particularly access to global markets have created additional avenues for funding civil conflict in the post-Cold War world. While approaching the problem of armed conflict differently, these scholars nonetheless also attempt to describe economically influenced warfare and violence. In more recent work both Keen (2006) and Duffield (2007) have noted the complicity of the West and the institutions of international governance in promoting unstable economic situations in the Global South and encouraging conflict through world-wide economic, military, and political policy. Other scholars have argued that local economic concerns, including micro-economic issues on the ground among those most affected by poverty and violence, as opposed to international or national level economic considerations, also promote conflict dynamics by incentivizing participation in violence (Berdal and Keen 1997; Peters and Richards 1998; Brett and Specht 2004; Kalyvas 2006).

Together this literature has brought a new recognition of the importance of economic factors at all levels of conflict. Economic motivations on the part of states, armed groups, and individuals have been brought into the debate regarding conflict, conflict resolution, and post-conflict peacebuilding. In response to these findings, a number of scholars have incorporated economic reforms, diversification of exports, anti-corruption measures, controls over the export of resources, and sustainable economic development in general into their conceptions of how to create peace and stability within transitional states (Collier 2000; de Soysa 2000; Boyce 2002; Pugh 2005; Nitzschke and Studdard 2005; Mansley 2005; Zandvliet 2005; Jackson 2005; Williams and Picarelli 2005). After all, if economic motivations play a major part in dynamics that lead to or sustain conflict, the argument follows that economic policies must be important in the cessation of conflict and the maintenance of peace. It is for this reason that economic policies have become central to peacebuilding, and indeed, in the dominant conception of peacebuilding today – the liberal peace – economic policy plays a central role. Indeed, to Paris (2004), "marketization" is one of two central lynchpins of the peacebuilding agenda (together with democratization).

The government in power in Sierra Leone today, led by the APC's Ernest Bai Koroma, has taken these lessons very seriously and focused quite intently on this "marketization" as peacebuilding approach; attracting foreign direct investment, diversifying exports, creating jobs, and increasing the tax base of the state. President Koroma came to office in 2007 on a platform that promised exactly such measures in the first free and independent elections run by Sierra Leoneans since the war, and he has since pushed forward dozens of large FDI projects in both mining and agriculture. These are geared to convincing foreign investors that the country is now stable and secure, to prove to his constituents that the country's economic future will be better than its present, and to provide the large number of unemployed youth in the country with employment opportunities (see Cubitt 2012: 43–51, 169). As I was told by a senior member of a national NGO in Makeni in October 2012, the government is concentrating on employing the youth to avoid conflict in the future; nothing else is important if that is not accomplished.

Within this context, the FDI project I discuss in this book must be seen as one plank in a broader liberal economic approach to creating a sustainable peace in post-conflict Sierra Leone. The project arrived in the rural north of the country in 2009, to conduct the initial survey of the available land and in 2010 the first physical work began on a sugar cane nursery in one small corner of the eventual land-lease area. After this, the work progressed swiftly, if not always smoothly, and the plan current during my fieldwork in 2012 was to plant approximately 10,000 hectares of sugar cane in "pivots" – circular fields fed by rotating irrigation arms anchored at the center-point of the field – before the end of 2013. These pivots are distributed throughout the 40,000 hectares, which both provides for more efficient irrigation and allows the company to leave space between the pivots in which villages can remain. However, each pivot is circumnavigated by, and all of them are connected by, wide dirt roads carved by the company so that earth-moving and sugar cane harvesting equipment can be easily moved around the project. In addition, for irrigation purposes a number of pump stations and dammed aquifers have been constructed along the river that forms one of the project's borders and irrigation pipes have been buried which will transport water and fertilizers to the growing sugar cane. Therefore, even though only 10,000 hectares of the land will be planted with sugar cane, the nature of the land itself – even that not under cultivation – has been significantly altered by the arrival of the company and though no villages have been forced to move, most have been forced to relocate their farmland, which has proven to be very difficult for local communities.

In recompense both for the 10,000 hectares that will no longer be available for local farming and for disrupting local farming on those lands which it will not itself be planting, the company has initiated a number of programs to compensate the communities. In total the company is paying $5 *per acre* for the land that is leased, $3.20 of which is paid to the male heads of land-owning families in each village while $0.72 goes to the chiefdom council, $0.72 goes to the district council, and $0.36 is paid to the central government in Freetown. In addition, the company claims that after construction of all roads, irrigation pipelines, and pivots are complete, it will still employ 2000 local people. The company argues, therefore, that it will pump approximately $3 million dollars annually into the local economy. The project design also includes a program to provide rice for three years to the communities whose land has recently been appropriated by the company and to train farmers to produce rice more efficiently. In addition, by processing the waste material from the sugar cane after ethanol is produced, the company will also be able to sell 15 megawatts of power annually to the national power grid.

In these various ways the government and the company claim that the project will be sustainable and will contribute to peace and stability. The company itself also claims that it will improve employment opportunities, food security, educational attainment, and medical outcomes on the project. Indeed, the company has a long list of metrics that they are required to track over the years of the project to record their social and economic effects. This will be accomplished through a bi-annual socio-economic Monitoring and Evaluation (M&E) process which they are required to complete due to the fact that they are largely funded by a consortium of seven different development banks who have, together, committed over €250 million to the project.

We can see, therefore, that the FDI project is the embodiment of the larger international liberal peace approach to creating stability in the post-conflict period, much like the TRC. It is an international intervention into the social and economic realities of transitional Sierra Leone, which claims that it will provide experiences of employment, opportunity, and empowerment. It has been funded and supported by both the state of Sierra Leone and the international community – through the development banks – and claims that its processes will contribute to one of the primary goals of the Koroma administration: youth employment. It therefore clearly embodies the economic aspect of the dominant liberal peace agenda: marketization. However, just as the local experiences of the TRC were significantly different from those predicted by reconciliation and transitional justice theorists, so the FDI project has had unpredictable effects. In the next four chapters, in Part II of the book, I will explore these impacts further, and illustrate why the ethnographic approach can be such a powerful tool for investigating not only *how* local people experience peacebuilding interventions, but *why* such interventions are experienced as they are by local people.

Part II

The four pillars of the ethnographic approach

3 Pillar I

Peacebuilding as experiential

This chapter will describe and illustrate the first pillar of the ethnographic approach to evaluating peacebuilding interventions; the necessity to see *peacebuilding as experiential* in order to evaluate *how* local people are impacted by international interventions. As argued in Chapter 1, there can be little doubt that the success of peacebuilding interventions will greatly depend on the experiences they provide to or inspire among local people. If criminal tribunals do not promote experiences of justice, if intergroup dialogue processes do not foster experiences of intergroup reconciliation, if democracy does not catalyze an experience of government accountability, or if economic reforms do not provide experiences of empowerment and opportunity, then the broader goal of building peace will be threatened. Further, in complex transitional states it is perfectly possible that institutions administered for the purpose of providing justice may be experienced as unjust, that those responsible for inspiring reconciliation can create division, or that those responsible for providing empowerment might be disempowering, and any such unexpected effects may have conflict-promoting as opposed to peace-promoting results.

However, counter to my concern with local experiences of peacebuilding interventions, Richmond and Franks note the "emphasis on institutionalization over local everyday life" and a "lack of concern with local experience" in the case of Bosnia and Herzegovina (2009: 61). Peter Uvin, reflecting on post-conflict projects in Burundi, similarly notes the disconnection between the international agenda focusing on "democracy, good governance, rule of law, and justice," and the local systems in which they intervene (2009: 79). Séverine Autesserre (2010) describes in great detail the professional, institutional, and cultural norms that limit the ability of interveners to effect any positive influence on the local experiences of conflict in the Democratic Republic of Congo. These are but a small selection of the dozens of studies that note similar issues throughout the world and, indeed, I argue that this is a prevalent weakness of the peace industry in both past and present cases. The field as a whole has largely focused on overly technocratic and institutional approaches to building peace and evaluating peacebuilding, largely ignoring how those institutions are experienced on the ground. Further, this failure to acknowledge local experiences of peacebuilding intervention serves to marginalize local voices as opposed to empowering them – to limit agency as opposed to emancipating it – and, in the end, might contribute as much to conflict as to peace. Put more simply, a focus on institutions without attention to experiences in evaluation will fail to provide a true assessment of the on-the-ground impacts of peacebuilding projects.

If we want to accurately assess what impacts such interventions have, we must understand *how* local people experience those interventions. The very nature of the peacebuilding exercise, therefore, demands that evaluators make a switch in their approach to evaluation – from measuring outputs and national-level impacts to comprehending how peacebuilding projects are understood, perceived, and experienced by local people on the ground within the complexity and confusion of transitional states. However, this switch is rarely made, either by administrators or evaluators. Instead, evaluators of peacebuilding interventions have generally: (1) conducted cross-case large-N quantitative studies that use proxy variables to simplify very complicated and culturally variable social phenomena; (2) conducted qualitative small-N but relatively superficial cross-case analyses based on national level data; or (3) conducted qualitative single case studies collecting data among elite members of local populations who are themselves involved in the administration of those projects and who are active members either of local government or "civil society."

For example, large-N quantitative studies have attempted to evaluate the impact of peacebuilding mechanisms at the national level; including research on democratization (Flores and Nooruddin 2009), criminal tribunals (Olsen, Payne, and Reiter 2010; Sikkink 2011), and truth commissions (Wiebelhaus-Brahm 2010: Chapter 7), but these studies have not investigated how individual people experience these processes. Instead such quantitative approaches identify patterns and trends at the national level across cases of transition. While such studies are able in some small way to infer how processes of peacebuilding in transitional states have affected larger nationwide dynamics, this approach does not allow us to understand what local people are experiencing on the ground during or after peacebuilding interventions or why they are experienced as they are.

Similarly, many who conduct small-N qualitative cross-case studies largely analyze national-level political, social, and economic factors; sometimes inferring, but rarely actually investigating the experiences of local people in response to peacebuilding processes. This is primarily the case for the contributions to edited volumes such as those by Rothstein (1999), Abu-Nimer (2001), Biggar (2003), Gobodo-Madikizela and van der Merwe (2009) as well as single-authored pieces such as Hayner's work on Truth Commissions (2002), Paris's (2004) influential evaluation of UN peacebuilding projects throughout the 1990s, and Wiebelhaus-Brahm's (2010) more recent evaluation of TRCs. The vast majority of the case studies included in such volumes contain analysis rooted solely in observations at the national level. As a result, and as Elin Skaar has recently noted, there are almost no "methodologically stringent case studies" on the "impact of truth commissions on reconciliation" on the African continent (2012: 77), and again, such studies fail to provide insight into how interventions are experienced and why.

Lastly, many scholars who do focus on the apparent impact of peacebuilding processes at the local level fail to evaluate the experience of the process among the local beneficiaries of that process, primarily collecting data instead among those who administer the projects evaluated. Regarding the effects of the TRC in South Africa, for example, Allan and Allan (2000) found that traumatized people have an "instinctive need to tell their stories," and, therefore, found that the TRC was beneficial to local communities. Their conclusions, however, were based on data collected not among the general populations of people experiencing the process, but among the staff of the commission and NGO workers who administered the process (ibid.: 462–63). Similarly, de la Rey and Owens concluded that "many conditions necessary for the healing of victims of political repression are present in the TRC process" in South Africa, but they also relied almost completely on peacebuilding and civil society professionals for their data (1998: 269). Presenting more critical findings, Joanna Quinn found negligible "social and political outcome[s]" in her study of the Commission of Inquiry into Violations of Human Rights in Uganda (2009: 175), but she too collected data among Ugandan elites (ibid.: 185). In such cases, micro-level data is collected and analyzed, but it is collected among those administering and not those experiencing the process (see also Cubitt 2012: 138).

There are a few examples of quantitative approaches that have attempted to overcome some of these problems by conducting individual-level surveys on issues pertinent to peacebuilding in transitional states. A series of studies by Mullet and his colleagues, for example, have examined forgiveness tendencies among individuals in a number of post-conflict states (Azar, Mullet, and Vinsonneau 1999; Azar and Mullet 2002, Kadiangandu *et al.* 2007; Mukashema and Mullet 2010). However, this research does not attempt to evaluate local experiences of specific peacebuilding intervention mechanisms. More important is the much-cited work of Gibson (2004), which attempted to evaluate individual experiences of reconciliation in direct response to the South African TRC, and research on experiences of disarmament processes by Humphreys and Weinstein (2007) and on experiences of truth telling in Rwanda by Brounéus (2010). However, while these studies provide useful insights as to *how* intervention is experienced, they have limited utility in understanding *why* peacebuilding interventions are experienced as they are by local people. Explaining why demands far more fine-grained understanding of the local social and cultural context than that provided by survey instruments.

In sum, understanding how and why local people experience international peacebuilding interventions as they do is central to understanding their success or failure. But few studies conduct extensive interviews with local beneficiaries on the ground in post-conflict settings or even attempt to understand experience within complex social and cultural contexts. Exceptions include the few studies taking a more ethnographic approach such as those by scholars such as Isaacs (2009), Shaw (2007, 2010), Theidon (2006, 2007, 2013), Autesserre (2010, 2014), Robins (2011, 2012), and Millar (2010, 2011a, 2012a, 2013), which are based on significant fieldwork studying local experiences of specific peacebuilding interventions. But while these authors do study *how* local people experience peacebuilding interventions and examine *why* through a deep analysis of social and cultural factors, with the exception of Millar (2010) and Denskus (2012), they have not presented this as part of a *structured methodology* of peacebuilding evaluation. This chapter takes on exactly that task, highlighting the central importance for substantive evaluation of seeing *peacebuilding as experiential.* First, we will consider more closely the expectations and experiences of both the TRC and the FDI project.

Expectations of the TRC

As noted in Chapter 2, truth commissions have developed significantly in the past 30 years, from a class of transitional justice mechanism thought to provide experiences of justice simply through the exploration of past atrocities, or what Biggar described as "vindication apart from punishment" (2002: 169), to a public performance of memory on the part of victims, witnesses, survivors, and perpetrators of wartime violence, thought to provide justice, reconciliation, and psychological healing, both individual and collective. The supposed benefits of the process have become so accepted that we have seen the development within international legal theory of a post-war "right to truth" (Antkowiak 2002; Naqvi 2006; Wiebelhaus-Brahm 2010: 9). This approach to justice differs markedly from the "duty to prosecute" assumed within formal approaches to post-war justice (Orentlicher 1991) and implies a different form of justice; one that claims to be restorative as opposed to retributive. This shift is very closely related to the processes of the South African TRC, during which "restorative justice and its basic principles became a process of international interest" (Menkel-Meadow 2007: 10.4) and which changed the entire approach of TCs (Freeman 2006: 24). Indeed, South African leaders argued that "restorative principles were uniquely suited to addressing the tensions of the transitional context" (Leebaw 2003: 27). Both Evenson (2004) and Schabas (2004) claim that the TRC in Sierra Leone similarly provided a restorative experience of justice which acted as a complement to the retributive approach embodied in prosecution.

This shift also evidences an implicit theory of change, the connection of truth commissions and their truth-telling processes not only to experiences of justice provision but to experiences of community reconciliation. In this model, accounts of past violations are considered central to the initiation of *healing* among victimized populations, and to a healing of the state as a whole (Tutu 1999). The collective psychological traumas of conflict are said to be undone by this intergroup reconciliation process. Indeed, Mendeloff highlighted 18 different ways that processes of truth-telling are considered beneficial in the literature and noted the implicit theories of change connecting truth-telling to justice, social healing, and reconciliation, the creation of an authoritative historical record, beneficial public education, institutional reform, democracy, and the preemption and deterrence of future abuses (2004: 358). While an institutional perspective may remain convinced of these implicit theories of change, investigating local experiences of such truth-telling processes forces us to recognize quite different realities.

Experiences of the TRC

If we are to approach peacebuilding as experiential, we must make a conscious choice to reject the top-down, institutional, interventionist, or technocratic perspective (see also Richmond 2012: 371). The task demands that we determine how the processes of the TRC were experienced; to evaluate if it was indeed experienced by the supposed beneficiaries as the theory predicts. To do this, we must ask a series of questions which seem, at first, rather simple; did the TRC provide local people with experiences of justice, with experiences of reconciliation, and with experiences of healing? In the case of Sierra Leone, at least for the town of Makeni, the answer to each of these questions, and for the majority of local people is, no. Quite to the contrary, and as I have reported elsewhere (Millar 2010, 2014), the truth-telling processes of the TRC hearings in Makeni were overwhelmingly experienced in one of two ways: either as a waste of time or as a provocation.

Over my ten months in Makeni in 2008/2009 I explored these questions with 50 different non-elite local people (30 sampled through snowball sampling and 20 randomly selected) and 12 local elites (sampled through snowball sampling). Specifically I was trying to find out whether or not the TRC hearings had provided what people needed in order to recover from the war in Sierra Leone. I did not use the words "justice," "healing," or "reconciliation" when conducting interviews. I learned from speaking to local people informally over my first few months in country that these words would be confusing for a number of reasons. Even among non-English speakers, the term "justice" was associated with the parallel and ongoing operation of the SCSL which people had been hearing about for some time through the SCSL's own sensitization campaign. Second, psychology as a discipline, a practice, or an industry, is nearly non-existent in the country, and so "healing" is not associated with psychic trauma but with physical ailments or injuries. And, third, similar to other scholars, I found that "reconciliation" is a very difficult word to translate, and while the TRC's own sensitization campaign had used the word quite frequently, I quickly learned that to most people it had no clear meaning (Esser and Vanderkamp 2013: 51). Instead, I explored local experiences by asking whether the TRC had helped people after the war, whether it had provided what was needed, or if it had assisted people to forget and to forgive those who had done bad things during the war. These questions were far more easily understood, but the responses were far from positive.

For example, Hanna, a 29-year-old housewife who had attended some of the hearings, noted that after the hearings she and her friends:

> Usually discussed how the TRC only came to add wounds to people. They just came to awaken people's wounds because if a certain thing is past and maybe you just remain as you are, it will be better for you. But recalling the past, it can be more dangerous.

She continued, arguing that:

> The TRC came when the problem had happened for a very long time and you came in just a single day for me to start back and unveil all what has happened, just like I said before, you are coming to *add pepper in my wound.*

Mamusu, a 40-year-old housewife and student at the Northern Polytechnic in Makeni, argued that, "to tell your story every time will not help you forget because at every point in time that you tell your story, so you remember." She felt that, "If there are no stories, people will forget, but if people are to be telling their stories, it is the more they will take it into their heart again." Instead, she argued, what was necessary was for people to be silent about what had happened. As she said: "If they don't tell any story, people will forget because they will find something else to do." This was a message repeated over and over again by my interviewees; that storytelling was a useless, if not a dangerous, process.

One young man we interviewed, Usifu, a 20-year-old still trying to finish secondary school because, like many, his education had been interrupted by the war, made this message very clear. He told us of the negative things that had happened to him during the war:

> The way we suffered for things to eat, you know that all we suffered, we never had something to eat, we were straining. Yes, and also a place to sleep also, some of us were sleeping under mango trees and the rains were falling down on us.

As a result, he said, telling his story was not helpful: "It is really not fine. Even me, now that I have said, I now begin to remember from afar the way we were suffering." Sallamatu, an older woman working as a petty trader in Makeni and who estimated her age to be 35 but looked much closer to 55, had even stronger views on this issue. As she said:

> Because the person that do the bad thing you can't revenge on him anymore, it will only just remind in your mind and it will never leave your

> mind, and in fact if you are able to identify the person as *soon as you see him at any time your heart beats*, because you always remember him and never forget him … you will not forget.

These negative experiences caused a number of people I interviewed to attend only the first day of the hearings – abandoning the process afterwards – and still others decided not to attend at all. Aminata, a 33-year-old housewife who lost her home during the war, attended only the first day, after that she had no more interest:

> Because I just felt that they just came to make me remember what they have done to me before and *I am feeling the pain*. That was why I don't just feel that it is necessary for me to go and attend there anymore.

Alpha, a 25-year-old Mende farmer, said that:

> That program, I don't see no reason to go there leaving my farm work, they have nothing to do for me and to go and sit there for nothing, idle. That was why I didn't go … Because *I don't see what they did for us*. What I get in my farm is far much better than going to sit at that place, that kind of nonsense.

Sadly, among the non-elite residents of Makeni the predominant experience of the TRC's public hearings process was that it was too much talk and not enough action. Osman, a 28-year-old teacher argued that:

> Most of the people failed to go because they just take it to be unnecessary just to go and talk. At the end of the day, you, you've been, you've made them to recall the bad things that happened with you, at the end of the day, they leave you that way.

Unisa, a 44-year-old Temne carpenter held exactly the same view. His statement on this point is worth quoting at length. He said:

> Well, I was having some other things to do, things that I feel would get me some much more benefits because I don't believe that this country, upon all the war we had gone through, we will also take a huge amount of money and spend it on things that I don't believe seeks the interest of many. For reasons that the people were hurt, and if you have been hurt, they need to help you. So if the money that was brought for it to be used for unity and peace and [if] they gave it to people, they would have been able to help people, but if you say that … to talk will make people have peace, I don't see that reality. So that was why I didn't go.

As I have argued elsewhere (Millar 2011a), what most people wanted to see was action. They wanted to see the money spent on physical needs. Amadu, a local area chief on the south side of Makeni, was quite vocal and outspoken on this point. He argued not that the TRC should have presented the stories of witnesses and victims, or even held people accountable through punishment. Instead he provided a list of things he felt would have helped "so that peace would be in the country." Among other things, Amadu argued that the TRC should have "come along with tractors because we have great fields," "sen[t] medicines for us because health is very important" and "help[ed] us to ensure we progress with our education," to "help us to see our children educated."

Even a woman like Sallamatu, already quoted above, who is not herself a wealthy woman, argued that the most needy should have been helped; that this would have been more useful. As she put it:

> You see them broken, you see them not having anything, and even for him to get food, it's difficult. You need to go helping them. Help them because when they came with the money, they did not ask you to put it in your box, but they said that you need to put help for people.

Hanna argued the exact same point. For her:

> To me, *the TRC is meaningless* because the money that was used to help them to go through their program, if they would have used it to give to the people who were directly involved, maybe some will forgive. Because if he turns and sees that what has been missing, I now have something to replace it, then he will be able to manage his life, but if you go to Freetown, you will see a lot of them in the street.

Perhaps the most worrying aspect of local experiences of the process, however, is that a number of interviewees felt that the provocative nature of the hearings process – its requirement that victims, witnesses, and survivors recount the violence of the past but receive no assistance in return – might lead to new conflict in the future. A 32-year-old Fullah trader named Abass argued, worryingly, that:

> Their relatives, what they see is happening to their relatives, and they have no encouragement, and then again maybe they will want to take revenge if they know the people that did those bad things to them … Myself, if any of my relatives would have been affected seriously and they show the person that did this and when the situation with my relative goes worse, I will avenge for my relative.

This echoes a story I was told by a journalist friend when I first arrived in Makeni late in the summer of 2008. He told me the story of an old Pa who had both hands amputated during the war and who had chosen not to attend the hearings because they were of no use to him. As you hear so often in Sierra Leone, this old man was coping; he had managed to press on after the war, to rebuild his life, to send his children to school, to forget *small-small* (slowly). But when he heard on the radio the voice of the man who had *chopped* his hands off, it all flooded back to him, hot and painful. The old Pa remembered how that man had hurt him, maimed him, and in that moment the hate and humiliation returned and he wanted to have revenge.

This is a story that captures in brief the general experience of the TRC's public hearings process among many of the non-elites I interviewed in Makeni. Sadly, while the theory attributes to the process of truth-telling the ability to provide experiences of justice, reconciliation, and psychological healing, the local experiences of the process among my interviewees in Makeni failed to meet that standard. Instead, the TRC's hearings process was experienced by most local non-elites I spoke with as either a waste of time, money and effort – something not even worth attending – or an actively provocative and potentially harmful experience. In this case, approaching peacebuilding as experiential allowed the evaluation to uncover problematic gaps between peacebuilding and transitional justice theory and local experience; gaps which seem to go unnoticed in national-level qualitative case studies or in large-N quantitative evaluations. An ethnographic approach, however, which explores local experiences, can uncover these problems and examine exactly *how* local people experience this intervention. The same is true in the case of the FDI project.

Expectations of large-scale FDI projects

As described in Chapter 2, a great amount of literature over the past 15 years has analyzed the complex relationships between economics and armed conflict. It found that economic motives and dynamics are regularly powerful drivers of violence through their influence on a variety of actors at all levels; international, regional, national, and local. Research focusing specifically on the conflict in Sierra Leone has pointed to the various economic dimensions of the war, including the corruption of national elites (Keen 2005), the crisis of the patron–client system in the final years of APC rule prior to the war (Reno 1997), the extraction of alluvial diamonds used to fund the war (Saunders 2000; Hirsch 2001), and the unemployment and lack of opportunity among the thousands of young people who joined the various armed groups (Abdullah 1998).

This research is consistent with significant literature on a variety of conflicts over this period, including those in Angola, Cambodia, Liberia, Afghanistan, and the Former Yugoslavia. In response to this evolving literature many peacebuilding scholars, policy-makers and practitioners have emphasized the importance of specific economic policies and reforms geared towards realigning economic motivations away from conflict, and towards peace. These thinkers see "a move toward a modern capitalist system of exchange as inherent to the development of peace" (Richmond and Franks 2009: 43–44), and see the primary purpose of economic reform as developing this system of exchange. As Ballentine has noted, peacebuilding requires policies to promote "longer-term strategies of economic diversification and poverty reduction" (2003: 280).

Such economic policies are thought to be beneficial to the development of stable peace for a number of reasons. For example, the management of natural resources that are available for export and profit is associated with conflict of various kinds (Ross 2003), and so the management of such resources is one of the greatest challenges of contemporary peacebuilding (Cater 2003: 35). Economic policies that diversify the streams of revenue a state can tap into, it is argued, can overcome the resource curse that threatens so many underdeveloped states.

In a related issue, as state weakness is another critical problem in contemporary Africa linked to the outbreak of conflict (Cater 2003: 26; Zartman 2005: 278), economic policies that increase the tax base and provide some way for states to fund security and social services can, theoretically, undermine conflict dynamics. Indeed, as Duffield has argued, the collapse of the Washington consensus has led to the "argument that human security requires effective states" (2007: 160), and effective states must be able to fund their provision of security and social services. From this perspective, economic development becomes central to the creation of a sustainable peace.

However, many observers have concluded that sustainable peace requires not only economic development, but a particular form of liberal economics. In this perspective, peace is seen as dependent on the privatization of economies and the development of open markets (Addison 2001; Li and Resnick 2003; Paris 2004; Jackson 2005: 174; Winer 2005: 72). Such theories demand the *opening up* of post-conflict state economies to foreign investment, including in the form of FDI projects such as those which specialize in the extraction of resources. And, indeed, significant FDI has entered post-war contexts in the past decade. One of the primary forms in which this has occurred, and that which is studied here, are what the media, and some academics (see Borras Jr. and Franco 2012; Zoomers 2010; Chu 2010), have called agricultural "land grabs," wherein large tracts of land are acquired by international actors, usually for the production of either food or bio-fuels for export to external markets. This has become a significant issue in Africa over the past 15 years, with over 50 million hectares of arable land in Sub-Saharan Africa leased or bought by non-African corporations or states between 2001 and 2011 (*The Economist* 2011). Based on data from the UN Economic Commission for Africa, those 50 million hectares account for 21.7 percent of the non-degraded arable land on the continent (United Nations Economic Commission for Africa 2009: 129).

Although such investments are sought by African governments as a path towards both modernization and the expansion of the local tax base

(Woodhouse and Ganho 2011: 3; Sesay 2009), many have also recognized the potential for new conflicts over land rights and food security to emerge in response to investment, and particularly in already politically and economically sensitive African states (Mansley 2005: 207; World Bank 2009: 153; Cotula *et al.* 2009: 43). Indeed, some have argued directly that post-war reconstruction based on FDI has the potential to aggravate old wounds or initiate new local conflicts (Zandvliet 2005: 187–89; Del Castillo 2011). Without a full understanding of the local interactions between politics and economics, the "conflict mitigating efforts of outside actors may have the opposite effect of what is intended. They may prolong conflict rather than prepare the ground for lasting peace" (Berdal and Keen 1997: 807).

Hence, while the currently dominant liberal peace approach to post-conflict peacebuilding demands that economies be opened up to market forces to provide empowerment to local people and support to local economies and governments, many question marks remain. As with reconciliation or transitional justice theories that promote TRCs, these theories hold within them implicit theories of change which are foundational to the currently hegemonic approaches to peacebuilding. As noted by Richmond and Franks, "[m]ost of the various approaches deployed by international actors claim to be emancipatory" (2009: 12), and the implicit assumption here is that liberal economic reforms and FDI lead to local experiences of opportunity, individual empowerment, and economic security. Unfortunately, as with the TRC, the outcomes theorized for local non-elites, at least in the case studied here, have not materialized. Again, an institutional perspective on peacebuilding might remain convinced of these implicit theories and quantitative large-N analyses largely fail to evaluate local experiences of the actual events on the ground, but the ethnographic approach uncovers stark problems with this particular element of the liberal peace among local people.

Experiences of FDI-led development

As with the case of the TRC, the central question that must be asked when evaluating peacebuilding as experiential remains: is the FDI project experienced in the villages within the land-lease area as providing opportunity, empowerment, and/or development? Unlike the case of the TRC, which completed its work in 2004, the ongoing nature of the FDI project means that many local opinions and experiences of the project are still being formed. What is presented below is, therefore, a snapshot of experiences as reported by local people in interviews conducted throughout June and July of 2012. These experiences may change over time as the project expands and progresses over the life of its 50-year lease. As of the summer of 2012, however, the experience is far from positive. Let me begin with the local experiences of opportunity within the land-lease area.

To many people, the great promise of the FDI project was the opportunities it would provide. Young people hoped that they would be among those employed by the company, would receive a regular salary, and be removed from the hard labor of subsistence agriculture. Elders, reliant on their children and grandchildren for support in their old age, hoped that their children would be employed so that they could, in turn, secure the economic future of the elders. However, though this was indeed the case for a handful of respondents – and the experiences of this minority will be discussed in Chapter 5 – the majority of those who live in villages where the project has been implemented at this time have had far less positive experiences. While the youth wanted to be employed and receive a regular salary, in reality few are employed permanently by the company and the salaries are far below a level sufficient to support their families.

Indeed, salaries have been both unpredictable and lower than expected for many of those employed by the company. Pa Abu Kamara, a 75-year-old Muslim man in one of the villages that has been engaged most actively by the company and is surrounded by a number of finished pivots, complained that the pay is unpredictable for the young men; "When it comes to payment," he said:

> when they pay for the month, it is half salary they will pay you … At times a worker will work for a whole month complete, they will only pay at times for fifteen days, or for some for five days.

Danda, a 28-year-old in the same village and employed by the company as a security guard on one of the pivots, echoed this complaint, saying; "Right now, we do not have a fixed salary yet … some months can be 250,000, some can be 300,000, some can be 350,000." This was reported consistently in other villages too. Another company employee, a 26-year-old father of two, named Idrissa, working as a field laborer clearing tree stumps from pivots still under construction in 2012 told us that "some months they will pay you 350,000 … some months they will pay like 420,000."

This unpredictability, combined with the fact that these are very low wages for men who might be supporting families of eight or ten people, means that, very often, these salaries cannot replace the value of the food the men would have produced had they simply stayed working on their own farms with their family. When I explored with individuals how much money they needed to survive with their families each month – to pay for food, clothes, rent, education, and medical emergencies – the figure most often cited was more than twice the value of most of these salaries; at about 800,000 Leone. Keep in mind that 800,000 Leone in the summer of 2012 was only about $200, so my interviewees were claiming that it costs about $200 per month to keep a family of perhaps eight or ten people afloat; or $20–$25 per person per month and less than $1 a day per person. These are not exorbitant figures. But the salaries that the company employees are receiving, usually reported as between 300,000 and 350,000 Leones, were only equivalent to between $70 and $81. In short, those who were employed by the company were often trying to support families of eight or ten people on $80 per month; perhaps $0.33 per person per day.

For example, one project employee I met in a village where the company had been working for almost two years described his struggles with his low wages. Rambo, as he asked to be called when I told him his identity would be protected by the use of a pseudonym, explained that he had nine people to look after in his house because though he himself only had a single wife and three children, he also looked after his brother's children. As he explained: "When they paid this money, a few days ago … three hundred thousand they gave me a few days ago, I escaped some of them because the money is insufficient." What he means by "escaped" is that he avoided seeing or talking to the family members he usually supports so that he would not have to share his insufficient salary. Pa Issa Conteh, the headman of another village, who is 52 with one wife and 11 children, put the problem this way; "For us in this country now … if they pay you like 250,000 or 300,000, if you go and buy one bag of rice, that money left is small, and the month is long." Here Pa Conteh refers to the price of the staple food in Sierra Leone, white rice, which, in the summer of 2012 was selling for about 120,000 Leone per bag, and the problem of feeding a family on just 300,000 Leones. His family of 13 would easily go through a bag of rice in less than a month, but after using up the small salary for other food, educational fees, emergencies, clothes, and other costs, they would have no money left to buy additional rice.

A 32-year-old father of three, Anthony, one of the few Christians I interviewed in the villages, explicitly argued that he would not take a job with the company because of the low salaries. As he said: "I don't yet want a job because what I eat when I do farmwork, [the company] wouldn't be able to pay me for that." He continued, describing the cost of food for a family:

> Palm oil is 5000, rice is 1000 for a cup, fish is 5000. [A family will] have to eat up to 20,000 for a day. When you work for [the company] they only pay you 300,000. Can this money which they pay us take care of us?

But unfortunately most of my interviewees were not as educated or analytic as Anthony, who had completed two years of Junior Secondary School, which made him one of the educated men in his village. Most young men want desperately to work for the company, assuming that a salary from a large Western corporation will cover their bills. They are then dismayed to discover how little their salary actually turns out to be.

And so we begin to see the problems associated with an institutional view of the local impacts of the FDI project. Yes, many individuals within the project area are being employed and paid by the company. The company's own estimate during the summer of 2012 was that 1700 local people were currently employed by the project. But is the local experience of the project one of opportunity if it is unable to support the families of those employees? If the salaries do not replace the value of the food that would have been produced on the land through subsistence agriculture, is this an opportunity? Is this empowerment? When I asked people whether they felt the project would spur development, the results were similarly uninspiring. Anthony, just quoted above, and citing the pollutants he believes the company to be expelling onto the land, argued that it could not produce development because, as he said, "When you get sickness and die, you will not develop again." He believed the project was development for the company, but would produce no good things for the people. Isatu, a 34-year-old petty trader and mother of four, felt that the project had failed to provide development, after promising that it would do so. To Isatu, "the arrangement, the way it came the first time, they say if they come into our village they will do this for us, they will do that for us. I have not seen that."

Indeed, for many, the project was seen to have gone back on its promises of development and assistance. I was regularly told that the company, and the representatives of the government who promoted the company to the people, had promised that it would provide healthcare and build schools, that it would take the people out of their poverty and improve their housing situation. And, indeed, at numerous community meetings that I attended between April and September of 2012, I heard statements by both government and company representatives that did make such claims (as will be discussed in detail in Chapter 5). However, most local people living on the project's land-lease area felt that the company had failed to live up to these promises and had, therefore failed to provide experiences of development (the reasons behind this will be explored more in Chapter 4).

However, one of the most damaging problems with the impact of the project is that, contrary to all liberal theory about capitalist economic systems and the liberating power of free choice in an open market, it has resulted not in the empowerment of the people living within the project area, but in the disempowerment of the majority. Theory would have it that the $3 million circulating each year through the local economy in the form of land-lease payments to "land-owners," salaries to workers, and contracts to local companies for construction services would empower people in these communities and give them the resources to do as they choose; make improvements to their land or house, send their children to school, invest in a business, etc. But within the project area, the vast majority of people seem not to be empowered, but to be disempowered by the project.

Most of those living in the area feel they are now dependent on the project for their livelihood. When I asked what the communities will do if the situation does not improve, Momadu, a 52-year-old farmer, described the situation this way:

> We will not stop [the company]. The reason being, if you have a place, and a company like [them] enter there, [and] they work with you good, you will get happiness in your life, because *you will live through them*. But if they are not working with you good, the way you were expecting them,

> it is dangerous, and we don't have anything, hardship is too much. *We are pleading.*

When I asked people directly, if they had power now that the company had come, or if the company had the power, responses were almost uniformly negative. "Well, what will we do, we don't have something to do," lamented Mabinty, a 35-year-old mother of five in a village not yet greatly impacted by the project. "The rich man and you the poor man are not the same, that is why we are just keeping quiet," argued Tutu, a clever and articulate young woman, a petty trader and mother of one in a large village heavily affected by the project. And most worryingly, Rambo stated that, "When a company like this comes, there is nobody who rejects it, because *everybody in the surrounding is surviving through it.*"

Similarly, and problematically, the lawyers chosen by the paramount chiefs to represent the people, but paid by the company, are widely considered to be working not for the people, but for those who pay them. As Pa Moreh Karoma, a 42-year-old farmer in a tiny village in the southeast of the project area explained:

> Who is more than you, is more than you ... *We don't have strength*, because if we have the strength, well, we will be able to take the lawyers for ourselves. But the man you have to fight takes for you a lawyer, is this a better thing?

Further, most people do not feel that they have any power to affect the decisions being made regarding the project. The important decisions are being made only by the government and the company itself. In the eyes of those on the ground, the company has been brought to the people by the government – particularly by a Member of Parliament whom I will call The Honorable Mr. Lansana – and, therefore, over and over again the people I spoke with described the project as something out of their hands; something coming from government that they simply could not question. As Momadu said, "If somebody says this thing is brought by the government, you have nothing to do ... since it *is a company, you cannot fight them*, how can you fight them?" Similarly Danda, the company employee working as a security guard, described the situation;

> Before, we have one of our brothers, [The Honorable Mr. Lansana] who brought this work here. When we want to strike, normally us the town people, he is the one that encourages us and says we should bear up [not strike].

In all, the experience of the FDI project is quite unlike what was expected and predicted by an institutional view of marketization as peacebuilding. To the vast majority of people living in the villages within the land-lease area of the FDI project, the experience has more been one of disempowerment, one more of subservience to or reliance on state and corporate interests than of individual empowerment. The dominant institutional perspective, on the other hand, implicitly assumes that the institution will have predictable and positive effects; building roads will give people more access to markets, paying taxes and regular payments to the regional and national government will fortify the state, providing jobs will be empowering. But evaluation that sees *peacebuilding as experiential* and actually investigates local experiences among "beneficiaries" on the ground brings to light the complexities and begins to highlight distinctions between the implicit theories of the international actors and the actual impact of intervention in local settings.

The added value of seeing peacebuilding as experiential

The data above provide us with evaluations of these two peacebuilding interventions that inform us of some of the local experiences of these large international projects. It should be clear that concentrating on local experiences of these processes provides insights quite different from those provided through the usual institutional lens. There are a number of elements to this approach that should be highlighted. First, the ethnographic approach does not operationalize concepts to be studied and then measure those concepts using proxies. In my research, I did not decide on a definition of justice, reconciliation, healing, opportunity or empowerment prior to entering the field. Instead, I asked local people about issues pertinent to their lives; did the TRC help them to move on after the war? Were perpetrators treated as they should have been? Did the hearings help them to forgive or forget? Do they feel they have power now that the FDI project has come? Do they have enough money to pay for food, etc.? These questions are not attempting to measure experiences of previously defined concepts. They attempt only to inquire about local experiences of the two projects. Both institutional approaches that assume predictable local effects and survey-based research that operationalizes predefined concepts fail to recognize that local concepts and experiences central to peace will vary from those the evaluators implicitly expect.

This is why, in my research during 2008/2009 in Makeni I avoided using the terms "justice," "healing," or "reconciliation." Put simply, those words may not have the same meaning in local contexts as they do in the peacebuilding theory or in a Western setting. The evaluator cannot know what images will be conjured up in another person's mind when they ask about justice, reconciliation, or empowerment. Will that term mean what it means to the evaluator? If you ask about healing, non-elites in Sierra Leone almost invariably think of physical as opposed to emotional healing, so is it relevant to ask people if the TRC provided an experience of healing? Although the situation has developed somewhat since, when I was first in Makeni in 2008/2009 there was one trained Sierra Leonean psychologist in the entire country and he was well past retirement age. In the only psychiatric hospital in the country, patients were regularly chained to beds and they received little in the way of actual psychological care or therapy. In such a setting, where the ideas of psychological trauma or healing so normalized in the West are simply absent (Furedi 2004), what is gained from asking people if the TRC provided "healing" or helped with their "trauma?" The ethnographic approach does not attempt to ask such questions, or to operationalize such concepts themselves, as to do so is to accept culturally variable concepts as universals, as will be highlighted in Chapter 6.

Instead, this approach demands that the evaluator comes to understand local definitions of concepts and by so doing identify the barriers that emerge between the expectations of theorists and practitioners, and the experiences of local people. The limitations of theories of empowerment through liberal economic policy imposed by the cost of living in rural Sierra Leone when compared to the meager salaries paid by the company, for example, point to a clear inadequacy with the accepted theory of change within the liberal peace model. Similarly, the problems with theories that describe truth-telling as the provision of justice to victims and survivors of war are highlighted by the depth of substantive information that is collected when we see peacebuilding as experiential and evaluate it as such. By actually asking local people how they experienced peacebuilding interventions, the evaluator can purposefully and consciously avoid assumptions implicitly reliant on very limited and culturally specific theories of change. Instead, the evaluator can collect data that informs her/him of local needs and local conceptions of healing, reconciliation, justice, opportunity, security, development, empowerment, etc.

Seeing peacebuilding as experiential, because it demands much more intense discussion and interaction with local people, also allows the evaluator to collect much more substantive data. Similar to the process followed in grounded theory (Glaser and Strauss 1967), the evaluator does not instruct the interviewee about what to talk about, but asks broad questions that allow the interviewee to direct the conversation. The evaluator then returns to points made by the interviewee to ask for clarifications and additional detail. When interviewing local people about their experiences of the FDI project, I did not ask direct questions such as "How much are you being paid?" "Has the project empowered you to make your own decisions?", or "Who benefits most in this village?" Instead I started each interview by asking, "Tell me what you know about [the company], why are they here?" After allowing the interviewee to say whatever they felt like saying in response, and to go on for however long they chose (sometimes a few words, sometimes a 30-minute rant), I then used the notes I scribbled while they were talking to return and ask for further detail on the points they had made themselves, showing interest in their own ideas and their perception of events. This approach has the effect both of building trust between the interviewee and the evaluator and allowing the interviewee to relax and feel confident enough to reveal information that goes unreported in surveys and more structured interviews. In rural Sierra Leone, among individuals often completely disempowered by the structures of authority in politics and economics, this is often the first time anyone from outside their family or village has shown an interest in what they have to say.

Finally, an additional added value of seeing peacebuilding as experiential is the ability to explore whether or not interventions are creating substantive experiences of "positive peace" or the simple absence of violence – Galtung's (1969) "negative peace." The substance of the qualitative data collected through the ethnographic approach allows the evaluator to explore local experiences of complex phenomena missed by other methods of evaluation. This strength is exemplified in the data described above, where the ethnographic approach revealed the failure of both interventions to provide local people with substantive experiences of positive peace. In addition, like grounded theory, this approach reveals many unexpected or completely untheorized phenomena, a quality absent in many qualitative case studies relying on national-level data and almost all quantitative studies of peacebuilding projects which have largely predefined their concepts prior to data collection. Chapter 4 builds on this strength and shows how the second pillar of the ethnographic approach – *ethnographic preparation* – allows the ethnographic approach to move from discovering *how* peacebuilding is experienced, to understanding *why* it is experienced as it is.

4 Pillar II

Ethnographic preparation

In Chapter 3 I described the necessity and benefits of shifting our perspective from one that sees peacebuilding through an institutional lens, to one that sees it as experiential. While truth-telling processes are theorized to produce experiences of justice, healing, and reconciliation, and open market reforms and large-scale FDI are thought to create experiences of opportunity, development, and empowerment, I described the significant differences between the theories of scholars and practitioners and local experiences of those projects in Sierra Leone. For example, instead of providing experiences of psychological healing, the TRC was often experienced as provocative, and instead of empowering, the FDI project is being experienced by many as disempowering. These findings highlighted the value of the ethnographic approach for understanding *how* peacebuilding is experienced on the ground.

However, the data used to illustrate these points in the last chapter does not fully explain *why* these processes were experienced as they were. The quotes used present local people's words, which clearly indicate how they experienced the TRC or are currently experiencing the FDI project, but these words alone do not allow us to fully understand the potential reasons behind those experiences, and, therefore, cannot help us to avoid such mistakes in the future. This chapter turns to the second pillar of the ethnographic approach and demonstrates how our understanding of local experiences of peacebuilding interventions can be enhanced by comprehensive *ethnographic preparation*. I will also argue here that this pillar cannot be considered to be optional but must instead be seen as a requirement for accurate evaluations of peacebuilding interventions in settings socially and culturally dissimilar to those within which interventions are theorized and planned.

To illustrate the importance of good ethnographic preparation in order to understand local experiences, this chapter will explore in further detail the local experiences of the peacebuilding projects in Sierra Leone noted in Chapter 3: the provocative nature of the TRC's truth-telling process, and the disempowering effects of the FDI project. The key cultural characteristic that sheds light on both of these experiences – which provides great insight into *why* these experiences predominated – is the prominence of the patron–client system in Sierra Leone (also discussed in Millar 2010, 2011b, 2014).

By choosing to focus on the patron–client system I am not claiming that other local cultural norms and beliefs are not equally important, but only that this particular cultural norm is useful for my purposes both here and in later chapters, in that it sheds light on how local experiences of peacebuilding are related to contextually and culturally specific expectations. So, what exactly are we talking about when we use the term "patron–client?" The next section will provide the reader with an overview of this system within the Sierra Leonean context.

The patron–client system in Sierra Leone

The term "patron–client system" is used to describe a particular type of hierarchical social organization. Wantchekon has described patron–client political systems as best "defined as transactions between politicians and citizens whereby favors are offered in return for political support at the polls" (2003: 400). But in Sierra Leone patrons need not be politicians and support from clients comes in many forms other than votes. Instead a patron may be anyone who controls resources (land, food, money) which he or she distributes to people (clients) who, in turn, provide support, services, labor or loyalty to the patron. In such systems the patron, or as they are called in Sierra Leone, the "big man," is *responsible for* the client, while the client is *responsible to* the patron. In such systems the client acquires a meal, an education, a job or other social good by supplicating themselves and providing services to the patron. In turn, the patron provides protection or resources to their clients.

Such social systems have been described throughout much of the world and, indeed, are probably far more common than the West's much lauded but somewhat mythical "meritocratic" systems. In reality, no society is fully meritocratic and no society is completely clientalistic. It is, however, accurate to conceive of a spectrum wherein some societies are *relatively* meritocratic and others are *relatively* clientalistic. On any such spectrum, Sierra Leone would be located towards the clientalistic end while countries such as Germany or Switzerland would be found at the farther reaches of the meritocratic end. Often elements of social life common within such patron–client systems are labeled as corrupt. The close association of patron–client systems with corruption is evidenced by Sierra Leone's rank on Transparency International's corruption index, where it is ranked at #123 out of 174 countries (Transparency International 2012). But, to classify patron–client systems as corrupt is to label them as the antithesis of some "normal" or universal meritocratic system that is taken to be preferable or even natural. The term "corrupt" implies that something pure has been degraded. But no social system is natural, normal, or universal and both meritocracy and patron–clientism are cultural artifacts. As a result, many scholars have identified various problems with this simple application of the corruption label to African contexts (Chabal and Daloz 1999; Treisman 2000).

Whether or not patron–client systems are best identified as corrupt or negative will be further addressed below. For the purposes of this chapter more generally, the point here is to highlight the deep-rooted strength of this paradigm of power and relationship within Sierra Leonean culture. Nyerges argued that particular characteristics of the Sierra Leonean ecology have led to human labor controlling a particularly high premium and that this led, in turn, to what he termed *wealth-in-people* (1992: 863). He claimed that "[o]n the frontier, the direct expression of and means to wealth is the control of persons, their reproduction, and labor" (ibid.: 863). Nyerges claimed, in essence, that Sierra Leonean society, experiencing throughout history regular waves of new migrants settling new villages and starting new farms (as described in Chapter 2), has been characterized by the constant need, among those who settled new sites, to attract labor and additional population to make their settlements viable. In such settings, the argument goes, a system developed wherein the individuals settling a site would provide access to land and protection for later immigrants to the area in exchange for their support and labor. Over time, such a dynamic led to the patron–client system. This theory, accurate or not, is clearly consistent with anthropological interpretations of Sierra Leone.

For example, Jones described the wealth of one powerful Mende man in the south of Sierra Leone as consisting "not only of goods (both European and African) and fine houses, but also of human beings whose services he controlled" (1983: 103), while Ferme, who has worked for years among the Mende, found that "the first indication of a rural Mende's wealth, be he chief or commoner, was the number of his wives, children, and other dependents" (2001: 172). Among the Mende of the Gola forest, along the border with Liberia, Leach noted that "a big person (*numu wa*) is a powerful patron on whom others depend for political or economic assistance" (1994: 60), while Bledsoe has observed that the control of women was particularly valuable because of the dual nature of their "productive and reproductive capacities" (1984: 456), an argument also supported by Chauveau and Richards (2008: 518–19). For the Temne – the dominant ethnic group in the north – Dorjahn argues that the "traditional ideal was that people should live in 'big households' with sufficient adult labor of both sexes to produce an adequate amount of food to feed all members" (1990: 171) and Bolton has recently reasserted these ideas, noting that "[w]ealth is measured in both people and material" (2012: 10).

However, it is important to recognize that while patron–client systems are hierarchical, with big men controlling the labor of those below them, they are also reciprocal. Consumption by the big men is "balanced by generosity and other benevolent forms of extension to their dependents and supporters," and in this way "big persons are understood as acting within moral limits" (Shaw 2002: 256). Such benevolence is a responsibility and, in many ways, a burden. Among the Mende, Leach describes how big men – big women are also possible in the south of Sierra Leone – often provide their dependents the money necessary for bride-prices, thus "giving them leverage over the labour [*sic*] of both the man and his new wife" (1994: 82), but also providing men with the means to marry. In this way there exists "the implicit understanding that a chief will give his protection to those who submit to his authority and place themselves in his hands" (Jackson 2004: 47). In addition, if big persons fail to carry out their responsibilities in relation to their clients, they risk stepping outside the bounds of the accepted reciprocal relationship. If they do not provide the requisite resources necessary to be seen as a benevolent patron, they risk being seen as consuming more than their rightful share and, therefore, earning the ire of their clients (Shaw 1996: 37; Jackson 2004: 47).

In Sierra Leone, the patron–client system is, therefore, one of mutual interdependence and the various social connections implied knit together individuals at different levels of society. Importantly, such patron–client relationships are the norm; they are the accepted practice. As a result, phenomena that make no sense or appear to be destructive to observers from other places make sense within that system (Chabal and Daloz 1999). What appear, to an outside observer, to be corruption and nepotism are perfect and prominent examples. Certainly from the Western perspective, neopatrimonialism – wherein patrons use the resources of government office to ensure the support of clients in the general population – counts as corruption. But given the locally dominant patron–client system in Sierra Leone, such actions are considered part of the normal practice. During my time in Sierra Leone I have learned that every NGO worker knows the anti-corruption rhetoric. They know that corruption is bad and that it is imperative for development that they "Kick Corruption out of Sierra Leone" (as promoted in a marketing campaign all over the country featuring soccer players on billboards "kicking" corruption). But when it comes down to it "corruption" is everywhere and a Sierra Leonean official who does not utilize his position to provide jobs and resources for his clients, and a lifestyle befitting a big man for himself, would be considered foolish.

One of my research assistants, Edward, once told me the story of the man who found a wallet full of money. The man in the story, along with his son, took the wallet to the police because it was "the right thing to do." He then proceeded to go home, where he realized that he had no money for food that night, so he sent his son to the local shop to buy food on credit. However, when the shopkeeper heard the boy request credit he denied it, because he would not help a stupid man and if his father had given away all that money instead of keeping it for himself and his family when they could not afford food, then he was a stupid man. This story reflects a certain cynicism regarding anti-corruption programs in Sierra Leone, but it is certainly warranted. The fact is that cultural and practical constraints impose themselves on individual decisions and force people to play the roles required of them: either patron or client.

Edward, along with many others I talked to, was of the opinion that there were two primary pressures on politicians forcing them to become "corrupt."

First, the patron–client system demands that important people in powerful positions are able to support large numbers of dependents even if their official salary cannot possibly support such large groups of people. As a result, given social pressures and often meager salaries, there is little to keep those within government or with access to public resources from taking more than they are formally allotted in order to meet those social obligations. Second, it is also assumed that patrons will live like patrons, and dependents like dependents. As Edward stated, if a politician or other big man in town has been in a high position for a year, and is still riding his bicycle to work, people will ask "what kind of man is he, that he cannot drive a car?" This is true even if the official salary for his position is nowhere near enough to allow him to afford a car. It is assumed that a big man has access to resources, and part of the role of a big man is to exhibit his bigness. If you do not perform bigness, you are not a big man.

This pressure even impacts on people much lower on the totem pole. A good friend of mine at the small NGO I worked with during my first three months in Makeni in 2008/2009 was always under pressure to provide for other people, simply because he was employed. When he went to Freetown on a work trip, he was expected to bring food not only for his family (a wife and two young boys living in an impoverished and flood-prone neighborhood), but for the neighbors as well. When his brother was contending for one of the chieftaincies in their home district, my friend was under enormous pressure to donate to the campaign so as not to be "left behind," and even in Makeni, where he lived in a single room in the NGO office without running water or power, he was under pressure to provide help to friends, neighbors, and extended family members who would stop by and "beg" for help. All of this while at the time making less than $100 a month. From this perspective, it is easy to understand how people in such positions skim a little off the top. The patron–client system and the process of "begging" (requesting help or resources from a patron) are not captured within or easily categorized by the western idea of corruption and, as a result, the term "corrupt" itself is largely inapplicable.

In the local perspective, patron–client relationships in themselves are neither negative nor positive. Citing Mbembe (1992a, 1992b), Karlström argues that in Africa "[t]he excesses of autocrats are cynically derided and parodied, yet at the same time applauded and emulated by their subjects" (2003: 59). This is because patron–client relationships are the accepted practice, they are the norm. Indeed, as will be discussed more in Chapter 6, Bolton has recently turned this debate on its head and described such systems in Sierra Leone as practices of love (2012). In this way, the application of a label, such as "corrupt," to institutions implemented within the context of patron–client idioms is inappropriate. Such systems are only corrupt if we assume universal norms, both idiomatic and infrastructural, of Western bureaucratic governance and individuated meritocracy which cannot be assumed in the case of Sierra Leone.

However, when peacebuilding interventions were designed, it seems few of those involved considered how those processes would interact with or be interpreted by people living within this patron–client system. But by introducing massive amounts of resources and importing or creating new patrons overnight, these interventions injected new actors, resources, and institutions into an already existing socio-cultural system. What this chapter will make clear is that such existing socio-cultural systems have significant influence on how peacebuilding interventions are experienced and, by extension, evaluators of peacebuilding interventions must understand local cultures if they are to correctly evaluate local experience. While the emergence in the past ten years of the idea of a "hybrid peace" as a function of local resistance has shown that such a complicated interaction is clearly occurring (Richmond 2010, 2011; Mac Ginty 2011), I illustrate below that the ethnographic approach – which includes ethnographic preparation – is the evaluative approach that can best understand such processes. Understanding *why* local people experience peacebuilding interventions as they do is only possible when significant ethnographic preparation is built into the process of evaluation. In short, local experience is always set within a context and you cannot understand the former without taking the time to understand the latter.

The TRC and the patron–client system

While conducting my research on the local experiences of the TRC in 2008 and 2009, one of the most alarming terms used was "provocation." As described in Chapter 3, many people felt that the TRC's public hearings process aggravated old wounds. One man described it as "pouring hot water over your head," while Hanna, the 29-year-old housewife quoted in Chapter 3, considered the process to have come to "add pepper in my wound," and Sallamatu said that "as soon as you see him [the perpetrator] at any time your heart beats." This attitude, echoed frequently by other interviewees, is the reverse of local conceptions of emotional calming, or what Shaw has described as the creation of a cool heart (2007: 195). But why was the process experienced as a provocation?

The first person I heard use the term which translated as "provocation" was Michael, the leader of one of the local polio victims groups in Makeni in 2008/2009. Michael was quite negative about the effects of the TRC process in general, feeling that it had not provided to victims and survivors as much as the DDR program had provided to ex-combatants. He, like most local people, had very clear reasons for considering it provocative. It was provocative, he said, because there was "no packet for people that suffered" and "nothing beneficial" for those who told their stories. Alpha, a 32-year-old Mende farmer, similarly felt that the TRC:

> Was just provocation as they talk it on the radio … Because they just keep talking about it all the time, TRC, TRC, and *I don't see what they*

> *have done for us*, so it seems as if it is only provocation to those that they seized advantage on during the war.

This comment was echoed by many, including Boubakar, a 48-year-old teacher, who stated: "Well, the TRC, it was just talk that they came and talked. What they talk, *they didn't even do it*. So I do not feel that they even came to help Salone [Sierra Leone]." This is a problem, as I will show below, of expectations. While most people had heard about the TRC before it came to Makeni thanks to its sensitization campaign and regular radio programs and jingles, what people in Makeni took away from the sensitization campaign was that it was going to "help" them, "encourage" them, or "consider" them. However, as I have noted elsewhere (Millar 2010), these are all words which, in Sierra Leone, are used to describe what we might call compensation in the West. Consistent with the norms of the patron–client system, to help, encourage, or consider means to provide financial assistance or resources. As the TRC's own sensitization campaign spent months informing the population that the TRC would "help" and "encourage" them, the vast majority of Makeni's residents believed, with very good reason, that they would be provided resources if they attended the TRCs hearings – food, money, construction materials, educational scholarships, training packages, etc. Many even believed that these resources would be provided immediately in response to the provision of testimony and were disappointed to see that, in fact, nothing was provided.

In short, many interviewees lamented that the TRC had not "encouraged" them and they did not understand this because the TRC was supposed to come and "help." Fanta, a 60-year-old Limba woman living in 2008/2009 at the Panlap amputee camp to the north of Makeni, lamented that "they said if we go and talk, they will help us." How could the TRC expect them to recover from the war if it did not help them? When we asked Hanna how she would have recommended the money for the TRC be spent, she stated that:

> The money should have been used to help the people that were directly involved in this saga, and then the second thing is to bring developmental things, things that will make the community forget about what has happened. Things like building schools or to help the teachers so that they will be actively involved in their service.

Alusine was a 26-year-old farmer and wheelbarrow-pusher. He had attended the TRC hearings but felt, in the end, that they were unable to help him because:

> That money, they came with it saying that they are coming to help the people … Those that are amputated, those whose parents have been killed, they should have been put to school and sponsored … The other amputees now are in camps but there is no feeding and medicines for them. Nothing at all.

Many agreed with Alusine. Samba, for example, another resident of the Panlap camp, believed that the TRC was one of the parties most to blame for the precarious position of the amputees in the post-war period. As he argued:

> The TRC talked very fine but just that talking and doing is not the same … even free medical, we don't get. Right now, go to the hospital, even if it is your child that is sick, you have to pay Le 5000 for clinic every time … TRC had stated that, even in these buses, they had told us that even the buses we should go there free, OK? So the medical business should be free, everything should be free, our children's business in schools should be free but, hey, instead of that they have asked us to pay. Every little thing, bring this, bring that, all of these … some will have to go and beg before they will get.

Douda, another amputee, reiterated this point. Echoing Samba's frustrations, he said:

> They promised us that they will help us for our school affairs. They will help us to come off the streets, not to be begging anymore. And that they will give us [a] little money that will help us sustain our lives … but the number of amputees whom have died in this place now is many. This is the punishment, because if they take you to the camp, and when you fall ill, the money you will pay is too much and you do not have money, and if your family also cannot provide, won't you die?

To each of these men, and to many residents of Makeni, any post-war project claiming to help survivors and victims must provide schools, medical facilities, roads, access to markets, housing, and food in order to bring peace. Truth-telling was not high on their list of priorities. For amputees in particular, living on the edge of society and, in many ways, on the very edge of survival, the idea of truth-telling as healing or as justice was anathema.

Within a patron–client system these frustrations with the TRC's process, with its failure to provide services and resources, must be seen as the frustrations of clients who expect their patron to provide support. The need for assistance from those above you was described by Sallamatu. As she said:

> Only when you have somebody that will be helping you bit by bit and after a while you will be able to forget, and this person plus the length of time this thing has taken place, this person that will come to help you, and after a very long time with the help you get then you will be able to forget a lot more of the things that they do to you.

Similarly, Unisa expressed his frustration with the lack of substantive help from the commission when he told us:

> If your house had been burnt down, if they had chopped off your arms, if they had killed for you, and they had done bad things to you, it should have been that you are being helped for the sake of reducing the loss you have had.

Boubakar too stated:

> I feel if they would have done those things, if they would have assisted that person, you will make him not to remember. If he will feel it, he won't voice it out again. He will say they have helped me for this small thing. He will talk every time how they [the TRC] have helped him to build a place. They won't talk about what they [the rebels] have destroyed for him.

While Kumba told us that:

> Our properties have been taken away, our business have been taken away, we were expecting that since they came to help us they give you money to do business so that you will be able to pay for your children in school … but up till now they always talk sweetly, this was a bad job.

Ejatu was the *Mami Queen* (ritual leader) of the women's secret society in Kalangba, a village about 30 minutes north of Makeni. She was very much in need of assistance in the post-war period and felt that if she had had the opportunity to attend the hearings, she would have received material assistance. But this was only because she too had received the impression, from the radio campaign and the TRC's sensitization efforts that the TRC was coming to provide survivors and victims with necessary resources. As she told us: "They have said it, anybody that goes to testify, they will help you and your children."

In each of these quotes we witness the operation of expectations primed by the patron–client system. The TRC was seen by local people as a patron; as a large organization arriving within the local context to provide to clients the help that they would "beg" for. We can see evidence of this directly in the testimonies presented to the commission at the public hearing in Makeni. At the end of every testimony the commission would ask the victim, witness, survivor or perpetrator if they had any questions for the commission. The leader of the commission's panel on each day would say something like; "It is now your turn to ask questions," and the person giving testimony would have this opportunity to ask questions of the commission. Almost all of the 26 witnesses at the Makeni hearings either requested some kind of aid or asked why they were not already receiving aid. The very first witness at the hearings in Makeni, Mrs. Isatu Jalloh, said, "We, the victims, are suffering but the perpetrators are taken care of. Why is this happening?" The second witness, Ya Alimamy Kogba, said, "I want to appeal to government for the education of my children. Our people are homeless and some live in the camps. I appeal to the government to build houses for them." The third witness, Adama Koroma said:

> This is all I have to say. We have no hands. We should be assisted. If we are assisted, we will have peace of mind. All our children can think for themselves now. They ask us who chopped our hands and feet. We have to make our children reconcile their mind.

And on it goes like this; witness after witness. Each of these requests is an act of begging, a supplication to a patron. As noted above, in Sierra Leone, the act of begging is standard practice; a normal process of requesting assistance from a big man. When a young man needs a job or money for school tuition, he begs his patrons; his uncles, his superiors, or the big men in town. When a family arrives in a village for the first time, they beg land from the headman and other village elders, asking to stay and to farm; to be their clients. This process of begging is the norm, it is not morally repugnant or disturbing but simply how clients approach patrons who are, if they accept this person as their client, rightfully responsible to provide assistance. And, therein lies the problem. To each of these local non-elites the TRC was not what its planners, funders, and administrators thought it was. To the majority of local people, the TRC was a patron and they expected it to act as one (the minority opinion will be discussed in Chapter 6).

A significant element of this problem is the status of those who represented the commission itself. As it was largely staffed by national and international big men, funded by the UN, and transported around the country in big white Land-Rovers, the TRC was automatically seen as a patron. Within the context of Sierra Leone's patron–client system, the conventional role of European, American or UN expatriates is to administer projects, drill wells, distribute food, build houses and community centers, provide resources, etc. Foreign workers, including the staff of the TRC, therefore, were expected to act appropriately as patrons. They were considered to have responsibilities towards the local people, and those responsibilities implied the provision of resources, not truth-telling. That rich Europeans would arrive in their big white trucks and talk – and only talk – was an affront to most local people. As a result, truth-telling failed to have the impact that Western scholars and practitioners expected of it. Instead of providing justice, healing, and reconciliation, it was considered by many to be a waste of time and by some to be a provocation.

The FDI project within the patron–client system

This section will explore further the issue of disempowerment among local-locals in the villages of the FDI project land-lease area and show how understanding the patron–client system allows the evaluator to better understand local experiences of this particular intervention in rural Sierra Leone. Again, here I want to illustrate how ethnographic preparation allows us to move a step beyond collecting impressions about *how* local people experience intervention, and to understand more about *why* intervention is experienced as it is. The issue of disempowerment, described in Chapter 3, is of paramount concern because it is so clearly at odds with the end goals and supposed strengths of post-conflict economic reform and FDI as a mode of peacebuilding. Such FDI projects are supposed to create individual opportunity and empowerment and spur individual creativity and ingenuity in order to kick-start national economies, provide resources for the state, and create positive opportunities for unemployed youth. So, why has this not been the case within the land-lease area of the FDI project? I will argue in this section that this local experience of the project can be explained if, again, we set these experiences within the local socio-cultural context, and particularly within the locally dominant patron–client system.

There are three specific ways that the FDI project, when set within the patron–client system, has resulted in experiences of disempowerment. First, there is the strictly hierarchical nature of the land tenure system governed by the paramount chiefs, wherein whole families are disempowered and, therefore, at the mercy of decisions made by those above them; the chiefs and the elder male heads of "land-owning" families. Second, there is the pattern of economic decision-making even *within* land-owning families that provides elder males with all of the power to decide whether and how resources will trickle down to younger and more junior members of families, thus placing young men, and all women, at the mercy of elder male decision-makers. And third, there is the tendency for a great number of local non-elites to see the company itself as a patron and, therefore, foster dependency on the company itself. I will first discuss experiences of disempowerment and the patron–client system as viewed through the prism of the land-tenure system.

The land-tenure system governing ownership of land outside Freetown and the Western District on the Peninsula rests ownership of all land with the state but custodianship of that land with the paramount chiefs. These chiefs hold the institutional memory of the land, remembering which families settled in which villages and work which land and which families arrived later and beg land from the original inhabitants. As such, the chiefs are usually the arbiters of land disputes and are also the only legally required signatories to formal land deals, whether for lease or sale. Therefore, while families who originally settled villages have a claim to the *use rights* of the surrounding land and the company running the FDI project refers to these families as "land-owners," these families are not land-owners in the sense of holding legal title but only insofar as they are vested with use rights of the land based on tradition and customary practice. This land-tenure system itself is clearly and intimately related to the patron–client system of governance in that the levels of hierarchy within this system mirror those of the patron–client system. The paramount chief is patron to land-owning families (his clients), and land-owning families are patrons to non-land-owning or "stranger" families (their clients).

It is this system into which the new FDI project has insinuated itself and, so far, produced a clear record of empowering those at the top of this system and disempowering those on the bottom. For example, those at the top of this patron–client system (the three paramount chiefs within whose land the project is located) had the most power in the decision to accept the project, those in the middle had some nominal power (the land-owning families), and those at the bottom (non-land-owning families) had no formal role in these decisions at all. This pattern also maps directly onto the pattern of benefits distributed by the project, which will see just three chiefdom councils split approximately $3,550,000 in lease payments over the 50-year period of the land-lease agreement (or about $23,666 each per year), the 250 or so land-owning families (this is an estimate assuming 2–3 land-owning families per village) split an estimated $16.8 million (or about $1,344 per family per year), and the non-land-owning families split exactly $0. Indeed, the only economic benefit of the project for non-land-owning families comes with the possibilities of: (1) land-owning families choosing to distribute money to them; and (2) employment with the project. But both of those potential sources of benefit are quite limited, as both the land-lease payments and job opportunities are largely controlled by the male heads of land-owning families and are distributed primarily to the sons of such families.

Isatu, for example, lamented that her husband would not get a permanent job with the company because "he is not a native here" (a member of a land-owning family), while both Danda, the 28-year-old son of a land-owning family, and Idrissa, also of a land-owning family, felt that it was their status as members of those families that had earned them their current jobs with the company. Danda said that you must have "*sababu*" (connections or influence) to get a job, and Idrissa said that in his town "the ones that are born there, there is no one that has not worked with [the company]." In this way, the non-land-owning families are completely sidelined in the process. They have neither a role in the process of decision-making, nor benefit equally from the project. Instead the non-land-owning families become further dependent on their neighbors.

Bai, a 65-year-old, male, non-land-owner in one of the two villages that have had the longest interaction with the project, a man with three wives and 17 children, said that "They do bring money for the land-owner, but we the strangers are not present where such meetings are held to collect the money. But if you are fit to get a little, the land-owners can give you." He said that they will give a small amount of money to strangers "who they want, like we that are old enough, they give to us. They split small and give to you like 10,000, 15,000 or 20,000 and that's it." In short, the land-owning families do not share most of the money they receive and what they do share is minimal. 20,000 Leone is only about $5 and enough to feed a family for one day (land-lease payments are once a year). In addition, few strangers, indeed, few people who were not elder male land-owners, had any idea where the bulk of the land-lease money was being spent. As Bai described:

> Our land-owners here, from our own observation it is only for their little problems, that's what I see they are using it for. For their little problems, that's what we see they are doing with it because they don't show they are sharing big.

So, as he said, "We, the strangers, are not included except if they give to you." In short, the strangers only receive what the land-owning families decide they should have.

The second issue to be explored is the disempowering effects of the patron–client system *within* families. Just as non-land-owning families are disempowered by the patron–client system, so youth and women are disempowered even within land-owning families. The way the payments from the company are organized requires three representatives of the land-owning families in each village to sign and receive the payment check for the entire village. In each village I visited, the three chosen representatives were elder male heads of land-owning families. It is, therefore, these elder males who both decided to accept the project and who control the distribution of one of the primary benefits of the project: land-lease payments. Much like the non-land-owning families, therefore, within land-owning families even younger males, and certainly women, have very little knowledge of where this money is going or what is being done with it.

Momodu, for example, is a 52-year-old member of a land-owning family who is not considered an elder because his uncles are still in control of family matters. When I asked him why they had agreed to lease their land at all, he said:

> Well, we are young men and they [the company] went to the elders, so the elders agreed with them. Because if they would have met us, we the young men, we would not have accepted them because we know what is going on. But when they met the elders, since they have agreed with them, we just have to stay behind them … After they have arranged, we have nothing to do. That's that.

Idrissa's experience was the most alarming in this regard. As described above, Idrissa is also from a land-owning family, but his own father is dead and the elders who collected the money in his village have not shared the money with Idrissa and his brothers. When I asked Idrissa why he did not have more of a say in how this money would be spent, he said:

> Well, I am afraid for my life because if I stand for that, if I vexed [annoyed] them for that, I am afraid for my life. They will kill me … if I talk, they will say, "This young boy, what is he after?" So if I talk, you will hear them say "You are young."

When I asked Tutu, the outspoken young mother introduced in Chapter 3, if there had been any conflicts in her village over how the money is being spent she replied:

> Well, all over these towns. Here, they have not yet fought over that, but those grudges are among the youths and the elders. When they are sharing [the money], the old people say they are now going [dying] and they are not looking for what is coming later. But our brothers and our husbands are thinking of our future, the young ones, because the old people say they are now on their way to the grave … so the youths thought that [the elders] are trying to imprison the future of those that are coming up. That is the grudge they have.

The limited role for young people is, therefore, a significant source of tension and potential future conflict within the villages. As young men are disempowered by the patron–client system in general, the manner in which the FDI project has engaged the local communities – directly through this system – has aggravated existing tensions between the generations.

Less concerning for future conflict, but just as damning regarding the FDI project's ability to "empower" local individuals, is the manner in which the decision-making has almost completely sidelined the voice of women. Not one woman I spoke to seemed to have had a role in either the decision to accept or reject the project, or in deciding what to do with the land-lease money. Instead, women talked about what their fathers, brothers, uncles, and husbands do or do not do with the money from the project and expressed their own lack of a role in the process.

When I asked Alima, a 35-year-old petty trader and farmer, and a member of a land-owning family, if she had any say in how the money was spent, she said that "the one that my husband brings to the house is the one I see after they share." Fatu, a 44-year-old mother of six said, "We are women. You, a married woman, have no power." Kaday also, when I asked if she felt the decisions the elders had made regarding the project were good, felt that she had no right to question them; "I came to marry here … we came to marry so whatsoever they say we will accept it. They own the town." The company's institutional solution to this problem of female exclusion was to require a single woman to be included on the "five-man committee" that represented each village at project-related meetings such as land-lease payment or sensitization meetings. But when I asked Mabinty, the 35-year-old farmer and mother of four introduced in Chapter 3, if the men on the committee would listen to that female representative, she replied; "They will not listen … they will not treat her well." But even if she were treated well, Mabinty did not feel that that single female representative would represent her. As she said; "She will not stand for me, because I don't know her." And so we can see that the interaction of the FDI project within the patron–client system seems not to empower, but to disempower both young men and most women. This disempowerment, unfortunately, must also be recognized as a potential source of future conflict.

The third and final way in which the disempowering local experience of the project can be understood through the patron–client perspective is perhaps the most difficult for the company to understand and to deal with. This is the fact that they are themselves now seen as patrons. Just as with the TRC before it, villagers fully expect the company running the project to act as a patron. Having reviewed the ethnographic literature on rural Sierra Leone, and understanding now some of the deeply rooted assumptions of the patron–client system, it should be very simple for the reader to understand how and why the company and its staff would be seen as patrons by local people in the villages. For example, local people felt that the company was clearly the powerful actor in the relationship. As Mariatu, a 65-year-old woman in one of the first villages to interact with the company, stated; "*We are under them* because they are educated and they bring the job to us. We do not call them, they came and meet us." Ekmatu held the idea that they would be happy for "*whatever they bring to us*, we are not educated." While Bintu, also 65, said that the company should be responsible for them because "if somebody has a land and they take it, *they should help you* and that help will make you happy."

Worse still, the local non-elites were of the opinion that the company had, like the TRC's promises of "help," promised the people improvements in their lives. Alima illustrated this quite clearly. She reiterated a proverb used by one of the expatriates who had worked since the early days of the project in sensitization and community outreach. As she said:

> They that came, they said their work is like a child. The proverb that they give to us. So their work, *as it is going, that is how they have to increase.* So, if you put somebody on your land and you see improvement [for them] you should think that *he has to help you for something*.

Alima here refers to a proverb which likened the project's development to that of a child, and which I did confirm was used by an expatriate member of the project's social outreach team to inform the people in the villages of the future benefits of the project. This proverb implies that the project will take some time to develop, like a child, but, like a child, in the future it will provide for you. Many of the local people reiterated this story to me, claiming that this is why they feel the project is responsible for helping them in their lives. They interpreted this message as a promise of "help," which, just as in the case of the TRC, was interpreted to mean resources and support.

Similarly, the power that the project exhibits on a daily basis sets it above the local people in these relatively impoverished villages. As Idrissa said; "The money that we want, it is they that own it. That is why *they have power more than us.*" And the people in the villages therefore expect the project to provide resources. The list of community projects people expected to see the company provide includes schools, hospitals, dry floors, community centers, water wells, and new roads. “As they came they should have made hospitals, built schools, and made community centers, and take care of our water wells. So if they do this we shall be happy,” said Anthony. Isatu even claimed that they are responsible explicitly because they have taken the land from the villagers; “It is to [the company] they hope, we all hope, because we don’t farm again. *They have taken our land so there we should hope.*” By “there we should hope” Isatu means to say that it is in the company that they have placed their hopes for the future or on which they now depend.

Over and over again during my six months of fieldwork in 2012, I heard this same interpretation of the project’s responsibility. They are a rich and powerful company. They came to us and asked for our land. Now we have less land. Clearly they are now responsible for us; to help us, to provide for us. The people in the villages had, in their eyes, performed the role of a client. For that reason they now fully expect reciprocation on the part of the patron. Unfortunately, the bulk of the land-lease payments appear to have disappeared into the pockets of a few elder males and most people have seen no benefit from that money. Whereas the company, and peacebuilding scholars, like to see FDI as a central linchpin of the liberal peace and as a process that will empower local communities, in this case, the project is creating a great amount of dependency. For their part, however, the managers of the project have no intention of becoming patrons. In my discussions with them I regularly heard different versions of the standard private industry mantras: “It is better to teach a man to fish than to give him a fish,” “we are not an NGO here to provide services, we are a company here to make profit,” and “if we start providing for them, where will it stop?”

What this means is that the local experience of the FDI project is, in many ways, mirroring that of the TRC. The prominent patron–client system primes local people to see this peacebuilding intervention as a patron, a provider of resources. The local-locals are more than prepared to play the role of clients, to provide the land, the labor, and their support to the project, but if those actions on the part of the clients are not reciprocated by the patron, as Shaw describes, the company will risk being accused of bad medicine (1996: 37), and of not following through on their responsibilities to their clients. I fear that if this problem is not taken very seriously, the project will result in conflict in the future – potentially between three different groups: (1) between land-owning families and non-land-owning families; (2) between youth and elders: and/or (3) between the local communities and the company. Hence, ignoring these complications may not only fail to build peace, it may actively provoke future violence.

The added value of ethnographic preparation

The aim of this chapter has been to illustrate the value of ethnographic preparation for an understanding of local experiences of peacebuilding interventions. The material presented added to that in Chapter 3 by providing an additional layer of analysis; describing in more detail *why* local people have experienced the TRC and the FDI project as they did by placing those experiences within a socio-cultural context. It should be clear, of course, that this added understanding would be impossible without ethnographic preparation. It should also be clear why such preparation should not be seen as a secondary or optional element of evaluation, but must be considered a requirement of evaluation. The unexpected experiences identified in Chapter 3 only become fully understandable when contextualized within the anthropological knowledge developed over decades by scholars with a deep understanding of Sierra Leonean society and culture. This second pillar of the ethnographic approach is, therefore, critical to accurate evaluations of peacebuilding interventions. Simply knowing *how* locals experience a peacebuilding intervention is not really the end goal of evaluation. The real point is to be able to develop more successful practices and for that we must understand *why* peacebuilding processes are understood and experienced as they are. As is noted also by Bush and Duggan (2013b: 21), this requires a far more thorough understanding of local culture than is usually included in evaluation efforts.

In addition, while this chapter has focused on one element of Sierra Leonean culture – the predominance of the patron–client system – and how that element has influenced local experiences – this is by no means the whole story. Indeed, I could just as easily have written a chapter about how experiences of peacebuilding interventions in Sierra Leone are influenced by the local power of religious belief (see Millar 2011b, 2012a) or the local "aesthetics of secrecy" (see Millar 2011b). Each of these important elements of Sierra Leonean culture has influenced experiences of peacebuilding interventions just as powerfully as did the patron–client system, but space demands a focus on only one such element. Indeed, it is more accurate to say that within any setting, a number of such socio-cultural dynamics interact and comingle on the ground and influence local experiences in complicated ways. The patron–client system cannot be fully disconnected from the "aesthetics of secrecy," the prominence and power of local secret societies, or local religious beliefs. No more than American democracy can be separated from individualism, capitalism, or the Calvinist cultural tendencies of the United States.

Such complex settings make for complicated and nuanced interactions between peacebuilding interventions and the local socio-cultural context. These interactions can, in turn, only be understood if the evaluator has gained the initial ethnographic knowledge needed to prepare for qualitative evaluation and to understand the complex relationships between cultural norms and local concepts and experiences. When evaluators try to evaluate and understand local experiences of peacebuilding interventions in complex foreign settings, they cannot be aware of such interactive dynamics without significant ethnographic preparation. As such, ethnographic preparation allows the evaluator to both collect more nuanced data and to make sense of the data she or he collects. Indeed, as I will describe further in Chapter 8, even quantitative evaluations can benefit significantly from more ethnographic preparation as only an understanding of local cultural contexts can allow evaluators to design and translate surveys and interpret responses to such instruments in the field.

It is important to recognize also that the case of Sierra Leone is not unique. Although other settings will not share exactly the socio-cultural dynamics illustrated in this chapter, cultural characteristics will play similarly important and powerful roles in mediating local experiences of peacebuilding projects in different settings. Throughout West Africa patron–client systems are significant, and throughout the upper-Guinea coast (Liberia, Sierra Leone, and Guinea) secret societies and animist religions are common, but in other contexts wholly different but equally powerful socio-cultural dynamics must be understood and integrated into the evaluator's analysis of the data they collect. This is why technocratic check-list-oriented evaluations that collect "standardized information" (Mac Ginty and Richmond 2013: 778) cannot truly assess the local experiences of peacebuilding interventions. It is also why the professionalized and technocratic approach to peacebuilding intervention fails to produce predictable outcomes. Misunderstanding the context, or failing to establish a sufficient knowledge of the local socio-cultural milieu, as is just as common, leaves both administrators and evaluators unprepared to work in social and cultural contexts dissimilar from those in which they were raised, trained, and learned their discipline. However, as I hope is now clear, ethnographic preparation on the part of the evaluator can begin to overcome this limitation.

5 Pillar III

Local engagement

While Chapter 3 focused on the need to see *peacebuilding as experiential* to understand *how* interventions impact local people on the ground and Chapter 4 demonstrated the importance of *ethnographic preparation* in order to understand *why* interventions are experienced as they are, this chapter builds on these points by illustrating the value of *local engagement* for understanding experiences of peacebuilding projects. Even if evaluators consider peacebuilding to be experiential and are fully ethnographically prepared, evaluations of peacebuilding projects on the ground are still greatly impacted by how the evaluator conducts their research, and, specifically, to whom they speak. If evaluators speak only to particular sub-groups of the supposed beneficiaries of any given project – only male ex-combatants demobilized through DDR while excluding female ex-combatants, only those who participated in TRC hearings instead of the broader audience of the hearings, or only residents of urban areas instead of including those in far-flung villages – then evaluations will not fully capture the local experiences of those projects. Indeed, they will only describe experiences among a sub-sample of the targeted beneficiaries.

As briefly mentioned in Chapter 1, this is the case with far too many evaluations of peacebuilding interventions, which are often conducted among the urban elite, the speakers of the language spoken by the evaluator, or even among those who helped to administer the peacebuilding project itself, such as international or national NGO staff. As a result, it is often very difficult to assess the validity of evaluations, as they are regularly based on data collected among individuals who represent only a small section of the beneficiary population. With illustrations from my two case studies, this chapter demonstrates how local engagement can overcome these limitations, uncover diverging experiences on the ground, help to explain multiple and contradictory local experiences, uncover patterns of experience within local populations, and provide some guidance for future policy, planning, and practice to overcome the limited and often unpredictable impacts of many peacebuilding processes on the ground. The key piece of this puzzle, however, is to first define what we are discussing when we use the term "local."

Defining the local

If those who speak English, live in capital cities, or assist in administering peacebuilding projects do not represent the "local," then why not and who does? Using the term itself can be problematic because we can too easily be seduced into considering the local as one homogeneous mass or as geographically bounded, timeless, traditional or essential. Just as problematically, discussing the "local" often results in its being considered only in juxtaposition or subservience to some homogeneous or universalizing "global." Defining the "local" and deciding whose experiences are valid or important can, therefore, be a contentious issue and talking about "local experience" or "local engagement" is difficult; as is true also in the case of "local ownership" (Donais 2012: 9–13). Clearly not all people located in any given village, city, region or country will have the same experience of a peacebuilding process. Further, the "local" cannot be confined to any such easily separated geographic spaces. In cases such as the Liberian TRC, which held hearings in diaspora communities as far away as the United States (Minikon and Shepler 2009; Steinberg 2011), individuals thousands of miles away are still experiencing the peacebuilding intervention. So whose experience counts as "local experience" and what does "local engagement" mean?

For the purposes of the ethnographic approach, the "local" must be defined specific to each task of evaluation. The definition is, therefore, dependent on the defined "beneficiaries" of specific peacebuilding projects and will vary from project to project. If we are evaluating the local experiences of a project designed to provide livelihood training to rural women under 18 within a particular region, for example, then the "local" in this case is rural women under 18 within the targeted region. The "local" is defined by the specific population to which the project itself claims to provide experiences. Similarly, if we are evaluating the local experiences of a criminal tribunal which claims to provide experiences of justice to a national audience, then the local is the nation; all ages, education levels, ethnicities, religions, classes and genders. In other cases, such as that of the FDI project discussed in this book, an intervention will claim to provide different things to different beneficiaries. The FDI project, for example, claims that it will provide tax revenue and 15 megawatts of power to the state. Such benefits need not be evaluated as experiential as they are measurable outputs. However, the project also claims to provide experiences to the communities within which they operate – of empowerment and opportunity – and those outputs must be evaluated as experiential.

Also, in the case of the FDI project, the "local" is geographically defined but demographically diverse, being composed of more than 25,000 men and women, the old and the young, stranger families and land-owning families, spread over the 40,000-hectare land-lease area. In such cases, with such large and heterogeneous beneficiary groups, the local must also be made manageable; substantive engagement must be possible. Local engagement in such cases, therefore, requires speaking to representatives of the multiple groups which comprise the supposed beneficiaries of the peacebuilding project. This is why evaluations that rely only on NGO staff, only on urban elites, or only on those who speak the language of the evaluator should not claim to be evaluating local experiences. The key word here, for the ethnographic approach, is *representativeness.* Local engagement in relation to projects with such large and heterogeneous beneficiary groups must be with broadly representative numbers of males and females, the old and the young, and members of diverse ethnic groups, religious affiliations, and income, occupation, and education levels. Indeed, evaluators following the ethnographic approach must recognize that there are dynamics within societies that demand purposeful sampling within a population if "local engagement" is to be achieved.

For example, in rural Sierra Leone, the vast majority of people are poor, uneducated, and unemployed or, at best, working outside the formal economy; those I have termed the local *non-elites.* Therefore, if an evaluator's interviewees are 90 percent urban, elite, and employed by NGOs or government and only 10 percent non-elite, then this is a disastrously unrepresentative sample. A sample that is 50 percent elite and 50 percent non-elite would still have to be considered highly unrepresentative. On the other hand, a sample of perhaps 10 percent elite and 90 percent non-elite is more reflective of the dynamics on the ground. If most of the population of intended beneficiaries are illiterate, then an evaluation in which 90 percent of the interviewees are literate cannot evaluate the experiences of the population at large. Similarly, as the TRC was supposed to benefit Sierra Leone as a whole and the hearings in Makeni were held for the population of Bombali district, evaluating experiences of the process among only the 26 individuals who were chosen by TRC staff to testify at the hearings would not be representative and could not evaluate the broader local experiences of the process among the beneficiaries as defined by the TRC itself. Clearly such evaluations can accomplish other ends and are valuable for other research purposes, but they cannot evaluate "local experiences" as I am defining them here.

Because the populations of supposed beneficiaries in my two cases are generally under-educated, under-employed, and marginalized from power, local engagement, as I describe it above, must privilege the voices and perceptions of local non-elites; those without access and influence, who have little education or opportunities for formal employment, and who are predominantly ignored or overlooked in evaluations of international peacebuilding processes. As such, local engagement within my evaluations of these two projects is clearly related to the political, economic, and social context of rural Sierra Leone. However, while this kind of sampling may also prove relevant in many settings in Sub-Saharan Africa or the developing world in general, in other settings such as Northern Ireland, the Balkans, or Cyprus, for example, local engagement may require different sampling. This does not undermine the argument that local engagement is critical. It simply means that the local, and who is representative of that local, are contextually defined.

In short, any accurate evaluation of local experience must represent the voices of those who were the target beneficiaries of the specific project being evaluated. In this chapter I illustrate the value of this pillar of the ethnographic approach by showing the added understanding that it allows. While it is true that local experiences vary quite considerably within the population of target beneficiaries, it is also true that there are patterns to this variation which local engagement can uncover. Further, these patterns, once observed, can provide guidance on how to better foster positive experiences among broader populations in future peacebuilding projects. For example, if we recognize gendered differences in experiences of post-war disarmament, such as those recently described in Sierra Leone by MacKenzie (2012), then we know, first, that evaluations relying only on engagement with male ex-combatants or with urban elites will not provide a sufficient understanding of local experiences, and, second, that future DDR processes in similar contexts must take these gendered dimensions of the problem much more seriously and respond accordingly.

Below I first define the differences between local non-elites and local elites in each of my research settings. I then describe the clear distinctions between the experiences of the two groups within the supposed beneficiary populations of the TRC and the FDI project. These findings illustrate the value of consciously considering how a peacebuilding intervention defines its beneficiaries, the need for evaluators to work actively to identify and engage with the diverse members of such beneficiary groups, and the ability of this local engagement to help identify and explore the nuanced nature of peacebuilding experiences.

Local non-elites and local elites

In both of the peacebuilding interventions I have evaluated in Sierra Leone the vast majority of those the projects claims as beneficiaries were what I call local non-elites, who can be compared to those Richmond has termed "local-locals," individuals often rendered invisible by the liberal peace (2009a: 334; see also Bush and Duggan 2013b: 8). These non-elites must necessarily be defined in comparison to a different group, which I will simply term the local elites. This division, between non-elite and elite, proves to be one of the most important in determining how these projects were experienced, and will be used here to illustrate the added nuances of understanding that can be gained through local engagement. However, just as beneficiary groups must be identified specifically for each project, so the pertinent divisions within those groups will differ from case-to-case and it is first necessary to describe exactly what is meant by "non-elites" and "elites" in the context of Makeni and the land-lease area of the FDI project.

Many scholars have argued that a central cultural trope in Africa is the "moral matrix" of power as consumption and "bigness" (Schatzberg 1993), which has also been described as an "aesthetics of power" focused on the "centrality of bodily metaphors" (Karlström 2003: 57). In essence, the powerful are those who can control and consume resources, and who display that control and consumption. This is very much representative of the conceptions and the practice of power in Sierra Leone, where it is said that big men "eat" when they consume resources (see also Bolton 2012). Another characteristic of such bigness, which sets big men in juxtaposition to local non-elites, are the close ties that bind together local elites. Carola Lentz has described what she calls the "different registers of power" that serve as potential gateways to "bigness," including the economic, traditional, and political gateways (1998: 48), and argues that there is a great amount of convertibility and complementarity between these registers (ibid.: 61). Similarly, Michael Schatzberg describes one of the key elements of power in Africa as its "unity and indivisibility" (1993: 449). In this way numerous avenues to bigness are available – economic, traditional, religious, political – and those avenues often complement and overlap with each other.

In Sierra Leone, for example, a local chief controls a lot of land and receives taxes from those who occupy the land, so he can afford to own a business. He may then become even wealthier and support many clients, so he will be able to run for political office. Similarly, a bureaucrat who has risen in the ranks of politics can gain access to government funds and may use those funds to start a business, to support clients, and to run for traditional office; perhaps one day becoming a chief. In this way, while there are different kinds of local elites – traditional, political, economic, religious – the network of big men is quite interconnected and bigness easily transfers among the various registers of power. This is true of elites both in Makeni and within the land-lease area of the FDI project.

In the case of Maken, the 12 local elites I interviewed were members of an interconnected group of males who "owned the town." Although they were political elites (the mayor), business elites (a drugstore owner), traditional elites (the paramount chief) and religious elites (the district chief imam and the Bishop), there was clearly a great amount of overlap between these "registers of power." In addition, few educated English-speaking men were not somehow tied into these economic, political, religious, or traditional registers and those with access to power and money are those who send their children on to secondary school or even university and so the children of these elites are later handed the keys to the registers of power. As a group, these local elites are easily contrasted with the local non-elites; those with little to no education, no direct access to the registers of power, and few sources of support or resources to send their own children to secondary education.

While I did interview a handful of relatively uneducated non-English-speakers who held some authority in different spheres – an Islamic sheik (teacher), a local area headman, and the *Mami Queen* of a women's secret society, for example – these people are differentiated in Makeni from the local elite by their lack of education, lack of English skills, and marginalization from the broader registers of power. These low-level functionaries are included in local religious or traditional hierarchies, but are not local elites. In addition, a handful of my non-elite interviewees did speak some English – a young policeman, a few young men and women who were struggling through secondary school in their twenties, and a couple of community teachers – but though they benefited from a few years of education, these young people were not connected to the registers of power that define the local elites. In addition, while some may identify these individuals as members of an emerging middle class located between the elites and the non-elites, the experiences they had of the TRC's process echoed clearly those of the solidly non-elite whom I interviewed, such as housewives, farmers, unemployed men, market women, wheelbarrow-pushers, petty traders, carpenters, and menial labourers; all of whom spoke little to no English and usually had almost no education.

In the villages set within the land-lease area of the FDI project, the distinctions between the elites and the non-elites are somewhat different, but they are nonetheless significant. In such settings – isolated, rural, and less heterogeneous than Makeni – local elites have traditionally been the elder male heads of land-owning families and the headmen, section chiefs, and paramount chiefs who are chosen from their ranks. In these settings, as described in Chapter 4, the elder males control access to and use of land, accept or reject new tenants, control the labor of young men and women – both of their own families and those of "stranger" families – and largely make the significant decisions regarding resources. These are the men who "own the village." In these villages, younger males, women of all ages, and even elder males from non-landowning families are traditionally excluded from exercising power and influence and, importantly, excluded from controlling the benefits of new initiatives such as the FDI project.

In this rural setting there were previously few resources to compete over other than land, food, and the money produced from palm oil gardens. However, with the arrival of the FDI project and the monetization of land and labor, local elites – exemplified by the three paramount chiefs involved in the project – have found themselves further empowered as both those whom the company requires to sign the land-lease agreements and those who control the benefits of those agreements. In addition, the arrival of the FDI project has created a new kind of local elite – those employed in white-collar positions by the company – who, while usually living outside the land-lease area, are nonetheless empowered to make significant decisions that affect the lives and livelihoods of the more than 25,000 people who live within the 90 villages. These new local elites have been handed significant influence by the arrival of the project, placing some of them in positions above even many of the traditional local elites within the project area.

The influence of these local elites within the land-lease area can be directly contrasted with the lack of influence among the local non-elites, who had power neither to influence the decisions regarding the land-lease agreements nor to control the benefits of those agreements. These non-elites are marginalized from the structures of power and are excluded from key decisions regarding the future of their land. While such non-elites vastly outnumber the elites and are supposedly the major beneficiaries of the project's land-lease payments and employment opportunities, the extent of the benefits they receive is controlled directly by the local elites. This mirrors experiences in other African settings where liberalization of the land market has compounded the marginalization of those who were already disempowered (Tsikata 2009: 15), and concentrated power in the hands of those who already dominated its use (Lastarria-Cornhiel 1997: 1318). While these descriptions of the elites and non-elites in each context are interesting in themselves, they are more important when seen as major factors in the local experiences of the two interventions because, in both Makeni and the villages within the land-lease area of the FDI project, I found distinct differences between the experiences of the elites and the non-elites. These distinctions provide clear lessons for evaluators hoping to understand local experiences of international peacebuilding interventions.

The results of engagement: heterogeneous experiences

The vast majority of my interviewees during my fieldwork in 2008/2009 and in 2012 had experiences of the TRC and the FDI project that diverge significantly from the experiences predicted by those who theorize about, plan, fund, and administer such projects. Whereas the literature predicts experiences of justice, healing, reconciliation, empowerment, and opportunity, most of my interviewees in and around Makeni experienced the TRC hearings as either unnecessary and a waste of time, or as actively provocative. Similarly, most people within the land-lease area of the FDI project are currently experiencing the project as disempowering and disruptive as opposed to empowering and stabilizing. However, in each case, I have also observed clear differences *within* the "local" experience; those who are local elites, in both contexts, experience the projects quite differently to local non-elites. I will look first at the case of the TRC, then at that of the FDI project.

Elite experiences of the TRC

As I have reported elsewhere (Millar 2010, 2011a) and so will only recap here, during my evaluation of the local experiences of the TRC in Makeni it became evident that a small group of people did have positive experiences of the project, or at least remembered it in a positive light, while the vast majority did not. In addition, those who had a more positive experience also *projected* that experience onto others; arguing that most had experienced the project as they had. Further, it became clear that there were quite significant demographic differences between those who reported a positive experience of the process, and those who reported a negative experience. Those reporting positive experiences spoke English, had finished at least secondary education, and were linked into the networks of influence and power within the areas of economics, religion, or politics; they were the local elites.

While these privileged few were not all of one profession, ethnic group, religion, or age, they were almost all male (one was female), educated, and English-speaking. Included here are the Mayor of Makeni, two unemployed graduates of the elite Fatima Institute (now the University of Makeni) who were active in civil society, a medical professional working at the Catholic Hospital on the North Side of Makeni, and a drugstore owner who was a youth leader during the war, active in civil society after the war, and who had, like the unemployed Fatima Institute graduates, participated in the sensitization campaign of the TRC. Also included here are a few people who had worked for the TRC itself, including a staff member, a volunteer, and the director of the local NGO which assisted in the local administration of the TRC within Bombali District. It became clear that this group shared a connection to the post-conflict peacebuilding community, shared understandings, experiences, and evaluations of the process which reflected the international discourse about post-conflict reconciliation far more than it reflected the experience of their non-elite compatriots, and projected that more positive experience onto those less privileged than themselves.

For example, when I asked Alimami, the director of the NGO, who had been involved in administering the TRC in Makeni, if the truth-telling process provided what was necessary in the post-war period, he responded:

> To many people even saying what happened to you is a healing process. It was very helpful, I can still remember some victims, when they were testifying publicly they were crying, and *that crying is also part of the healing process.* It was very much useful.

Similarly, Ali, one of the former students of the Fatima Institute, stated, in response to the same question, that:

> After saying the truth out of your mind, because of what had happened, then *because you've said what has happened, then you can be able to resettle and then reconcile.* From the reconciliation then you will be able to resettle down with the person that has done bad things to you.

Other elites specifically highlighted the power of perpetrators' stories and the effect it had on them personally. Mustapha, a youth leader and another former Fatima Institute student, claimed that:

> The testimonies I did appreciate, both from the side of the perpetrator and the victims. But what I admire the most was that, the mere fact that some, the perpetrators, had the zeal to come out before the audience and speak of what he had been doing to people.

He later said simply that the truth "*touches them, the minds of people.* It really touches the minds of people," and that "people were filled with awe." Similarly Matthew, who had been involved in collecting victim and perpetrator statements with a local NGO prior to the TRC and then volunteered to help administer the TRC process itself, claimed that:

> Most of them, when they listen to this, these types of stories, *they really accepted that they have done bad*, you know? I believe it very important because most of these things, because most of these things come out.

In this way, many of the elites reported positive experiences of the TRC and of truth-telling, not only for themselves, but also for others; claiming that others in the audience shared their own experience or opinion. Abdullah, who owned the drugstore in the heart of Makeni, echoed key themes of the academic reconciliation literature when he said:

> When you have a platform wherein you can pull out your anger or your frustration, your discouragement, maybe when something is within you and you have a forum to voice those particulars, then they will go off naturally. *It is natural for human beings to say or share their experiences when they have suffered, then that will release the tension within oneself.*

Similarly, Anthony, the medical professional working at the Catholic Hospital, argued that truth and revelation are necessary for people to overcome the violence that happened to them during the war because "when someone has something in his mind that he cannot reveal … it works within him." In short, many of these elites, in direct contrast with the experiences of local non-elites as described in Chapter 3, reported more positive experiences of the TRC process. But, perhaps more problematically, they *projected* that experience onto their less privileged countrymen.

Elite experiences of the FDI project

This dynamic is, worryingly, being reproduced within the land-lease area of the FDI project. In this case there are two different but significant elite/non-elite divisions that can be identified as marking clear distinctions in local experience. The first is the division between traditional elites (local male heads of land-owning families exemplified by the paramount chiefs) and the non-elites (women, young men, and stranger families). In this case, again, these local elites simply have very different experiences of the project than do the local non-elites.

For example, in comparison to the negative experiences of the majority highlighted in Chapter 3, one elder male land-owner I interviewed in the villages told me adamantly and repeatedly that he loved the company, and, like the local elites did with the TRC hearings in Makeni, he *projected* that experience onto the rest of his village. Pa Lima was 81 and claimed he had leased 1000 acres of land to the company. He argued that the company "stands to develop the country" and that "I want them to stay 100 years if this is the way they are working. I like them too much." He felt that the company had brought both money and jobs and said that "that is why we are blessing [the company] … because [the company] bring this good thing for us." Pa Lima was the most ardently pro-company person I spoke to, claiming he would thank the company a thousand times if he could. But while less effusive, a few others of his generation also felt that the project was having positive effects.

Some felt, for example, that the project was providing them with some economic security as it both provided funds through land-lease payments and it might employ their children. Thus, 65-year-old Pa Rok described himself as an old man who could no longer work and saw the company's arrival as his salvation; "Look at me" he said, "I'm old … I am sick, but if your child is working and you can get something better, you can have some hope in him." Pa Rok, along with others, believed that young people today do not work as hard on the farm as they used to and cannot be relied on to support their elders. As he said:

> The world we are [in] today is not like the previous one, wherein if you go to the farm in the morning, you be there till the sun set. They [the youth] have their own time. If they go to work … the time will be like 2:00 pm or 3:00 pm, they will leave the job.

Pa Rok was concerned that the youth no longer wanted to work on their farms and that they would no longer be able to support their parents. To him, the coming of the company provided a way for elders to secure their own future by providing young men with easier "white man's work."

Other elders felt that the project would take the burden of supporting their children off their hands. In rural Sierra Leone youth who are not working must be supported by either their peers who have some income or by their parents. Such youth are often considered a nuisance. Indeed, to be "idle" is considered a potential source of trouble. Hence, some elders felt that the company providing some youth with jobs was a double blessing. It meant not only economic security for their parents, but that the potential negative effects of idleness would be countered. Pa Mange described, for example, how the company is able to pay his son 450,000 Leone and this will be better than for him to be at home where "he will just make carelessness." Echoing Pa Rok's concern with the failing work ethic among modern youth, Pa Mange argued that employment with the company provides a check on the idleness of young men.

But these positive experiences on the part of a few elders of land-owning families in the villages seem minor compared to the experiences of the paramount chiefs. While male heads of household are local elites within their villages, paramount chiefs are elites over large regions that comprise hundreds of villages and tens of thousands of acres of land. As such, the three chiefs involved in the FDI project accrue massive benefits from the project and experience it as hugely positive. These paramount chiefs receive substantial economic incentives for their acceptance of the project. For example, they control the chiefdom councils, which receive 20 percent of every land-lease dollar paid by the project; estimated at $23,666 per year for each chiefdom council if this money were divided equally between all three chiefdoms. This amounts to more than 12 times the yearly salary for a laborer on the project. They also receive substantial payments in the form of "transport costs" (reported to be about $90, or more than one month's salary for a laborer) for their attendance at each community meeting. Finally, they directly benefit from the project as they are themselves the male heads of powerful land-owning families and receive land-lease payments for the large tracts of land which they themselves control.

These traditional local elites have quite simply been both the primary beneficiaries and the prime promoters of the project, convincing non-elites repeatedly that it has come for their benefit and will help them to "develop." At meetings with the community, for example, at which the company, the villagers, the government, and the traditional leaders always had representatives, either the chiefs or their representatives spent the bulk of their time thanking the company for coming, praising them for helping the local people, and encouraging the non-elites in the audience to respect the work of the company, not to get in its way, and to thank it for the good things it is bringing. At the very first such meeting I attended in April 2012, the chief thanked the company for respecting tradition and inviting him to participate, for being transparent and carrying out community meetings, and for being better to work with than the mining companies that also were operating in the area. However, he also reiterated to the non-elites that the company was in its early stages – that it was not yet earning profit – and so that they must wait for the real benefits of the project to become apparent. This message clearly echoes the "company as child" parable I described in Chapter 4 and further builds local expectations of the project's role as a patron.

At another meeting I attended, the second of the three paramount chiefs attempted to preempt any complaints from non-elites in the audience by arguing that only the chiefs can play an intermediary role between the people and the company and that they will "cool the situation" and convince the local people to "*hold their hearts.*" He directly said that those employed by the company should not cause problems with the company over their salaries, they "should not grumble," he argued. Instead, any problems "should be brought to the chiefs." However, when in the field, I came across people who had taken their complaints about the company to the chiefs, I was repeatedly told that nothing was done for them; that the chiefs always side with the company and tell the local non-elites to "bear up." For example, when I arrived in one small village included in my initial random sample, there was a conflict between the young men and their headman. The young men wanted to tell me about how the company had taken a large piece of their land without asking and without an agreement to do so, and had mined it for sand to construct a new road. They wanted to complain about the company, to have me hear their anger. But the headman said, no, they were not to tell me this story and that he could not talk to me because he has already taken that problem to the paramount chief and he was told to "leave it to God," to "bear up," not to complain. This headman was fearful of speaking out of place because his chief had told him to be quiet. I, in turn, was forced to sample a different village for the research.

Indeed, over and over again, the chiefs proved to be deaf to the fears and concerns of the non-elites and aligned themselves with the corporate and government actors. They were, of course, powerfully incentivized to hold that position and were benefiting personally from the project. Knowledge and control of land are the primary resources of the paramount chiefs, as their power largely rests on their status as custodian of the land, and any monetization of that land therefore results in an increase in their economic and political power. As such, these traditional elites benefit hugely from the arrival of the project. In turn, however, they also have every reason to support the company, to ignore the negative experiences of the non-elites they supposedly represent, and to largely report the bright side of the story to external evaluators or researchers who ask them for their opinion.

This dynamic is clear also among the new local elites who work for the company as managers and white-collar administrators. Such actors recognize the benefits for themselves in promoting and defending the company and have aligned their own interests with those of the company. I first became aware of this by witnessing a number of problematic dynamics when working alongside these managers and supervisors during the six weeks I assisted the company with their own M&E program between late April and early June 2012. At that time there were a handful of villages that were holding out against the company; the male heads of land-owning families in these villages were refusing to sign the land-lease agreement. Such resistance was considered a major problem by the company's foreign managers because any such resistance delayed land-clearing and pivot construction, which eventually functioned to delay the project's profitability.

The response from foreign managers – i.e. frustration – was understandable. But the response from the new local elites was more striking. In a number of exchanges and in general office conversation, I heard these new local elites describe their local non-elite countrymen as ignorant, as confused, and as trouble-makers. Indeed, on a number of occasions, one of the two most senior local company staff members within the team primarily responsible for community engagement was sent to one of these villages to overcome the resistors and get these communities on-board. When they failed to do so, they were angry at the non-elites and frustrated at their own failure to make them accept the company's contract. I thought this was interesting, but not particularly problematic, until I realized the extent to which these new local elites tried to *manage* the local communities with whom they were supposed to be *engaging*.

For example, as part of their general sensitization and community outreach programs, as well as for the purpose of distributing land-lease payments, the company holds large community meetings in each of the three chiefdoms attended by the "five-man committees" from each of the villages within the land-lease area of that chiefdom. At these meetings the presentations are in Temne (the local language) unless an official or the media is present from Freetown, in which case the presentations are in Krio and translated into Temne, or a white person is present, in which case the presentations are primarily in English and translated into Temne. At such meetings, it is the role of the new local elites who work for the company to translate, thus, supposedly, ensuring that the communities are fully informed and that details are clearly transmitted from the speaker to the audience and vice versa. However, it became clear, from attending these meetings with my own research assistant who speaks fluent Temne, Krio, and English, that many things were simply not being translated for the audience. These new local elites were selectively translating into Temne only those elements of the Krio or English that they wanted to translate – primarily, it became clear, those elements that appeased the audience and did not provoke disruptions or protests.

So, for example, when I myself was speaking at one of these meetings to explain why the company was conducting a socio-economic survey of the area (discussed in detail in Chapter 8), I stated clearly that this survey would not be used in any way by the company as a guide for the distribution of resources. I explained that the company was not here to distribute food, clothing, or scholarships and so there was no use in providing strategically inflated or deflated responses to the survey questions. However, when this was translated into Temne, the local audience was told to respond truthfully to the survey, but the piece about the company not distributing resources was never translated. The former serves the interests of the company and the new local elites, while the latter would not. Indeed, translating the latter could potentially result in disruptions and protests at the meeting as the local non-elites very much expected the company to provide such benefits to the communities, as I described in Chapter 3. It was, in essence, in the interest of these new elites to maintain a sort of *functional ambiguity* regarding the potential benefits of the company. As long as the people felt that the company *might* provide real benefits, then they would toe the line

Consistent with the usual patron–client system, these new local elites have primarily been identified for company employment by the paramount chiefs, who suggest such hires from among the local people with secondary or tertiary education qualifications. As such, these new local elites are connected to and their interests are aligned with the traditional, political, and economic elites in and around the project's land-lease area. All told, these local elites, whether the traditional elites or the new elites working for the company, had far more positive experiences of the project than the average non-elite local and so their evaluations of the project are understandably more positive. Indeed, when I was looking to speak with one of the primary such elites, the Honorable Mr. Lansana, the Member of Parliament who had attracted the company to his home area, I was unable to do so. I was informed that he was currently enjoying a trip to Europe, at the invitation of the company.

Just as elites in Makeni who were employed by the NGOs that flooded into Sierra Leone in the immediate post-war period had a more positive experience of peacebuilding interventions generally and of the TRC specifically, it is easy to see why local elites within the land-lease area of the project have more positive experiences of the FDI project. Rather simply, they actually benefit more from its processes. Even male heads of household – while enjoying less status than chiefs and white-collar company employees, experience some positive aspects of the company's presence. Elder males can secure their financial future and feel they are securing that of their families as well, as the company has promised to employ their sons. They feel the land-lease payments have been a great boon for their villages, allowing them to improve their housing and expand their village. While certainly not the majority, those who control the money do seem to have a more positive experience of the FDI project's process. On the other hand, most women, young men, and members of stranger families had neither a say in decisions regarding the acceptance of the project, nor any influence over how the benefits it provides will be distributed.

The added value of local engagement: explaining diverging experiences

It is not difficult, therefore, to see why elites would experience these two projects more positively than non-elites. The local elites in both cases did actually accrue significant benefits from the projects. In this sense, their experiences are indeed more positive. These elites are the people who have both the power to influence peacebuilding interventions, whether through their support or their participation in management, and also those who directly benefit. They are also those with the social and human capital to make the most of additional resources that enter the local setting; starting businesses, building homes, investing in agriculture, etc. This, in itself, highlights the added value of local engagement and should be instructive for evaluators. Different elements of the local audience experience projects differently. But it will be very difficult to understand *how* or *why* without engaging with multiple actors in the local setting and actually exploring their varying interactions with and benefits from a particular peacebuilding intervention.

Hence, while ethnographic preparation provides the first step towards understanding local experiences, local engagement allows a more nuanced analysis.

Further, the problem for evaluation is not only that these two groups (simplified to some extent as the "elites" and the "non-elites") have experienced the TRC and are experiencing the FDI project differently. The primary problem for evaluation is that the elites *project* their experience onto the wider population. They see their own experience as prominent in the local environment or representative of the local experience generally. I am relatively confident that many of my elite interviewees actually did believe that most others, including their non-elite compatriots, shared their experience of the events that have occurred or are unfolding. Some readers may feel that elites are instrumentally declaring the broader benefits of these projects (particularly the FDI project) so as to defend the benefits they are accruing and that they are not actually convinced that these projects will benefit the wider population. And probably some of this is occurring. But the situation is not always that simple. I do not believe that elite's projection of their experience onto their non-elite counterparts can be so easily interpreted as disingenuous or as primarily strategic.

Instead, I believe it must be seen as a product of their particular positionality in relation to the projects being administered and their significant but unrecognized *dissociation* from the experiences of local non-elites. In the case of the TRC, for example, the positive experiences of the elites are rooted in the different levels of understanding of the process which they acquired through participation with the TRC itself and with its sensitization campaign. As many of these elites were involved in the administration of the TRC hearings process or had been invited to the sensitization workshops and planning meetings that occurred before it was administered, they understood the process far more than local non-elites and were, as a result, less likely to experience it negatively.

For example, while the local non-elites felt that the TRC had been a provocation because it had not provided what was needed after the war, local elites were well aware that the TRC would only make recommendations for future government action and that it would not directly distribute resources or reparations. The access that local elites had to the process, and the discourse about post-war reconciliation to which they were exposed, provided them with additional understanding, and this understanding allowed them to experience the processes of the TRC more positively. While the expectations of the non-elites ran rampant due to their near complete lack of knowledge and understanding about the project, the expectations of the elites were controlled by their understanding of the recommendations element of the TRC and their internalization of the rhetoric of reconciliation communicated by the sensitization process. The fact that the TRC did not immediately hand over resources did not impair elite experiences of the process as they knew that this was not its purpose.

Similarly, there is a clear difference within the land-lease area of the FDI project between local non-elite and local elite ideas about the role of foreign companies and the concept of "development" which greatly influenced the expectations and evaluations of local people. During my 2012 fieldwork I asked most of my non-elite interviewees what "development" meant to them. Although most people had heard the word, as it is constantly repeated on the radio, most non-elites said they did not know what it meant, because they do not speak English. But when I asked people what they imagine in their head when they hear this English word, the answers echoed, distressingly, non-elite ideas about the role of the TRC. Development, to local non-elites, was when "fine things" come; "something better" that will help you. Fobi, for example, a 65-year-old mother of 13, told me:

> If someone say he is bringing development for you, if he meets you in hardship and takes you out of it, so he put you into good condition, so you get from him development. This is the one I know.

Such interpretations of development, as someone coming and taking away your hardship, map directly onto prevailing social norms of patronage and mutual responsibility, as described in Chapter 4. Such interpretations also require that the company act as a patron and provide for the people, a role the company is in no way prepared to play.

In contrast to the local non-elites, however, the local elites, and particularly the paramount chiefs and the new elites working for the company, have a much more accurate conception of the role the company plans to play. They understand the *modus operandi* of a private company is profit, not patronage. They realize that the benefits that will accrue to those in rural Sierra Leone will be unequal but believe, just as the local elites in Makeni believed in the power of truth to initiate healing and reconciliation, that free-market economic policies will produce generally more positive economic conditions for everyone. In short, just as the local elites in Makeni understood the TRC through the prism and rhetoric of the West – internalized during the sensitization campaign – so the elites involved in the FDI project today understand it through the prism and rhetoric of the company and of free-market capitalism in general. Unfortunately, that prism is unrelated to the worldview of the local non-elites, who see the company primarily through the frame of patron–client relationships and so experience the project as failing to meet the implicit responsibilities of a powerful patron.

These findings highlight just how important it is to commit to local engagement as described in the first section of this chapter, because they make clear the risk of relying on limited subsets of beneficiary groups for evaluations of local experience. If evaluators speak only to English-speaking elites, to land-owning elder males, to paramount chiefs, to staff of NGOs, or to government authorities, non-elites will be further marginalized instead of empowered. In addition, as elites tend to project their experiences onto their non-elite countrymen, evaluations among elites will not only fail to reflect the experiences of the non-elite, but may erroneously extend the experiences of the elites onto those they claim to represent. Any accurate evaluation requires not only that we listen to the voices of both elites and non-elites, but, indeed, that we privilege those whose voices are so regularly excluded, both by the structures of power and, due to the difficulties of access and communication that evaluators often seem to consider insurmountable in the field, from common evaluation methodologies. We must remember, as was recently noted by Denskus (2012: 151) and Bush and Duggan (2013b: 9), that processes of evaluation are themselves implicated in the workings of power, and can, therefore, further compound inequalities and dynamics of disempowerment if not appropriately aware of local dynamics.

Clearly, attempts to facilitate an emancipatory peace must both recognize such dynamics and work to counter the inherent inequality within post-conflict settings. For evaluation processes the lessons should be clear. The ethnographic approach requires *local engagement* not only with elites, with those who speak English, with urban dwellers, or with NGO staff who claim to represent the impoverished or the marginalized, but with representatives of the heterogeneous groups who comprise the population of supposed beneficiaries of any particular peacebuilding intervention. This draws attention to one of the challenges of the ethnographic approach; the selection, training, and use of interpreters and translators during the research process. As noted in the Introduction, it would clearly be beneficial if those using the ethnographic approach to evaluation of peacebuilding interventions were themselves fluent in the local language in settings of intervention. However, this would be asking too much of scholars, practitioners, and evaluators engaged in comparative research across cases, or even in evaluations of national-level processes in most settings of contemporary conflict which occur in states characterized by a great amount of linguistic diversity. Instead, scholars and evaluators must carefully utilize a well-trained and sensitive interpreter during interviews to access the voices and needs of local non-elites. Such scholars, evaluators, and practitioners must, therefore, spend enough time in the local setting both to train an interpreter and to identify and interview representatives of these various groups and to understand these complex divisions and differences on the ground.

In turn, local engagement further contributes to the emancipatory potential of peacebuilding in general by ensuring that a more diverse selection of voices is included in the debate and that a more accurate picture of past successes and failures is developed. Evaluations conducted based on data collected only or even primarily from NGO staff, employees of foreign companies, local government officials, or even local headmen and chiefs, will not – cannot – accurately reflect what local people are experiencing of peacebuilding projects on the ground, nor what they need to experience in order to "buy into" or feel "ownership" of post-conflict peace. As a result, such evaluations are extremely unlikely to promote the emancipation of such groups. The ethnographic approach, in reaching out to usually marginalized and disempowered groups, can provide an outlet for the voices that are almost always missing from evaluations of peacebuilding intervention. In this way, the third pillar of the ethnographic approach, local engagement, can develop new pathways towards an emancipatory peace and give voice to often ignored actors.

6 Pillar IV

Appraisal of one's own implicit assumptions

This is the final chapter in Part II of this book and it presents the final pillar of the ethnographic approach. However, this fourth pillar is somewhat different to the first three and the pages that follow are certainly of a different tone than those that precede them. While Pillars I–III can be seen as progressive steps whereby the evaluator begins with a commitment to see *peacebuilding as experiential*, completes *ethnographic preparation*, and then employs *local engagement* in the field, the fourth pillar is not simply a fourth step in this process. Similarly, while each of the last three chapters described one of these first three pillars and then illustrated its value with quotes and examples drawn from my two evaluations in Sierra Leone, this chapter draws more from theoretical work and requires a little more patience on the part of the reader. But, I would like to stress here at the beginning that this pillar is – though described last – the foundation of the ethnographic approach. The willingness of the evaluator to question and critique their own implicit assumptions underpins the entire approach.

As described in Chapter 1, the field of peacebuilding, including both its academic and practical components, is undergoing consolidation and professionalization. In this process young future peacebuilders are being ever more trained and directed to consider the social goods provided by peacebuilding projects as predefined and specific; to see justice, reconciliation, democracy, security, empowerment, development, and even peace itself as products of a defined set of technocratic solutions. Professional training in graduate programs throughout the "developed" world provides definitions of retributive, restorative, or reparative justice and how to provide them, for example, while research centers, think tanks, and consulting firms publish guidebooks and best-practices for intergroup dialogue and reconciliation processes (Bloomfield, Barnes, and Huyse 2003). At the same time international organizations such as the World Bank, the International Monetary Fund (IMF), and the Organization for Economic Co-operation and Development (OECD) provide statistical analysis explaining the failures and successes of past development programs and how development can be fostered in the "least developed countries." This technocratic approach to the field of peacebuilding takes as its core responsibility the definition of problems, the design of solutions, and the administration of projects "for them" located "over there."

Similarly, these same professional training programs are continuously pumping out graduates skilled in evaluating how many women have participated in "livelihood" programs, how many convictions have been handed down by a criminal tribunal, how many guns have been destroyed through disarmament, how much money has been spent on a development project, or how many people have participated in "good governance" training programs; all of which are outputs; numbers easily observed. This approach can adequately evaluate certain things. For example, it is quite simple to evaluate whether truth commissions have or have not published their findings, or to count how many people attended their public hearings or how many statements were collected among witnesses, survivors, victims, and perpetrators. However, it is much more difficult to evaluate the substantive outcomes of such projects; to determine if disarmament is experienced as fostering security, if convictions are experienced as providing justice, or if and how good governance training actually affects local experiences of governance, the quality of that governance, or whether it is considered legitimate and authoritative by local non-elites.

More worrying still, however, is that the new graduates of such programs and seasoned professional peacebuilders in the field rather uncritically consider these easily collected numbers to be *proxies* for more substantive experiences – whether of justice, healing, development, or transparency – apparently unaware that such measures cannot tell us much about actual experiences within the world of those living in most contemporary post-conflict settings. Proxies, by their very nature, are chosen *a priori* by the evaluators – not the beneficiaries – and are, even at their very best, very rough indicators of complex social experiences. It will hopefully be clear, at this point in the book, that an evaluator's own definition of such experiences cannot be the starting point for evaluating whether or not peacebuilding projects provide local people with the social goods they are often theorized to provide. If peacebuilding as a discipline and a practice hopes ever to contribute towards an emancipatory peace, the first step must be to stop defining what justice, reconciliation, or development will be for those who have survived war. Only local conceptions of those social goods can be the starting point for accurate evaluation, or for that matter, for peacebuilding.

While Chapter 3 illustrated that peacebuilding processes attempting to catalyze experiences of culturally variable social goods often fail to do so and, therefore, that evaluation must see peacebuilding as an experiential as opposed to an institutional project, and Chapter 4 demonstrated that ethnographic preparation is necessary because we can only evaluate local experiences of such social goods if we understand what these concepts mean in local settings, the cases of the TRC and the FDI project in rural Sierra Leone also highlight a much deeper lesson. They show not only that concepts of justice, reconciliation, empowerment or development are variable between settings, but that much more fundamental conceptions of self and sociality which buttress local conceptions of these social goods are themselves variable over space and time. This chapter argues, therefore, that ideas of justice, reconciliation, or empowerment are secondary concepts, built on foundations of more fundamental schemas or "mental maps" of the world in which we live, and – importantly – that these foundational conceptions vary between the social and cultural homelands of those who plan, fund, design, and administer such projects, and those of the supposed beneficiaries.

I therefore argue that the evaluator must do more than question their own ideas of the social goods supposedly provided by peacebuilding projects, such as those of justice, reconciliation, opportunity, or empowerment; they must question the foundational concepts that underpin these secondary concepts or, as Jayawickrama has recently argued, you must "seek an awareness of your own culturally based assumptions" (2013: 34). As has been indicated in the previous chapters, the local experiences of the TRC and the FDI project were closely related to culturally specific ideas about the relationships and responsibilities between people which give definition to the dynamics of the patron–client system. I will argue here that secondary concepts are shaped by the very concepts of self that govern such relationships, responsibilities, and social action in Sierra Leone, which are, in turn, wholly different from those in the West.

This chapter, therefore, ties the previous three together by exploring more closely the deeply engrained unconscious conceptions underpinning the common misunderstandings of international actors working in Sierra Leone and explains how such deeply engrained but nonetheless culturally variable concepts can undermine accurate evaluation. In addition, I will show that what must start as a willingness to recognize the boundedness of one's own perspective and an appraisal of one's own implicit assumptions must then evolve to allow more accurate assessment of the data collected. This data, in turn, further reinforces the imperative to question basic assumptions. I will return, at the end of this chapter, to provide a very short conclusion to this part of the book before moving on to Part III.

Self, society, and implicit assumptions

In what follows, I am attempting to make five rather simple points. I argue; first, that conceptions of self and society are culturally variable; second, that there is a clear distinction between such conceptions in the privileged Western societies in which peacebuilding projects are theorized, planned and funded and in most contemporary post-conflict settings; third, that these foundational theories have a significant impact on the practices of peacebuilding that are eventually administered; fourth, that the dominant conceptions of self and society in Sierra Leone, which give rise to particular notions of relationship, responsibility and mutual interdependence, underpin many of the negative evaluations of the TRC and FDI project described in prior chapters; and fifth, that any evaluator, therefore, who hopes to accurately assess local experiences of peacebuilding projects in settings socially and culturally dissimilar to their own must make a full appraisal of their own implicit assumptions in order to understand those of peacebuilding's "beneficiaries."

Culturally variable conceptions of the self

In order to follow the argument below it is important to first understand the distinction I draw between the *self-concept* (who we each consider our-selves to be) and *conceptions of the self* (the culturally normative ideas of what selves are). Both are important to secondary concepts such as justice or empowerment and underpin patterns of sociality and responsibility such as exist in both patron–client systems and Western "meritocratic" systems based on ideas of individuality and autonomy. However, the distinction between the two is important. Each person's self-concept is understood here as constituted by their collection of autobiographical memories and experiences. Together these memories and experiences create a person's impression of who they are or who they consider themselves to be. As Singer and Salovey have described, "each person has a unique collection of autobiographical memories" and "these memories can be examined in an effort to define who a person is" (1993: 12). In this way "ordinary everyday events may yield up much of the raw materials from which self knowledge systems are constructed," (Barclay and DeCooke 1988: 120). My own memories of childhood, family, relationships, triumphs and failures, for example, form an image in my head of who I believe my self to be. This is, as I am defining it here, my *self-concept*. But at the same time, this self-concept, or anyone's self-concept for that matter, emerges within a setting amenable to certain collectively or culturally defined conceptions of the self.

Those moments and events that form the milestones and moments of my autobiographical memory, and which together form my image of my self, are recognized and remembered always within a cultural milieu that promotes and values some particular milestones and kinds of memories, while completely ignoring, repressing, or failing to value others. My conception of myself as successful, for example, is closely related to my knowledge of myself as an individual with a collection of degrees, a career, and a relatively healthy credit score. This self-concept is, therefore, related to my society's recognition of university degrees and economic security as acceptable markers of success. Alternatively, if I had been raised in a different socio-cultural context, having a PhD and a good credit score might not be considered as valuable and my self-concept would be different. In this way we work to define what we consider as our selves in relation to the context of our memories, actions, and existence – "our identities and memories are two sides of the same coin" (Neimeyer and Metzler 1994: 105) – and our self-concepts are constructed within the rules of our society. Our self-concepts are, therefore, bounded by their acceptability within broader socially accepted conceptions of the self;

within the borders of potential self-concepts valued or allowed within a given society's moral matrix. As Moghaddam has said, such selves develop "through active participation in collective life, and in the collaboratively constructed and collectively upheld versions of social reality that come to dominate society" (2008: 882).

However, because this self-concept is, for all intents and purposes, the only self a member of any given group can conceive of, this self is real, or – more accurately – real based on its construction and acceptance within an inherently narrow understanding of which selves are allowable. The socially constructed nature of this self – its reliance on outside acceptability and affirmation (see Goffman 1959) – becomes invisible and we become unconscious to both the constructed nature of our selves and the variable construction of selves across time, space and culture (see Bourdieu 1977; De Certeau 1984; Foucault 1990). If I had never travelled to other socio-cultural settings and perceived myself through the eyes of, for example, Sierra Leonean villagers as opposed to my family or my academic colleagues, I would never have had an experience of shifting self-concepts. I would not be aware that the self I experience as my self is a social construction and that conceptions of self more generally are culturally variable.

There is no shortage of theoretical and empirical literature supporting this argument. For example, we can witness the patterned construction of selves in different culture's varying definitions of goals, values, and success orientations. Shweder found, for example, that children assign value to their experiences based on the cultural norms in which they are raised, and that these norms are defined within their first five years of life. "[W]hen it comes to judgments about what is right and what is wrong" among American and Oriya children, he argued, "there is virtually no correlation between the judgments of the five year olds in the two cultures" (1991: 190). This is due, as Miller points out, to the relentless "flow of social and moral messages" (1994: 159) that form our collective or "social memory," described by Roseman as memories attached to social group belonging (1996: 843). Children, therefore, do not individually or autonomously define themselves – they define themselves within a context bounded by culturally defined norms. As Bourdieu recognized, "[b]etween the child and the world, the whole group intervenes" (1977: 167).

Moghaddam more recently argued that "we tend to reconstruct the past in biased ways, using selected bits of information," or the use of "cognitive shortcuts" (2008: 885), and we can see how such unconscious selectivity leads to the trimming and pruning of the self until it fits with collective social expectations and norms; until we are what we think we should be. In fact, McAdams argues that each person has;

> by the end of adolescence or shortly thereafter, consolidated an ideological setting for his or her identity story ... the ideological setting situates the action of the person's evolving story within a particular locus of belief and value – a locus shaped by society's conventions regarding the good

> and the true and the individual's struggles to find meaning within or outside of conventions.
>
> (1989: 165)

Similarly, Barclay and DeCooke found that "accuracies and inaccuracies in autobiographical memories result from judgments about what could or should have happened in one's life" and that "[p]eople grouped their own memories into conceptually distinct and coherent categories of meaningfully related events" (1988: 120–21). Similarly, Gergen states that "[o]nce a valued endpoint has been established, it will largely determine the subsequent contents of the personal memory" (1994: 91). In this way, our culturally defined goals determine the very memories we later recall as establishing those goals in the first place.

These cultural influences on each of our personal self-concepts are very powerful and impose themselves even upon our most intimate opinions and emotions. In a cross-cultural analysis of personality differences between the US and Mexico, for example, Holtzman, Diaz-Guerrero, and Swartz note that "[c]lear and uniform differences were found across the two cultures for many psychological dimensions and test scores" including "most of the personality and attitudinal measures" (1975: 355). Similarly, Averill showed how cultural values can differ even on such basic ideals as romantic love (1985: 107) and LeVine showed among the Hausa that so strong are the culturally determined "normative ideals of sociability" that "conformity with their respective cultural ideals is achieved even during pain and stress" (1982: 27).

These examples all show that there are cultural differences in goals, values, ideals and success orientations between groups. They each clearly support the argument that conceptions of the self – ideas about what selves are or should be – emerge out of collectively shared values and norms, and that these norms are variable between cultures. Indeed, what would the discipline of anthropology be if this were not believed to be the case? However, what are the implications for peacebuilding policy and practice?

Conceptions of self in the West and the Rest

Having shown that conceptions of self are culturally variable, the second step is to show clearly that there is a particular distinction between conceptions of self within the Western world, the setting from which the vast majority of peacebuilding theorists and practitioners emerge and who dominate the planning and administration of peacebuilding projects, and those settings in which these projects are primarily administered. A few caveats are necessary here before proceeding. First, I do not want to imply that there are no non-Western theorists or practitioners of peacebuilding, or that there are no Western settings of peacebuilding administration. But nor do I want to avoid the fact that in the contemporary period there are very few wars occurring in the "developed" world from which the vast majority of peacebuilding professionals emerge, while there are dozens of violent conflicts in the "developing" world in which the recipients of the largesse of such professionals primarily reside. There is clearly a transmission of "know-how" and technocratic solutions from the core to the periphery, to follow Paris (2002) in the use of Wallerstein's terms (1974).

Similarly, I am not trying to promote or imply an essentialist notion of "us" and "them," nor would I contend that any such approach would be an accurate reflection of the complex interactions that occur between those who administer and those who experience peacebuilding interventions. I am also well aware, as discussed in Chapter 5, that many local elites actively participate in administering peacebuilding interventions, that there is a rise in the participation of non-Western actors such as India and Brazil in peacebuilding and development processes, that there is significant resistance from local communities themselves to the interventions of the "West" (see the various contributions to Shaw, Waldorf, and Hazan 2010; Mac Ginty 2011), and that there are many local "grass-roots" or "traditional" processes of conflict resolution, reconciliation, justice, and peacebuilding that are utilized on the ground in conflict zones (see various contributions to European Centre for Conflict Prevention 1999; Quinn 2009). However, none of this counters the still solid argument that the West (Europe and its former settler colonies) governs the vast majority of international peacebuilding interventions and both trains and deploys the bulk of the "experts" who administer the projects and programs theorized to build peace in transitional states. Further, though there are certainly some less doctrinaire peacebuilders, most such experts assume that the social and psychological space occupied by the beneficiaries of peacebuilding projects – the way they see, understand, and act in the world – is similar to that of the experts themselves.

Unfortunately, ample research tells us that this is simply not the case (Jayawickrama 2013: 39). Indeed, empirical studies of ethnic groups and the manner in which social norms determine what and how we each remember events indicate that Western culture contains within it a distinct definition of the self as individual and autonomous, which seems at odds with that in many other settings. Again, decades of research and theory support this contention, most famously (but also simplistically) in the form of Hofstede's characterization of Western Europe and its settler colony offshoots (Australia, Canada, New Zealand, the US), as individualist societies compared to the more collectivist societies of Asia, Africa, the Middle East, and even Southern Europe and Latin America (1980, 2001). In such typologies individualist cultures are said to value "independence, autonomy, self-reliance, uniqueness, achievement orientation, and competition," while those in collectivist cultures value "a sense of duty toward one's group, interdependence with others, a desire for social harmony, and conformity with group norms" (Green, Deschamps, and Páez 2005: 322).

A study of American and Chinese adults, for example, found that Americans were more likely to remember individual events and to focus on their own emotions and roles, while Chinese were more likely to remember social and historical events and to place emphasis on social interaction in those memories (Wang and Conway 2004). Moreover, and importantly, such memory selectivity in individuals produced "stories that they use to define and articulate themselves" (Wang and Conway 2004: 31). In this study, American adults were seen to actually remember events differently and to focus more on their own role and emotions within those events than were Chinese adults. In another study, Wagar and Cohen (2003) found that Asian-Canadians recognized personal traits encoded with reference to the self more slowly than Euro-Canadians, as opposed to those coded with reference to the collective. They argued that "cross-cultural differences on memory measures were presumably driven by differences in long-term self-concepts," (ibid.: 474). In essence, the authors argued that culturally defined conceptions of the self as individuated (or not) primed the respondents to remember events through that particular lens. They concluded that the Euro-Canadians were significantly more individually oriented than the Asian-Canadians.

In another more ethnographically oriented stream of research we see practices of memory which purposefully prioritize and construct not individuated identities, as in the West, but collective identities. Carsten, for example, describes the phenomenon of "genealogical forgetting" in Pulau Langkawi, Malaysia, and the manner in which "small everyday acts of forgetting" form a "*collective construction of identity*" (1995: 331; emphasis added) wherein the individuated self is subservient to the needs of the group. Elsass similarly described how the underlying organization of a culture in relation to conceptions of the self and society determines how memories of trauma will be experienced and what treatment will be needed. In individualist societies (in Elsass's study, this was the case in Colombia), autobiographical memories of trauma will be prevalent and individual therapy may be necessary. However, in a more collectivist society (Peru, for Elsass (2001)), such individual psychological interventions might be inappropriate because trauma will not be stored as individuated memory.

Additionally, Battaglia described the ritual of *segaiya*, performed by the Sabarl of Papua New Guinea after a death in order to forget "the dead and the debts that survive them" (1992: 5). In this ritual, the acts performed accomplish forgetting and allow "constructive social effects" and "cultural revaluation." The performance itself, she argues, "constitute[s] an ideology of personhood" in that the ritual performed centers on the forgetting of the individual as well as the gifts and debts related to that individual that are central to Sabarl conceptions of selves and their role in society (ibid.: 15). Similarly, Taylor argues that the Jivaro of the Amazon practice rituals of mourning specifically oriented to perform "losing the deceased" in a collective effort of depersonalization (1993: 662), i.e. to forget the individual who has passed. In Jivaro cosmology, "so long as the dead are remembered as recognizable and specific individuals ... the virtualities of existence they occupy remain unavailable" and because there are a finite "number of unique potentialities of life" available for "filling in," no new life can be born until the old one has been forgotten (ibid.: 658). In this case again, the practices of memory demand a dis-remembering of the individual in order to serve the collective memory and identity of the group.

Specific to recovery after collective violence, Orta (2002) describes the intricate connection of various commemorative rituals of the 1921 "massacre of Machaqa" among the Aymara. She describes the acts of remembrance and the appropriation of space, as constitutive of modern-day Aymara collective identity in the state of Bolivia. She notes the manner in which acts of memory were seen as legitimate or based on implicit conceptions of Aymara sociality such as the valuation of transparency and reciprocity (ibid.: 488), as opposed to individuality and autonomy. Similarly, Honwana has described the rituals of reincorporation following Mozambique's civil war as rooted in local approaches in which "the whole symbolic array of spirits, family traditions, and prayers to God" were brought into the rituals (2006: 121). She highlights that cosmology is embodied in the actions within ritual, such as the manner in which returning soldiers are "forbidden to look back" on their return to the village, because their reintegration in to society must be a complete break from their past (ibid.: 112).

Hence, though such simple dichotomies as Western vs. Other are problematic (Kirkpatrick 1985: 225; Lu 1998), the conceptions of the self that have dominated Western thought over the past centuries have primarily presumed a self isolated, atomized, and independent of social forces: rational and detached. Such rather simplistic conceptions of the individual as inherently autonomous underpin the ideas of influential Western social theorists such as Rawls (1971) or Nozick (1974) and conceptions of the self within most psychological literature harkening back to Freud, which hold similar ideas of the self and, problematically, often *assume the universal nature* of these conceptions of the self (Fromm 1974: 7; Ossorio 1985: 30; Gergen 1994: 79; Seigel 2005: 654). Through all of this literature, emerging from philosophy, psychological, and anthropology, we can clearly see how Western society has defined its conceptions of the self; a conception that has risen to prominence and is today the central foundational linchpin of "international" practice, while being quite distinct from many other ways of conceiving of the self in societies around the world in which that practice is applied. Indeed, such a conception of the self is largely unrelated to ideas of the self in many settings which today are experiencing war and instability and in which current and future peacebuilding projects are or will be administered.

Conceptions of self and the practice of peacebuilding

So, how do these Western conceptions of the self affect the practice of peacebuilding and why is this important? Let me provide a clear example of the impact of our ideas regarding the nature of the self and sociality by examining a particular section of the transitional justice literature; that which promotes the dominant, retributive mechanisms of justice. This literature demands individuated punishments for what are overwhelming seen as individuated crimes. They therefore accept, usually without substantive consideration or critique, a conception of individuated selves as the pertinent, even the only possible, actors responsible for wartime atrocities or human rights abuses (Orentlicher 1994: 426; for a more nuanced discussion, see Teitel 2000; Mani 2002). Within such literature both the victims and the perpetrators of crimes during conflict or authoritarian regimes are considered autonomous independent individuals. As such, autonomous individuals are also those either deserving of redress or requiring of punishment. These individuated conceptions of responsibility and punishment are prime examples of the problematic relationship between theory and practice within the peacebuilding field and they show us clearly how conceptions of the self accepted in the West are reified in practice and applied in non-Western settings.

The conceptions of the self which underpin retributive notions of justice are central to traditional international legal thought – dominated of course by the descendants of European philosophy – which concentrates on the rather narrow notion of the *physical integrity* of the individuated person as the primary right deserving both of protection from infringement and, therefore, of legal mechanisms for redress. It is considered legitimate, as we can see in the mandates of the International Criminal Tribunal for the Former Yugoslavia (ICTY), the International Criminal Tribunal for Rwanda (ICTR), and of the International Criminal Court (ICC), to hold individuals accountable for the infringement of other individuals' rights to physical integrity; for crimes pertaining to death, imprisonment, and torture. These legal bodies largely only deal with such crimes against individuals by other individuals, and assume that justice will be done with the punishment, again, of individuals.

However, as Fletcher and Weinstein (2002) point out, different situations will demand redress for the infringement of rights based on different needs. In some situations and some contexts, physical integrity may indeed be central, but in other contexts rights to psychological integrity as it has become dominant in the Anglo-American world (Pupavac 2004: 379) may be paramount. In still others, the "higher order manifestations of need" attended to by truth commissions may be primary, such as "empathy, forgiveness, and altruism" (Fletcher and Weinstein 2002: 625). Very often in contemporary conflicts in the developing world, however, we can assume that the very base needs at the bottom of Maslow's (1954) hierarchy will be important for creating peace: rights to shelter, food, water, security, education, and health. But the dominant paradigm of transitional justice, emerging from Western conceptions of the self and largely excluding alternative non-Western voices (Mani 2002: 49), leads to a practice of transitional justice which minimises these alternative conceptions of justice because they are not so simply grounded on individuated rights and responsibilities.

This is a clear example of how theory guides practice. The ideas we carry around in our heads about the world – the "ideologies, rules, rituals, assumptions, definitions, paradigms, and standard operating procedures" (Autesserre 2010: 11) – tell us how to operate in that world. Among those with the power and influence to design peacebuilding projects, Western conceptions of the atomized self are predominant, and so the administration of projects and programs in transitional justice predictably focus attention on the individual. To demand that legal protections be provided for social or collective rights – also supposedly protected under international law – has traditionally been considered outside the bounds of those same transitional justice mechanisms that make such a show and spend so many hundreds of millions to apply individuated justice. There is no clear reason for this distinction other than the predominance of Western conceptions of the self and sociality among those who hold the power and make the decisions. Under this approach, rights to a long list of violations including social, economic, or cultural freedom are rarely seriously considered as needs worthy of protection against infringement (Brooks 1999: 7; Forman 2002: 129; Bell and O'Rourke 2007: 34; Arbour 2007), nor of redress, because the victims and perpetrators cannot easily be individuated.

This becomes uniquely problematic when applied to the socio-cultural environments of contemporary wars, within which it is conceivable that, as Mani argues, everyone should rightly be seen as a survivor, and it is hugely problematic to draw distinctions between victims and perpetrators (2002: 123). The idea that individuals, not structures, must be held accountable is related to a concern with what Osiel calls "administrative massacre" (1995), in which nobody is considered guilty because we all are. If it is simply society's fault, if we are all collectively both victim and perpetrator, then guilt cannot be assigned; "collective guilt absolves everyone of responsibility for past wrongdoing" (Fletcher and Weinstein 2002: 599). The problem of course arises if, predictably enough, sometimes society is both at fault and its own greatest victim. In such a case, where social forces have played a major role in the prevalence of past violence, the traditional international legal paradigm's inability to account for or forcefully address problems with larger social and collective forces impairs its ability to play a constructive role in the peacebuilding process. There are clearly times when, as Fletcher and Weinstein note, "individual agency is superseded by other influences that profoundly determine what actions an individual may take. This raises the questions of whether or how they can be held responsible for their actions" and forces us to "question the assumption of the primacy of individual agency" (2002: 605). As a result, we are forced to realize that post-conflict recovery cannot be achieved always and everywhere through currently normative mechanisms of individuated justice and we should consider alternatives.

This lesson is pertinent for many peacebuilding practices and projects. Indeed, we can see similar problems arising in any situation where Western norms are uncritically assumed to be operative. In short, the conceptions of needs, rights, infringements, and redress that compose the conception of justice dominant in international law and transitional justice practice are all secondary concepts based on the foundational conception of self as atomized and autonomous. This is true also of dominant concepts of reconciliation, security, empowerment, opportunity, and forgiveness that are the purported contributions of a host of other contemporary peacebuilding processes. Such institutions, planned, funded, and administered by international actors – often with the help of national elites – are very often prepared only to deal with such atomized selves; selves thought, at their core, to be the same as Western selves. But, as described in the preceding sections, this turns out to be a massive and problematic simplification.

Individuality and responsibility in Sierra Leone

It should be clear at this point, first, that conceptions of the self – the normative ideas of what selves are – are culturally variable. Second, that conceptions of the self in the West are quite distinct from those in much of the developing world in which a great amount of contemporary conflict occurs. And, third, that these foundational conceptions of self – culturally variable ideas of what selves are possible – have a significant impact on the practices and projects of peacebuilding that are eventually administered, such as the dominant mechanisms of transitional justice. Here I turn back to the particular case of Sierra Leone, and describe the specific nature of selves and sociality in this setting and how these alternative conceptions underpin significant cultural characteristics, including the patron–client system, which, as already described, undermined the operation of the two externally designed peacebuilding interventions I have been discussing in this book.

As noted in previous chapters, the local experiences of the TRC and the FDI project were closely related to culturally specific ideas about the relationships between and responsibilities of people within the community which give definition to the dynamics and expectations inherent within the patron–client system. In essence, because local people saw both of these projects as patrons, they fully expected both to provide resources and support and their experiences of both projects were negatively affected as a result because these expectations were never fulfilled. A critical reader might simply respond that the problem then is patrimonialism; often associated with corruption. The response may be that we should undermine local structures of authority and hierarchy; that everyone everywhere wants to be free and independent, and that Sierra Leoneans are being held back and marginalized by their own elites and perhaps even by their own culture. But this is exactly the response that proves my point and is the reason why an evaluator must work towards critical appraisal of their own implicit assumptions. We must dig deeper and engage in a more substantive analysis. As I will show, expectations of patronage are not themselves foundational concepts and cannot be so easily "undermined." They are built into more deeply ingrained conceptions of the self in Sierra Leone; conceptions which are distinctly unlike the Western notions of the atomized and autonomous individual and which make such simple institutional and technocratic responses quite inappropriate and potentially disastrous.

As described in Chapter 4, in rural Sierra Leone, selves are seen as entangled within networks of obligation and expectation. As was described, the patron–client system is one of hierarchy in which the client is *responsible to* the patron and the patron is *responsible for* the client. The reader will recall that such systems involve intricate connections of mutual reciprocity, whereby the patron provides resources and assistance to his or her clients in return for support and labor. These relationships serve to bind together communities but have also led to the prevalence of *wealth in people* wherein big persons attempt always to attract more clients so as to both control and project more influence and power. In addition, while such mutually reciprocal relationships are often viewed by Western eyes as proof of West Africa's endemic corruption, in the local setting, these relationships are accepted, normal, often perfectly functional and, as has been described by Shaw (2002) and Bolton (2012), regulated by culturally prescribed norms of behavior and propriety.

But patron–client systems are themselves built on even more foundational conceptions of the self which dominate Sierra Leonean culture. There are many ways to engage with these ideas, but I will do so through the perspective of *relationship* and juxtapose the Western idea of the self as autonomous (requiring no relationship) against the Sierra Leonean idea of the self as relational (existing only in relation to others). By this I do not mean to imply that there are no individuals in Sierra Leone, or that there is no such thing as community or collective identity in the West. Nor do I mean to imply that all people in Sierra Leone are defined only by their relationships and no people in the West are defined by their relationships. Instead, I mean to use this individualist/collectivist dichotomy as a lens by which to understand more easily the distinction between selves and sociality in these two settings. It will be helpful here to refer to well-researched non-Western models of self and society, such as the relational conception of Ubuntu in Southern Africa or Confucianism in Asia.

The term "Ubuntu" springs from the isiXhosa proverb that says; "a human being is a human being only through its relationship to other human beings" (Marx 2002: 52). As described by Desmond Tutu, Ubuntu means that one's "humanity is caught up, is inextricably bound up," in that of others (1999: 31). Ubuntu means not, according to Tutu, that "I think therefore I am," but that "I am human because I belong. I participate, I share" (ibid.: 31). Chinese Confucianism is similarly believed "to glorify and promote collectivism with its emphasis on the collective good and social harmony as the ultimate goal" (Lu 1998: 94), and shares with Ubuntu the central values of "community, the desirability of ethical partiality, and the idea that we tend to become morally better when we grow older" (Bell and Metz 2011: 80). Within Confucianism, Lu argues that the value of *yi* is associated with "morality, benevolence, righteousness, and faithfulness" (Lu 1998: 93), while Leung, Koch, and Lu note that this does not appear to be a characteristic of classical

Confucian doctrine, but of a secular cultural collectivism dominant in modern China (2002).

But no matter its source, such a philosophy implies a conception of self as reliant on relationship and community which mirrors that of Ubuntu in its promotion of harmony and mutual responsibility and interdependence, and which echoes the findings of the studies comparing Chinese and Western self-construction cited earlier in this chapter. While Ubuntu has been privileged by great attention in recent academic literature since the South African TRC and because of the prominence of South African scholars in comparison to other African voices, and Confucianism is often referenced due to the rising influence of modern China, in tone and substance both echo and can act as prisms by which to understand conceptions of the self alternative to the Western norm prevalent throughout the modern world. Indeed, as Bell and Metz point out, it is most likely the case that the Western norm of the individuated self is the global aberration and far more societies are built on collectivist characteristics than individualist ones (2011: 78). Indeed, these alternatives are clearly more in tune with conceptions of the self in Sierra Leone.

For example, Bledsoe argues that the simple terms "patron" and "client" do not fully communicate to the Western reader the actual import or meaning of these positions within Sierra Leonean society, and that the relationship is one of mutual reciprocity whereby individual persons "do not seek a dangerous state of independence" (Bledsoe 1990: 75) but instead seek to foster interdependence through their everyday actions. She describes how "the notion of clientage is the notion of 'being for' someone else or other people" (ibid.: 75). In this way individuals seek to construct a relationship with a powerful big person who can mediate the dangers of the world on their behalf; they place their future in the hands of another. In this perspective, the work of forming one's self is the work of situating one's self in relation to others and creating a place for oneself in the world through those others.

This creation of the self in relation to others, and the emphasis on the "everyday" maintenance of interdependence is closely related to Ferme's ideas of how "big-ness" is created through the ongoing use and manipulation of objects associated with power. Such use allows certain people to perform the status and role of big-ness in relation to those for whom they are performed. Consistent with a great amount of other anthropological literature on secrecy in Sierra Leone (Murphy 1998; Shaw 2002), Ferme also identifies the exchange and control of knowledge as a practice used to enhance big-ness through performance (2001: 160), and, thereby, to construct social status through exchange with others. Both Bledsoe and Ferme, therefore, describe the development of a self in relation to others – both on the part of the patron and of the client – through the strategic management or manipulation of information that authors such as Shaw (2002) and Jackson (2004) have also described in the case of Sierra Leone.

More recently Bolton has interestingly illustrated this dynamic by describing Sierra Leonean relational personhood as built on "love" and "eating."

She describes each as one side of a single coin of interaction, whereby individuals construct their identity in relationship to others "through the everyday actions of productive living" (2012: 4), i.e. through practices of love and/or eating. In this conception "love" is a practice, not an emotion, and it is seen in the many small actions of "investment, trust, and interdependence" that Sierra Leoneans conduct everyday with those around them to develop themselves as clients under the protection of a patron (ibid.: 7). On the other side of the coin, individuals attempt to "eat" (or consume resources) when possible (ibid.: 9) – sometimes just enough to progress *small small* (slowly), sometimes enough to attain big-ness – but to do so without stepping outside the lines of what is allowable by others. In this way, selves in Sierra Leone (both clients and patrons) are constructed always in relationship to those below, above, or parallel. Much as conceived in Ubuntu, they "are" only in relation to others; they are not stand-alone autonomous selves.

It is this relational aspect that distinguishes Western conceptions of the self from those in Sierra Leone and problematizes simple, and in the end often misguided, technocratic solutions that assume that individuals everywhere will react similarly to institutional changes or to particular individual incentives. Quite to the contrary, as both Bledsoe (1990) and Bolton (2012) note, being individuated or atomized is a dangerous and fearful state for a Sierra Leonean. Nobody would want to be separated, isolated, or alone, and everyone seeks constantly to develop and nurture relationship, in order to "be for" others and to construct themselves as someone "worth having" (ibid.: 153). This is the conception of the self in Sierra Leone which underpins the practices of everyday interaction as well as significant cultural institutions such as the patron–client system and secret societies. Within this setting, secondary concepts such as those of justice, authority, respect, development, dignity, security, and empowerment are not built on the conceptions of the self dominant in the West. While these terms in the West refer to secondary conceptions constructed on a foundation of an individuated self, in Sierra Leone, and perhaps in most of the world outside Europe and its settler colonies, analogous ideas that might be easily translated as justice, authority, development, empowerment, etc., are actually constructed on very different concepts, constructed on a foundation of a relational self.

In practical terms, the effect of planning and designing peacebuilding practices based on ideas of justice, reconciliation, development, or empowerment that are themselves founded on concepts inconsistent with those which dominate the context within which peace will be built, is clear. When such local foundational concepts differ markedly from the Western norm, local expectations of and reactions to the administration of peacebuilding projects will differ significantly from what would be expected among Western actors. Processes such as electoral reform, good governance and transparency trainings, anti-corruption programs, truth-telling processes, criminal tribunals, and development initiatives are all experienced through cultural lenses built on the foundational conceptions of self that are accepted within the local society and culture. They are, as a result, experienced in ways that individuals from the West – the society from which such institutions have sprung – cannot predict and, even worse, may not even be able to imagine. Further, the evaluator, in any good faith effort to understand *how* intervention is experienced on the ground and *why*, must be able to recognize these inconsistencies, but will be unable to do so unless he or she can take stock of their own implicit assumptions regarding such foundational concepts.

The added value of appraising one's own implicit assumptions

It is for this reason that we must, in our evaluations of peacebuilding intervention processes, conduct a thorough appraisal of our own implicit assumptions. While I have been able to glimpse, after significant fieldwork in Sierra Leone, how local people experience everyday life – the constant management of communication, massage of information, and the shifting sands of relational selfhood – I cannot truly understand how it is experienced. My own quite Western self-concept is fully integrated into my psyche. I cannot step fully outside of my own social positionality and experience the world as local Sierra Leoneans do. After years of study I can only glimpse – as if through my peripheral vision – what seems to me to be a shadow surface on which selfhood is constructed and experienced. However, having spent years studying the country, more than 18 months living in rural Sierra Leone working alongside and talking to hundreds of Sierra Leoneans, and having studied decade's worth of substantive ethnographic data from the region and from Sierra Leone in particular, I have at least come to recognize that my engrained, culturally defined conception of the world is most definitely not universal.

In addition, based on my experiences in Sierra Leone, I also know that just as I cannot fully understand their experience, my friends in Sierra Leone – people I have worked with on and off for seven years – do not really understand my own experience. Their positionality too, their integrated self-concepts and conceptions of self, do not allow them to step outside their reality and perceive accurately the way an over-educated, white male academic from Ireland, educated in the US, and living in Scotland views his world, his self, and his society. The very norms by which we live our lives become invisible in the processes by which they are imparted to us, and as Foucault describes so clearly, are more powerful for their invisibility; for being normalized (1995: 183–84). Even if intellectually we recognize that our implicit assumptions about the world are constructions, we are driven in our everyday interactions, in our jobs and our friendships, our hobbies, and our passions, to act "as if" the world is what those assumptions say it is.

But it is exactly this "as if" approach to the world that is dangerous when transported into the planning, administration, or indeed, the evaluation of peacebuilding projects. Our tendency to respond to and in the world as if it is what we believe it to be, and as if all people everywhere define themselves and experience the world as we ourselves do, can be disastrous when evaluating peacebuilding projects in socio-cultural settings clearly unlike those in which the evaluator has been acculturated. It is exactly such processes, for example, that lead us to choose inadequate proxies for the measurement of culturally variable complex phenomena. If we believe in the West, based on centuries of legal tradition, that punishment by trial will be experienced as justice, then we might use a count of the number of trials, trial years, indictments, or judgments as a proxy measure for experiences of justice. If we believe, based on a full century of Western psychological traditions, that talking about one's past victimization or disempowerment will heal psychological wounds, then we might use a count of the number of people who testified at a trial, during TRC hearings, or the number of counselling hours provided by a psychological service as proxy measures for experiences of healing. But these proxies are measurements chosen "as if" people within this post-conflict setting will experience those events as the evaluator believes they should experience them.

Similarly, if we believe that economic independence is the route of opportunity or experiences of empowerment, then we might use GDP per capita, new local job opportunities, or unemployment levels as proxy measures for opportunity or empowerment. If we believe that the nuclear family is the normal and universal economic organizational unit, then we may use the income of male heads of household or land ownership as proxy measures for economic security. However, what will any of these proxy measures mean if the individuals and communities among whom evaluation is conducted do not share with the evaluator basic foundational ideas about the social world and those in it? Indeed, I hope it is quite clear at this point that such proxy measures, and evaluations that rely on them, might prove to be badly misinformed and dangerously misleading. It is for this reason that a full appraisal of our own implicit assumptions about the world is a requirement for successful evaluation of local experiences of peacebuilding processes in contemporary transitional states (Jayawickrama 2013: 36).

It should be clear now why this fourth pillar underpins the entire approach. In many ways, this fourth pillar, the willingness to interrogate the implicit assumptions that we carry with us and believe to be "common sense," is the beginning of any good ethnographic approach to evaluation. If an evaluator does not already have some latent anthropological imagination, and has not already at least recognized the potential for significant cultural diversity, then they are unlikely to commit to or be able to succeed at pillars I–III. However, it is also true that conducting the first three pillars will push the evaluator further down the path of substantial self-critique and more accurate understanding of local experiences. As a result, in the final analysis, substantive evaluation of the experience of "the other" begins and ends with evaluation of ourselves. Peacebuilding may be conducted "for them" and "over there," but it is very much conducted "by us" and "right here." As a result, evaluation must begin with honest and critical self-appraisal. In practical terms, this demands constantly asking ourselves how our questions are being interpreted in the field, how local people are defining these concepts, what assumptions am I unconsciously accepting? But most plainly it demands that the evaluator ask local people directly; what have you seen? What have you felt? What do you know, understand, appreciate, and value? What would peace be to you? Again, only by taking local people seriously, by listening to their words about their own experiences, can evaluation contribute to anything approaching an emancipatory peace.

Conclusion

This concludes both Chapter 6 and Part II of this book. While Part I outlined the ethnographic approach (Chapter 1) and the context and setting of my two studies (Chapter 2), Part II has described in far more detail the rationale and value of each of the four pillars; seeing *peacebuilding as experiential* (Chapter 3), *ethnographic preparation* (Chapter 4), *local engagement* (Chapter 5), and *appraisal of one's own implicit assumptions* (Chapter 6). I hope that each of these chapters has been helpful, has made my points plainly and illustrated them clearly. I also hope that they have inspired the reader to recognize the challenges of international intervention in contemporary transitional states and to understand the value of an ethnographic approach to peacebuilding evaluation. Part III moves on to explore some additional problems and strengths of this ethnographic approach.

I will first describe, in Chapter 7, the practical and ethical challenges to this approach to evaluating peacebuilding in sensitive transitional states. This chapter describes many of the important questions that must be asked by anyone considering conducting this kind of evaluation and illustrates the reality that, unfortunately, this approach is not for everyone and may, in fact, be quite burdensome or even impossible for many scholars currently writing about post-conflict peacebuilding in transitional states. I will then, in Chapter 8, squarely address the problems and limitations of quantitative evaluation and the potential for a multi-methodological approach – combining the quantitative with the ethnographic – to overcome these limitations. As I will show, the very serious challenges to quantitative evaluation in transitional states can make findings from such studies all but meaningless. However, when complemented with substantive and rigorous ethnographic evaluation, such studies can be useful and informative. And finally, in the last chapter I will provide, first, a synopsis of the argument presented throughout the book and then proceed to make a case for the incorporation of the ethnographic approach not only into peacebuilding evaluation, but also into project planning, design, and administration.

Part III

The details and challenges of incorporating the ethnographic approach

7 The challenges and limitations of the ethnographic approach

The vast majority of peacebuilding work has and will continue to be conducted in settings of violence, poverty, disease, and hardship. However, most of the people who are today conducting evaluations of peacebuilding projects are academics, staff members of NGOs and funding agencies, consultants, and other predominantly Western expatriates, all of whom are ever more disciplined and professionalized to think and act in a particularly technocratic, solution-oriented mode; this, after all, is the point of training and professionalization. Most such evaluators have scant local knowledge and are instead, as Autesserre (2014) describes, hired for their technical training and professional proficiency. In addition, most of these professionals have little desire to spend six months or more of their lives in uncomfortable and potentially dangerous transitional states. These are some of the reasons so much evaluation consists of desk research, quantitative analysis, checklists, surveys, and perhaps a short "field trip." Spending time in an impoverished post-conflict setting, and asking local non-elites what they are experiencing can be an arduous, exhausting, frustrating, and difficult task.

While some peacebuilding work is conducted in relatively developed settings such as Northern Ireland, the Former Yugoslavia, or the Basque Country, the majority of contemporary conflicts, and therefore, contemporary peacebuilding processes, occur in states such as Afghanistan, Iraq, Angola, Nicaragua, Peru, Haiti, Nepal, East Timor, the Democratic Republic of Congo, Sierra Leone, and Liberia, just to name a few. In the near future, peacebuilding projects will begin (or continue) in the countries of the Arab Spring such as Egypt, Libya, and Syria, as well as in Colombia, Myanmar, Sudan, Somalia, and Mali, and in the coming years peacebuilding processes are likely to occur within the many potential settings of state fragility and failure, among and within states torn apart by resource wars, environmental conflicts, distributional inequalities, and conflicts driven by dynamics we cannot yet even predict. Peacebuilding itself, and the process of conducting ethnographic evaluations of peacebuilding processes, will not get easier, and those who make the decision to commit to this form of evaluation must, without doubt, be prepared to deal with unpredictable and often dangerous fieldwork conditions. Therefore, as much as the ethnographic approach to evaluating peacebuilding intervention is necessary in complex, sensitive, and culturally variable transitional settings, it is also hampered by the very sensitivity of such settings (Bush and Duggan 2013b: 6–7).

This chapter is divided into three main sections which try to address some of these challenges with illustrations and reflections from my own fieldwork. The first and longest section describes the practicalities of dealing with challenges to one's own physical safety and security in transitional settings often characterized by high rates of disease, crime, and violence. The second section attempts to address the psychological challenges of working with and among marginalized populations often suffering from poverty, illiteracy, and hardship. Both of these sections will provide practical suggestions on how to *avoid* threats to one's physical safety and how to *manage* threats to psychological security. The third section discusses the challenges related to research ethics and the evaluator's responsibility to the populations among whom ethnographic evaluations of peacebuilding interventions are conducted. This section will include reflections on my own role as an evaluator recording and reporting on the lives of the disempowered in Sierra Leone, and the questionable and personally problematic relations of power and status that dominate that role. Hopefully, this chapter as a whole can provide some insight and practical guidance for others willing to do this kind of work.

Many scholars have noted in the past the difficulties and dangers of working in settings characterized by risk (Williams *et al.* 1992; also see contributions to Nordstrom and Robben 1995; Ferrell and Hamm 1998; De Soto and Dudwick 2000; Lee-Treweek and Linkogle 2000; Sriram *et al.* 2009; Robben and Sluka 2012), and even in relatively "developed" countries affected by conflict, it is clear that there are particular concerns with security (Sluka 1990). A great amount of this literature is written by and directed towards an academic audience, and primarily towards anthropologists and sociologists, those academics who traditionally engage with impoverished and marginalized communities, whether at home or abroad. However, as a result, this literature is largely unread by professionals working for large international organizations, future or current staff of national and international NGOs, and the broad array of academics from international law to economics and from political science to psychology who operate directly or indirectly as part of the peace industry. Those who engage regularly in peacebuilding evaluation have not read this literature. This is a critical problem as anyone who wants to engage in this approach will need to have a greater awareness of and be prepared to deal with the many challenges unique to this form of ethnographic evaluation. I will turn first to physical challenges in the field.

The physical challenges of the ethnographic approach

The particular physical risks that threaten the evaluator in any conflict or post-conflict setting will clearly vary. Obviously the challenges of working in rural Columbia in the summer will differ to those of working in northern

Afghanistan in the winter. But there are characteristics common to both and the risks of falling afoul of any such threats rise with the duration spent in a sensitive transitional setting. For example, it is highly likely that both these settings will be very different to the evaluator's usual environment and, as a result, the evaluator will find themselves challenged by unexpected or unpredictable situations, including environmental hazards like heat, cold, or disease; a lack of government services such as clean water, electricity, sanitation, security, or medical assistance; the prevalence or threat of organized violence from ex-military or paramilitary groups; the prevalence or threat of non-organized violence from criminal groups or individuals looking for an easy target; and unfamiliar hazards related to lowered, non-existent, or unenforced construction or transportation safety standards. All of these problems are related more to the levels of economic, social, and institutional development that characterize contemporary transitional states than they are to any particular setting. As such, we can discuss these challenges of the ethnographic approach in a way that makes lessons from one setting pertinent to many others.

Sleep, sickness, and disease

For me, one of the key challenges to conducting ethnographic evaluations in Sierra Leone has been maintaining my own state of health. In 2008/2009, I, like almost everyone in Makeni, contracted malaria and spent a few days with a terrible fever, of which I remember very little other than that I was completely unproductive for a week or so. In 2012, I contracted malaria and typhoid at the same time and, though the malaria fever was not as bad the second time, the experience of having both of these diseases at the same time was exhausting and debilitating. These were, of course, temporary situations of intense physical discomfort and not extended periods of illness, but they were nonetheless dangerous, rather common among expatriates in Makeni, and very disruptive of my work. However, while it may appear that contracting diseases like malaria and typhoid are the serious health risks, much more problematic have been seemingly less dangerous but persistent health issues.

For example, during the hot and humid rainy season in the north of Sierra Leone, the temperature is rarely below 80 degrees Fahrenheit and, for many from the northern hemisphere, sleep can become a serious challenge. In 2008/2009, I lived in Makeni for ten months with no power, no running water, and of course, no air conditioning. Sometimes for weeks at a time there were few nights cool enough to allow me to get any deep sleep. On such nights I would roll out of a sweat-soaked bed at about 2 a.m. and take yet another bucket shower to clean off the sweat before heading back to bed and hopefully catching that sweet window before dawn when the temperature breaks just a little. But on most nights, and for weeks in a row, I would only get four or five hours of unsettled sleep. This kind of ongoing persistent sleep deprivation only added to other health hazards as my body become generally drained and less able to withstand more dangerous diseases, such as malaria, typhoid and dysentery.

In addition, such difficult conditions can aggravate any existing health issues that a researcher may be able to manage much more easily in the West. I have chronic bronchitis, for example, which flares up once or twice a year when I am drained from overwork, stress, or lack of sleep. While working in Sierra Leone, as might be clear by now, all three of these are common. As a result, bronchitis is always a threat to my everyday health in Sierra Leone. In addition, while a bout of bronchitis in Europe simply means I have to work less, relax more, get additional sleep, and head down to the pharmacy for antibiotics, in Makeni, most of these options are unavailable and the entire setting sometimes seems to counter any efforts to maintain good health. Again, while not all conflict or post-conflict settings will threaten the researcher with malaria or typhoid, or deprive them of sleep, the added stress of working in an unfamiliar setting, combined with a lack of adequate medical services, poses a significant threat to physical health over the course of six, eight, or ten months of fieldwork.

There are no clear solutions for these problems of climate and disease, but there are ways to minimize risk, some of which are simple, perhaps even obvious, while others are less so. For example, before you head to the field to conduct an ethnographic evaluation, be sure to understand the environmental and climatic challenges in the setting to which you are traveling – and *be prepared*. It may seem like such an obvious point that it need not be said, but it is very easy to underestimate the simple problems of living in an impoverished or transitional state. Most people traveling to West Africa know that they must prepare for malaria, that they should start taking a prophylactic prior to leaving home, and that they should bring treatment medications. Similarly, most know to bring rehydration salts in case of dysentery, typhoid, or general diarrhea. But few seem to pay attention to the little details that can stop them from ever contracting these diseases.

Many expatriates I knew in Makeni, for example, both in 2008/2009 and 2012, were infected with malaria three or four times over a six-month period even though they were on prophylactics. I even know people who have had malaria six or seven times within a year. While I do not take prophylactics, I have only had malaria twice over about 18 months in country. The difference is that, while many expatriates arrive in the country armed with prophylactics, most then proceed to sit around at night, outside bars, smelling of perfumes that attract mosquitoes, with low-cut tops, sleeveless shirts, unprotective flip-flop style sandals and ankle-baring pants; practically asking to contract malaria. As you might expect, they regularly have malaria. While they know to take prophylactics, they often fail to take the much simpler step of wearing long sleeves and pants, high collars, socks and mosquito repellent. Similarly, in 2012, a good friend of mine, who will remain nameless, could not figure out why she kept contracting typhoid over and over again; she seemed never to fight it off. Then one day someone with 40 years experience in Sierra Leone asked if she was brushing her teeth with tap water from the tank above her house, and, indeed, she was. Instead of washing her teeth with bottled or bagged water, she was, every night, reintroducing contaminated water into her system. Again, she knew that she had to have rehydration salts to treat typhoid, was prepared to go to the hospital to receive treatment if her health deteriorated enough – and had done so on two different occasions – but hadn't taken the simple step of avoiding the intake of contaminated water. These are clear examples of expatriates knowing the risks, but failing to take the very simplest steps to avoid them.

I have four basic suggestions to avoid such issues and to avoid losing time out of a busy research schedule dealing with medical emergencies. First, before leaving for fieldwork, spend an hour talking to a couple of people who have lived wherever you are going for an extended period. Whether by internet, phone, or in person, a conversation with people who know the lie of the land, the dangers to be encountered, and the simple ways to avoid disease can be invaluable. Ask them directly what you can do to avoid contracting whatever disease is prevalent in the pertinent environment. Such people can give advice on the basics of maintaining everyday health, as opposed to the obvious advice that everyone knows. Second, within your first few days in a research setting, locate the nearest source of reliable medical care, register at that place, introduce yourself to a doctor or nurse, put their phone number in your phone, and carry your registration card for that medical center or hospital with you at all times. Having a personal connection to medical professionals provides access to knowledge, advice, and a medical opinion that may be necessary at any time, for you or for the people you work with on the ground.

Third, be conscious about your interactions with animals, children, water, and food. It may seem obvious to avoid drinking contaminated water or eating uncooked meat, but in many post-conflict and transitional settings it is just as important to avoid touching your face, mouth, or eyes after shaking hands with children or interacting with animals. While such good health habits are also important in the West, they are far more important in settings that may harbor dysentery, typhoid, cholera, Lassa fever, or worse. While you do not want to be paranoid and avoid all contact with the environment, you must learn to be prudent and maintain a heightened vigilance and awareness of environmental hazards – carry a small bottle of hand sanitizer with you at all times and use it regularly. And, finally, be vigilant and *do not procrastinate.* A medical issue that can be a small problem at home may easily become much more serious in an unfamiliar transitional state with limited medical resources. The best advice that can be given is to be constantly on guard, pay attention to your body, get rest and sleep when you can, and respond immediately to any potential health threats. While the potential health hazards will clearly vary, the threats of climate and disease are noted by scholars working across cases (Sarsby 1984: 104–5; Madden 2010: 91), and the simple precautions listed here should be relevant to every case.

Crime, violence, and accidental injury

Another major concern in conflict or post-conflict settings is the threat of crime, violence, and accidental injury. While these threats do, of course, have their parallels in any setting, in a post-conflict setting they are often significantly increased. In such settings there may, for example, be a threat of violence from military or paramilitary groups, from ex-combatants, from individuals seeking to profit from the legal and normative ambiguity of transition, or from individuals simply trying to survive. For whatever reasons, conducting research in conflict and post-conflict settings inherently exposes the evaluator to an increased threat of crime. It is quite likely that any researcher will be the victim of opportunistic theft committed non-violently – losing a cell phone, a digital recorder, or some money – but more serious and significant crime and violence are also possible. There are cases of researchers being violently mugged, kidnapped, raped, and even murdered in conflict settings (Sluka 2012a: 238), and while scholars have been quite concerned about the implications of these violent settings for the collection and interpretation of research, there is much less attention paid to the practical ways researchers can avoid violence in the field (Kovats-Bernat 2002).

In my experience, the best way for any researcher to deal with the threat of crime, violence, or injury in the field is, quite simply, to *avoid it*. In Sierra Leone, I have regularly been the target of thieves; from the pickpocket who managed to unzip my wife's backpack and almost earn himself a free roll of toilet paper in Eastern Freetown, to the lucky young man (I imagine) who took a brand-new football right off our front porch, or the daring individuals who cut open the corrugated iron roof of our kitchen to steal my $80 generator. Crime is simply going to happen where relatively wealthy expatriates are present in a setting where many people are poor. However, in all of these situations I could have done better to avoid these attempted and/or successful thefts. We should never have left the football on the porch, for example, and I should have stored the generator inside the house, instead of in the small generator room attached to the outdoor kitchen. Indeed, in most cases, I think I must have successfully avoided crime, as I have fewer stories of crime and theft than most.

But there are also many instances where I could have been involved in far more violent events if I had been less conscious to threats. Violence is regularly quite close at hand in Sierra Leone. At the two lorry parks in Makeni where cars and trucks pick up passengers for trips between cities – as described in Chapter 2 – there are regularly violent interactions between drivers fighting over the passengers for whom they compete. Football matches too regularly descend into blows between competing teams, and sometimes between the fans and players, and I once watched, embarrassed, as my own team chased a pickup truck down a dirt track as the young men in the back of the pickup swung shovels at the heads of the players running behind. The truck, emblazoned with the logo of the Catholic Mission, had initiated this near manic display of hostility simply by crossing the field while play was ongoing, but from the reaction of my teammates you would have thought some major blood-feud was playing out. Violence is simply not a distant or remote possibility in Sierra Leone, as it is in much of the West.

In Makeni, it is common to see women beating children or young men fighting in the street. It is not uncommon for men to hit their wives or girlfriends, for parents and teachers to beat children, for older children to beat younger children, and for the police to beat the citizenry. You regularly see people of all ages throwing rocks at dogs or beating them with sticks. Such acts do not necessitate social response or sanction; they are taken as relatively normal events. I was once sitting talking to a friend, in his twenties at the time, about the education system in Sierra Leone, when he told me, with a worried expression on his face, that his younger brothers were not learning anything at school. They were not taking advantage of the education system, he said, because the teachers were not allowed to beat them any more; how would they learn, he argued, if they were not punished for not learning? On another occasion, one dry hot day in early 2009, my housemate and I rescued a dog from a group of perhaps 15 young boys who were jubilantly beating it with sticks as one of them dragged it by its tied paws down the road. They were beating it, they said, because it was a bad dog. It was bleeding badly and died in a convulsion about 24 hours afterwards on our neighbor's porch.

There have regularly been occasions, during my fieldwork, where I felt a strong compulsion to intervene in such scenes of violence. These include the many times I could hear the screams of a child being punished or two men about to come to blows over a few thousand Leone at the lorry park. At such times I have wanted to try to calm the situation and avoid violence, but have instead chosen to avoid the situation and walk away. This is, I believe, the appropriate response. Just as the best way to stay healthy in Sierra Leone is to avoid shaking every child's hand or brushing your teeth with contaminated water, or the best way to avoid getting robbed is to avoid leaving your possessions on the porch or showing off your shiny new tech gadgets, so the best way not to become involved in violence is to *actively avoid it*. When I see men fighting at the lorry park in Makeni, I turn away and walk somewhere else. When I see an adult beating a child, I say nothing, as hard as that is. When two rival football teams come to blows, I shake my head and walk off the field. I do not want, at any point, to give anyone a reason to see me as an active agent in any form of violence. Very simply put, violence is best avoided by pro-actively setting yourself apart from it. Particularly when you are in a social and cultural environment you are only coming to understand, the best option is to threaten no one and give no one the chance to see you as a potential threat; as either a source or a target of violence.

However, one area that cannot be fully avoided, and perhaps for that reason is the area I think is actually of most threat to researchers in the field, are accidents, and particularly traffic accidents. Just as most contemporary conflicts and, therefore, post-conflict settings are in impoverished or failed states, so most peacebuilding processes are carried out in states which lack – or simply fail to enforce – laws regarding construction codes and transport regulations. Hence, in many such settings the greatest threat to life and limb will not be a paramilitary group, a coup, or an armed criminal gang, but an accident. Any particular researcher is very unlikely to be shot at or embroiled in a violent protest, but they are quite likely to be harmed in some kind of transportation accident.

Transport infrastructure and regulation in Sierra Leone are particularly limited. You regularly see young men riding on the roofs of vans and trucks already loaded with goods twice the volume of the vehicle itself. I have seen four grown adults riding on a single motorcycle and even, quite a few times, young men riding on the hood of cars, their backs against the windscreen as they race down the highway between Makeni and Freetown. The three major forms of public transportation common in Sierra Leone – motorcycles (called *okada*), minibuses (called *poda-poda*), and taxis – are each extremely dangerous in their own way. The small underpowered *okadas* are dangerous because they are far too easy to fall from and the bikes zip in and around moving traffic, inches from colliding with one another or with the larger vehicles on the road. Riders in Sierra Leone are required to wear helmets, but the helmets are cheap plastic shells no better than a pretend firefighter's helmet you might find in a kindergarten; accidents are common and injuries are ubiquitous. The *poda-podas* are similarly dangerous, but for completely different reasons. Drivers cram between 20 and 25 passengers into a space that would, in the West, be reserved for perhaps 12, and while using such transportation is relatively safe in a busy city with slow-moving traffic – though extremely restrictive, humid, and stifling – when traveling at 70 miles per hour on the highway these vehicles are cumbersome, difficult to maneuver, and slow to brake. Further, when accidents do occur, it is difficult to extract the survivors from the vehicles.

Taxis are not much better, either in Freetown or on the highways. In Freetown most taxi drivers dodge around slow-moving traffic and speed down tightly packed lanes, while bush taxi drivers cram as many as nine people into ancient Honda Civics and Toyota Corollas, often with five people in the back seat, two sharing the passenger seat and, if he is particularly "skillful," two also sharing the driver's seat. Around these many bodies are packed bags, bundles, and perhaps a chicken or two; nobody using a seatbelt and certainly nobody too concerned about speed limits. When accidents do occur, fatalities are common. While I have had many close calls, I have somehow avoided such accidents during my time in Sierra Leone, but many people are not so lucky and, indeed, I would say that accidents are the most common danger to a researcher in this particular setting. While this may not be true for all post-conflict settings, it is quite likely that the lack of infrastructure and regulation enforcement in contemporary transitional states will create a situation unlike the very heavily managed transportation infrastructure in most Western states; a situation that the evaluator must be prepared for.

But, as I noted above, this is hardly avoidable. As the ethnographic approach requires the evaluator to get out into the community and to travel and engage with local people, you cannot avoid traveling on public roads, if not actually on public transportation. For my own part I have also tried to avoid associations between myself and any NGO or government agencies in the local setting and have, therefore, never had access to safe private vehicles when traveling to conduct interviews. During my fieldwork within Makeni in 2008/2009, I walked everywhere in town, plodding from house to house and often returning to the same places at pre-arranged times in the evening when people would have more time to sit and talk on the porch. This approach, if it is possible, seems the safest, as it allows you to avoid using public transport as much as possible and to be very visible in the community, while also avoiding association with a large, rich, powerful organization which would only further your identification as another big man.

However, my work in 2012 among the villages within the FDI project, which are spread throughout the 40,000-hectare site, required a vehicle and I spent many hours zipping up and down the highway or bumping along the rutted dirt roads of the project area moving from village to village on an *okada* which I bought and had my research assistant and translator drive. On many occasions I was uncomfortably close to disaster as Mohammed and I were regularly caught in major rainstorms while flying down the highway at 60 miles per hour or caught unawares by a company truck or a goat as we came around a corner on the dirt roads within the project. On many occasions I simply closed my eyes and hoped for the best. But the alternative was to only go into the project area with the few NGOs who are conducting their own oversight of the project, and it would have been very difficult to avoid being seen as an employee, or more likely a big man, of that NGO. This, in turn, would greatly affect the expectations of the people I interviewed and their responses to my questions.

So, at least in my case, it was not possible to avoid fully the dangers of accidents. In cases similar to Sierra Leone, where traffic accidents probably pose the most serious threat to physical security, I would advise researchers to bring a motorcycle helmet from home, avoid traveling in bad weather, hire a known and trusted driver, and demand forcefully that the driver follow the speed limit, no matter how much he or she laughs at you. If traveling for reasons other than research, try to travel in a private vehicle instead of on public transport, but, if you must take public transport, be selective. Choose the newest-looking car, ensure that it has seatbelts and then pay for two so that you can sit alone in the front passenger seat and actually *use your seatbelt*. These are suggestions for this particular setting. But again, comparable suggestions can be heard from other researchers who have worked in other post-conflict states. As with avoiding disease, before conducting an evaluation using the ethnographic approach, talk at length with someone who has previously worked extensively in the setting to which you are traveling, and again, ask them directly, which small everyday practices can help avoid accidents.

Psychological challenges

The physical challenges noted above are in many ways easy to identify and commonly acknowledged. The psychological challenges of working in post-conflict and transitional states, however, are far less commonly acknowledged and are much more difficult to avoid. Clearly threats to physical security create their own psychological challenges, which can then take a toll on the research being conducted and even affect how evaluators collect and evaluate data. In addition, the fact that most peacebuilding processes occur within impoverished and in many cases highly unequal societies may place particular stresses on individual researchers. All of these challenges must somehow be managed and, indeed, Sarsby argued that such challenges may pose the greatest difficulties for researchers in the field (1984: 104). At the same time, however, I believe that these are not challenges that should be avoided in the same way that physical threats should be avoided. Indeed, the dynamics of the setting that give rise to such challenges are exactly those that the researcher must come to understand and appreciate if they are to begin to understand the local experiences of peacebuilding processes. Hence, the correct response to psychological challenges is not avoidance, but *management*.

For example, in my experience, the physical challenges of ill-health, insecurity, and mild sleep deprivation create additional and problematic psychological strains that affect my ability and desire to go and do the actual work of qualitative research; traveling to villages, conducting interviews, writing field notes, transcribing interviews, etc. The stress of constantly worrying about your own health or safety will, inevitably, negatively affect your work. For example, after that rainy night when someone cut through the corrugated tin roof of our outside kitchen to steal my generator, I went weeks without sleeping much at all. As the thieves had used the noise of a heavy rainstorm to cover the sound of their activity, each night it rained heavily – and in the rainy season that is most nights – I simply lay awake listening to the scratching of the mango tree branches on the roof and the pounding of the rain. As the roof of the house was the exact same material as the outside kitchen and there were vastly more valuable items in the house than there had been in the kitchen (laptops, cell phones, iPods, etc.), there seemed little reason to think that the house would not itself be easily entered at some point. Whether my worries were simple paranoia or not, I didn't sleep very much for weeks on end and, as the reader can imagine, my productivity and enthusiasm suffered.

Although this is only one particular example from one particular case, it is quite likely that the stresses and pressures of living for months in unfamiliar and unsettled transitional states will have, at some point, similar effects on most researchers. For this reason, it is imperative that researchers take breaks from the field or, more accurately, breaks from the dynamics that are causing such psychological strain. During my time conducting research on the TRC and later on the FDI project, I usually tried to leave the particular settings of the research at least every six weeks. This has never meant leaving Sierra

Leone, but simply involved a weekend at the beach, a trip to one of the national parks within the country, or a weekend in Freetown. Such trips serve to get me out of the usual context, break the monotony, and refresh the spirit, and have always allowed me to get back to work much more calmly and productively when I return.

Similarly, I believe that it is imperative that researchers have a home that is protected, at least to some extent, from the context of the research. If you cannot retreat, at the end of the day, to a moderately comfortable and secure environment, somewhere that provides at least some comforts and memories of what is "normal" for you, then the everyday grind of the ethnographic approach in a post-conflict setting can become overwhelming. This was advice given to me before I first went to Sierra Leone in 2007, by someone who had worked with the TRC a few years before. "You cannot live as the local people do," he told me, "you will always be sick and won't get any work done." I found this to be true, at least in the case of northern Sierra Leone, and, whereas this may not be exactly replicated in all post-conflict or transitional states, the general lesson will probably hold. No matter in what post-conflict or transitional state your research is occurring, you must have somewhere to retreat to, somewhere to feel comfortable and secure and where the various physical threats are less immediate. This, in turn, will provide some relief from the psychological challenges.

However, as noted above, some psychological stresses should be accepted as a productive part of the work, a way to come closer to understanding the local experience. Witnessing the violence, poverty, inequality, and hardship that exist in everyday life in many post-conflict settings is a central part of coming to understand the local context. At the same time, it can foster difficult and negative reactions on the part of the researcher. Living in Makeni in 2008/2009 and then traveling extensively in the villages of the FDI project's land-lease area in 2012 exposed me to the endemic poverty and malnutrition with which local people deal on a daily basis. In turn, this allowed me to understand, at least in some way, what they mean by words like "hardship," or when they say, with heart-breaking understatement, that the "situation is very difficult." You cannot understand local experiences of development projects, government initiatives, or even the patron–client system, without understanding clearly the actual objective poverty with which most Sierra Leoneans contend. Such exposure is, for this reason, productive.

But at the same time it can also be psychological debilitating. I'm sure the experience varies from person to person, but, speaking only for myself I can say that I have a very real psychological reaction to certain dynamics of Sierra Leonean poverty. Some may react with tears; upset to see malnourished children or blind beggars on the street. Some may react with depression; perhaps feeling inept to deal with the magnitude of such problems. Some may simply repress their emotions, as seems quite common among expatriates in Sierra Leone, retreating into alcohol and long nights at expatriate bars. For my part, I respond with a mixture of deep frustration and anger. I get angry at the international actors; at those who control the money, make the decisions, and seem never to visit their supposed beneficiaries. I get deeply frustrated at the waste of life, time, effort, and potential that poverty allows. And I become increasingly infuriated at the local and national big men who try to convince you that everything is being well managed and taken care of. This kind of anger is not an optimal mindset for research. Again, while I know not everyone will respond in the same way, I do believe that everyone will have some form of psychological response to witnessing such situations in post-conflict settings; psychological responses which will then affect the actual research being conducted and the eventual analysis.

The challenge then is to manage that response. While I believe each person will have to find their own solutions, the key is to be conscious of the psychological effect – your own response to what you are witnessing in the field – and to respond accordingly. I, for example, have largely minimized my need to interview elites; whether local or international. My research questions have never particularly required much engagement with elites to begin with, as I am primarily trying to evaluate experiences among proportionally representative samples of the population who have supposedly benefited from peacebuilding projects, as described in Chapter 5. But since I have recognized my own rather negative response to the class dynamics I witness in the field, I have moved even further towards evaluation among populations who are overwhelmingly non-elite. This allows me to interview people I can identify with, feel empathy for, and feel proud to represent in my publications, as opposed to the elites I often cannot help but see as part of the problem.

Other forms of research demand that researchers do not respond to what they see in the field by altering their methodology. In quantitative studies concepts should be operationalized, survey instruments designed, and research protocols simply followed in the field. But in the ethnographic approach this cannot be the case and evaluators must be flexible on the ground. Evaluators following this approach must be welcomed into communities, project no hostility, anger, or fear, and empathetically listen to the stories and narratives of men and women, young and old, educated and illiterate alike. They must, therefore, find creative ways to engage substantively with their interviewees. To unconsciously carry one's own psychological burdens into such interactions would directly affect the quality of the data collected and, therefore, the findings produced. It is imperative, therefore, that evaluators following the ethnographic approach actively reflect on how the setting is affecting them psychologically, on how those responses might be manifest in the research endeavor, and initiate efforts to *manage* these responses during research. Similar responses may be required in response to ethical concerns.

Ethics and responsibility in the field

One of the most troubling challenges with the ethnographic approach to evaluating peacebuilding intervention is closely related to the inherently grounded empathetic approach to data collection that is built into the method. As the approach demands engagement with local non-elites, the evaluator is placed in a position that administrators rarely experience, a position of responsibility towards the supposed beneficiaries of the peacebuilding intervention. This position of responsibility raises significant ethnical challenges. For example, the most difficult experiences I have had in conducting this kind of research are when my interviewees themselves challenge me on the supposedly neutral position of the "evaluator." When I conducted my evaluation of the local experiences of the TRC, this was somewhat less of a problem, as the process had completed its work four years prior and I could do nothing to improve its processes or communicate to the TRC the voices of those it was supposedly trying to help. However, there were still people who asked me to represent their needs to the government. As many people felt that the TRC had promised help and support, many asked that I make sure the government was aware of their needs. The big men had forgotten them, and so I was a potential conduit for their complaints.

This was an even more pronounced challenge during my 2012 fieldwork in the land-lease area of the FDI project. As this project is ongoing and people see it as a process that can be influenced, changed, or affected, they are looking for any way to influence the policies and practices of the company. A 34-year-old man named Amidu, for example, who was a successful farmer and trader in his village, very much wanted me to convince the company to provide all that he felt they had promised. As he said directly to my research assistant,

> I am not talking to him to come and help [the company], I am not talking to him to come and help my people, I am talking to him so that what [the company] commit [to], let them be able to do it for us and our people.

Another young man, a 26-year-old Mende who had traveled from the south in search of work with the company but found himself unable to secure employment because he had no *sababu* [influence, support, connections], similarly stated, "if you will be able to help us … for us to be able to get a job I think that will be necessary … right now we have nothing even to eat today, we don't have anything." Pa Burehma, a 79-year-old retired farmer, most directly questioned my allegiance, asking me "to try very hard for all of us, the land-owners, to form a group in order for us to make one unit wherein nobody will get to lose." This is what he was requesting of me. At a later point in the interview he asked quite directly, "we and [the company], who do you support?"

Such moments highlight the distinct power differences between the "beneficiaries" of peacebuilding interventions and the evaluators of those processes. No matter how marginal their position within their organization or how small their PhD stipend, expatriate evaluators of peacebuilding processes will almost always be far more wealthy, educated, connected, and mobile than their interviewees. As such, they will be put in challenging ethical situations perhaps not identical to that described above, but of a similar scope. I have found that the standard ethical protocols applied by research ethics boards fail miserably to address these issues of power and the resulting expectations among local people. Even having explained to interviewees that I work for neither the company nor the government, and after describing clearly that I have no influence over the process, the majority of local people still assume that I can influence the project. This is clearly related to the patron–client dynamics of the local environment, within which I am identified by local non-elites as a big man. Just like the TRC and the FDI project staff, I am seen as someone with influence. They therefore turn to me as a potential conduit for their complaints, their problems, and their requests.

Of course, every researcher must do their best to fully inform their interviewees – technically the subjects of the study – of the potential risks and benefits of participation, and I do so quite ardently. I try to impress on all of my interviewees that I have no power to affect the government or the company, that my research will result in publications that will be read by other researchers in the West and perhaps by some government workers, but that there will be no direct benefits to the interviewee except the small *kola* (a sign of respect and ritual exchange) I provide for their time (Le 4000 or $1 in 2012). But this is somewhat meaningless to largely illiterate subsistence farmers in rural Sierra Leone to whom all white people appear to be members of a rather small group of privileged and powerful people. It is no surprise, when you consider the distinct power dynamics between the local and the international actors, that it proves impossible to overcome completely local expectations. In essence, any attempt to do so is an attempt to dissociate the interviewee from their very knowledge of the world. The evaluator's very presence, appearing on the scene, asking questions, inquiring about what is happening, implies that they will act as patrons; that they will act to remedy the situation of local non-elites.

Just as with the examples provided above regarding health, disease, crime, violence, accidents, and psychological stress, and the various ways to avoid and/or manage these challenges, this example may be unique to my particular research. But it is representative of the kinds of complicated ethical positions that the ethnographic approach to peacebuilding evaluation will produce. This approach is not anthropological ethnography, exploring the minutia of how people engage with and act in their world and with each other, nor is it a brief sojourn into the field as one small element of a largely quantitative or desk-based evaluation project. On the contrary, it is evaluation of local experiences of a particular international intervention specifically through engagement with often impoverished and needy local actors in a time of instability and transition; a moment of particularly heightened and keen stresses wherein anger, animosity, tension, and expectation may be only inches from the surface. As a result, while the ethical dimensions of such situations may be diverse, they will almost assuredly be complicated and complicating, and the usual ethical guidelines required by an institutional review board or university ethics committee will not cleanly overcome, and will often seem quite ignorant of (see Bourgois 2012), these complexities.

So what to do? At what point does the researcher choose to become an actor or to affect her or his subject of research? Clearly, in these kinds of sensitive transitional periods, and particularly when the evaluation is of an ongoing project, simply conducting research affects the subject. In the case of the FDI project, if I ask people how they are experiencing the process, they reflect on their experience of the process. If I ask if they have enough income to feed their families, if next year's palm-oil harvest will provide enough money for their children's education, or if they feel their land will still be available for use in the coming years, they will be forced to reflect on the impact of the FDI project on their lives. Hence, I have already, simply by conducting research and asking questions, affected the local non-elite experience of and opinions about the project. The ethnographic approach, therefore, automatically puts the evaluator in a non-neutral position.

It is for this reason that I have considered turning to "action research," wherein the researcher both studies and affects the subject of her or his research for "some social purpose (i.e. cultural salvage, political or social action, development)" (Clammer 1984: 80–81). The field of anthropology has wrestled with the potential ramifications of such socially or politically active research, both in terms of its ethics and effects (James 2000: 83–85; Lassiter 2005: 72; Madison 2012), and in terms of the security problems it may pose for researchers (Sluka 2012b: 290). A more activist fieldwork method allows the researcher to work towards emancipatory goals both for individuals and groups as opposed to maintaining the fiction of the neutral observer (Boog 2003), and seems, therefore, directly pertinent to peacebuilding's objectives regarding emancipation. Action research provides one way for research to contribute to social goals, and for the researcher to coordinate activity with concerned civil society groups, government agencies, or local people themselves. While I have not yet taken steps in this direction, action research does seem an obvious extension of the ethnographic approach.

Action research may, therefore, be one way to respond to these ethical dilemmas. Without question it demands serious reflection on the part of the researcher about their responsibility. Does the researcher have the responsibility to represent those they study? What if the research identifies legal or moral problems, human rights violations, for example? Does this demand action on the part of the researcher? If your research were to uncover such problems, how do you respond? Do you hand over your data to domestic or international actors with the power to intervene? What if these actors are themselves complicit, and what if you have guaranteed your subject's anonymity? How do you protect subjects you cannot identify? If you decide that you will not hand over your data, but will provide reports to NGOs, civil society groups, government agencies, journalists, and international watchdogs, what happens in the meantime? Analysis and writing of data can take months, publication can take years, how much more suffering will occur if you wait until your "findings" are clear and unassailable before you hand them over to agencies with a mandate to act as opposed to watch?

All of these are questions that the evaluator must address for themselves, in each case, as they have significant further impacts on the very practical considerations of research. For example, such considerations will affect decisions about grant applications. Many funders will expect academic publications to be the primary output of research, shunning activist approaches. Others may prioritize the social impact of research. The source from whom you acquire funds to conduct your research will, therefore, greatly affect your eventual options for publishing your findings. This is certainly the case if you conduct peacebuilding evaluation as an employee of an NGO, government agency, or an international organization. In such instances, the researcher themselves may not have much input into decisions about where, how, and to what end the findings will be used. Indeed, if the evaluator is working for a corporation, they will probably not own the collected data or the copyright to the eventual work. Therefore, great consideration must be given to the funding sought to support ethnographic evaluations of peacebuilding processes.

Similarly, different kinds of peacebuilding interventions, or the time at which the evaluation is conducted, may give rise to different ethical challenges. Evaluating a project after the fact, similar to my own evaluation of the TRC, for example, can avoid many of these problems. Evaluating a project with few human rights implications, perhaps a small-scale intergroup dialogue process or processes conducted for or among relatively empowered communities, similarly avoids some of the more pressing concerns about the evaluator's ethnical responsibilities. Hence, the evaluator's own choice of what to study and when, will have significant implications for the eventual ethical challenges to be faced. At the same time, this means that the evaluator's own willingness to take on responsibility must affect their choice of topic. An activist researcher may choose to take on more responsibility, to engage with ongoing processes among marginalized people as opposed to completed processes among empowered people, and to put themselves in positions where they can affect peacebuilding policy and practice. On the other hand, a more traditional, non-activist research may, for good reason, choose to avoid such problems.

I feel it is important to note that the central principles of the ethnographic approach bring with them new ethical challenges that have largely been ignored in peacebuilding evaluation. The approach demands that the peacebuilding community challenge powerful interests which work against any cogent and coordinated representation of local non-elites in post-conflict and transitional states; interests which have long undermined any such representation and which have, as Richmond and Franks make clear (2009), undercut the ability of peacebuilding to facilitate emancipatory experiences of peace (this will be discussed further in the conclusion). Anyone who commits to the ethnographic approach must recognize that they are, through that very choice, making an ethical and political decision. To listen to the voices of the disempowered and marginalized and to publish reports and academic articles that represent those voices, is already an inherently political and ethical decision to work towards something more emancipatory; to give voice and to represent. The researcher's responsibility, therefore, is to reflect on each of the problems and questions outlined above, and many others pertinent to particular cases, and determine, for themselves, how to respond in relation to their case.

Conclusion

There are, without a doubt, significant challenges to the ethnographic approach to peacebuilding evaluation. If there weren't, perhaps a book like this would be unnecessary as many more people would be conducting grounded ethnographic analyses of peacebuilding interventions. However, as it is, even scholars such as Mac Ginty and Richmond (2013) and Donais (2012), who demand more attention be given to local ownership and local experiences of peacebuilding projects, do not generally conduct extensive fieldwork in transitional states. The findings of those who do conduct such fieldwork, such as Veena Das in India (2007), Kimberly Theidon in Peru (2013), Danny Hoffman in Sierra Leone and Liberia (2011), Severine Autesserre in the Democratic Republic of Congo (2010), and others, seem to be sidelined in the fields of policy and practice and within disciplines (sometimes their own disciplines) with the greatest influence over future peacebuilding endeavors, such as political science, international relations, international law, and economics. These are all disciplines where extended fieldwork has not traditionally been considered necessary in order to understand a problem even if that problem is located in societies and cultures wholly unlike those of the researcher. The primary demand is, instead, for the supposed "generalizability" and "legitimacy" of quantification.

But simply asking that these disciplines conduct more fieldwork and engage with local "beneficiaries" is not enough; and will for the most part be ignored. Nor is it sufficient to ask anthropologists and qualitative sociologists to engage more actively with policy and practitioner communities. Indeed, anthropologists – some of whom are listed above – have been making recommendations pertinent to peacebuilding practice for years, and scholars within international relations and conflict resolution have engaged in a sustained critique of the liberal peace approach and called for increased attention to the empowerment and inclusion of local actors for almost two decades (see Lederach 1995). For the most part, however, this has not produced significant change in how projects are planned and administered, which remains largely by "us" and for "them." Hence, something else must be done. There must be some new approach to bring the anthropological imagination and perspective forcefully into the theories and practices of the good governance experts, the transitional justice gurus, the economic development technicians, and the democratization promoters.

I believe that the first step must be a widespread acceptance and commitment to the ethnographic approach – or something that looks much like what I have presented in Part II of this book. While Oliver Richmond has called for a "post-liberal" (2009a) or an "emancipator" peace (Richmond 2006), and many have called for "local ownership" (Chesterman 2007; Sending 2009; Richmond 2012; Donais 2012), there have simply been no operational instructions or clear guidance on what this would look like or how this would come about. How do you avoid the tautological problem of simply making "ownership" something "we" design for "them?" How do you avoid the external implementation of "emancipation?" I argue that the first step is two-fold; first, find out how local people experience what we are already doing "for them," and, second, ask them what they believe should be done instead, in addition, or not at all. The ethnographic approach provides a way to achieve both of these steps and can, therefore, serve as the first step towards an emancipatory peace. While the challenges are great, both structurally within the discipline and practice of peacebuilding and individually for each researcher and in each case, as described above, the rewards are well worth the effort and the results may be the first steps towards a new form of peacebuilding.

8 The limits of quantitative evaluation and the potential for multi-methods approaches

My aim, throughout the past seven chapters of this book, has been to convince the reader of the value of the ethnographic approach to peacebuilding evaluation even if, as noted in Chapter 7, the approach also raises significant challenges. However, perhaps the most convincing argument for the value of the approach is rooted in the far more persistent and pervasive challenges to quantitative evaluations of peacebuilding interventions in contemporary post-conflict settings. Just as the practice of peacebuilding has come to be dominated by "tool-kit" solutions supposedly applicable across all cases, so procedures of monitoring and evaluation (M&E) have largely taken the form of either quantitative assessments of project outputs, or qualitative assessments relying on state-level observations of individual cases. As I have argued throughout the prior chapters, I am of the firm belief that neither of these approaches truly evaluates the local experiences of peacebuilding projects on the ground.

However, my critiques of quantitative approaches to evaluation have often been met, by academic colleagues, with assurances that I'm simply getting it wrong; I am being critical because I do not understand how statistics work. If I understood how quantitative scholars can control for sampling and measurement error, I'm told, then I would see that quantitative findings are valid and generalizable. I find myself always wanting to sit down with these colleagues for an hour or so, particularly those who primarily analyze secondary data, to explain exactly why I believe that quantitative approaches to evaluation in transitional states are so problematic. I want to explain that I don't have a problem with surveys administered in contexts in which the concepts governing sociality and relationships mirror those in the minds of those who design and administer surveys, but with those administered in non-Western cultures where survey instruments usually prove to have clear cultural and conceptual biases and are rarely validated for use in the local setting. Further, I want to explain to them that my concern is not with quantitative methods *per se*, but with quantitative methods that do not recognize and cannot control for the systematic and quite fundamental limitations of human and technical capacity in often impoverished transitional states. Needless to say, I rarely have the chance to explain these points.

While I started my academic career with training in both quantitative and qualitative methods, my focus on local experiences of peacebuilding projects – on outcomes as opposed to outputs – has affected my methodological choices over the past decade. However, while conducting my own fieldwork I have also had first-hand experience with two quantitative surveys in Sierra Leone which brought to light substantial problems with the collection of quantitative data in transitional states with often degraded national infrastructure and human capital. More worrying still, however, is that the people tasked with managing these research projects on the ground – the first for a major international NGO and the second for a consortium of seven different international development banks – were unaware of the systematic research errors they were committing, and though my presence during the administration of these two projects was accidental, I was the only one with any previous knowledge of how to design a research process and both collect and analyze the resulting data. Those tasked with managing the process of collecting and analyzing data did not have sufficient training in research methods and yet, even in the extremely trying circumstances of post-conflict Sierra Leone, were tasked by international actors to produce reports that would guide future policy and practice.

And this is, of course, my key concern. I have no interest in purely academic debates regarding research methodologies. My interest is in the role that research methodologies and their results have on those who make decisions about funding, planning, and administration. Similar to Jerven's recent observations within the field of international development, quantitative evaluation presents policy-makers with supposedly generalizable evidence and false certainty in the form of figures, tables, and graphs (2013: 5), instead of more nuanced representations of experiences, perceptions, and understandings. It is in response to this supposed generalizable certainty that toolkit solutions are developed. Only with a quantified picture of state failure, of internal displacement, of child soldier recruitment, of arms transports, etc. can programmatic solutions be devised and administered. The system is, therefore, incentivized to support and fund quantitative assessment projects, to come up with generalizable images of the problems peacebuilding should tackle, and to devise, in turn, standardized projects and programs of intervention. But, as I hope I have shown throughout this book, when transported from one post-conflict setting to another, these programs do not provide the predicted results.

In this chapter, therefore, I hope to highlight the serious problems I have observed with quantitative studies in transitional states and, in the end, describe the potential for a combined, multi-methodological research agenda in peacebuilding to overcome many of these problems. The first section briefly introduces the two quantitative projects with which I was involved in Sierra Leone and describes some of the most glaring problems identified during each. In the second and longest section, I provide a more structured breakdown of nine major problems I have identified with quantitative work in rural

Sierra Leone, with illustrations from the 2012 project. As usual, while I do not know if these problems would be found in all transitional states, I see little reason to believe that most of them would not be replicated in many other contemporary post-conflict settings. In the third section I describe briefly a potential multi-methodological research approach which could provide more accurate analysis of peacebuilding interventions and more helpful guidance for future policy.

Quantitative evaluation on the ground: two studies

On two occasions while in rural Sierra Leone I have had the opportunity to see how quantitative data is collected on the ground. The first project occurred in November and December of 2008 and was a survey administered among head-teachers, teachers, and a sample of students in 68 elementary schools in one region of northern Sierra Leone. The project was funded by a large well-known international development organization and carried out by a national NGO which focuses on children's health and welfare and with which I volunteered for three months when I first arrived in Makeni. While the NGO focuses its work on child welfare, which was pertinent to a survey hoping to measure child health, safety, and security in the schools, nobody at the NGO had particular training in designing or administering surveys, nor in analysis of data. As might be expected, there were many problems with the administration of the survey.

For example, the survey instrument itself had been taken from another country and it was presumed that it would be applicable also to Sierra Leone. In one question it asked, for example, if students knew their rights as a child and in response the child could choose "yes" or "no." The survey then proceeded on to the next question. It was assumed that this question would measure students' knowledge of their rights under the UN Convention on the Rights of the Child. But this question does not measure whether children know their rights, only whether the child believes they know their rights. In the rewrite of the survey, I added an additional question after this to confirm what this meant. The follow-up question asked the child to name three of those rights, thus confirming, or negating, the initial answer. In response to this added question we were able to gain real insight into which children really did have knowledge of their rights and which only believed they did. For example, a child might say that "yes" they did know their rights as a child, but on the follow-up question report that they had the right to respect their elders, the right to clean up after themselves, and the right to be punished if they misbehaved. This revealed that they had been informed not of their rights, but of their responsibilities. Others said yes to the first question but then proved unable to name even one "right" in response to the follow-up question. In this way, and in many questions, the survey was asking for information which was much needed but doing so in ways that simply were not appropriate. The real problem, however, is that no one at the small NGO tasked with administering the survey would have thought to make these edits to the questions on the survey they were provided by the international organization.

Another problem was related to the relationship between the national NGO conducting the surveys and the population of schools in which they were collecting the data. In the case I observed, the same individuals who carried out the survey engaged with many of these same schools for their regular programming (distribution of soap and water buckets, sensitization about health and safety, etc.) and, I later learned, regularly distributed these services in such a way as to appropriate resources while ensuring that the international NGO's evaluators would never find out. In essence they distributed far less than the international NGO demanded of them but just enough so that the head-teachers of the involved schools would not want to disrupt their own access to those resources that were trickling down by reporting the national NGO to the international NGO. The same people hired to collect valid data, in short, were regularly lying to the international organization for whom they were collecting the data. Smaller NGOs were chosen to conduct the survey in particular areas where they had operational experience (which seems rational), but that operational experience meant that the teachers and head-teachers in these schools were most likely influenced in their responses by their history of interaction with that NGO; a history which was, at least in this case, far from innocent.

The second survey occurred in April and May of 2012, when I was working in the offices of the large FDI project for six weeks, assisting them with their own M&E program to monitor the social and economic impacts of their project in the land-lease area. This survey consisted of extensive household surveys collecting information about household income, demographics, education levels, agricultural production, and household commodities, and involved the training of a 15-person survey team. The survey was designed to measure the social and economic impacts of the FDI project within its land-lease area and would be administered every second year throughout the 50 years of the project. The company wanted to survey every single household inside the project area and had hired a South African consulting firm for the purpose of organizing and managing the process and training the survey team. This firm was primarily involved in Geographic Information Systems (GIS) technology but the company believed it was also qualified to conduct large-scale social surveys.

There were various problems with this survey which will be described in the next section, but I will provide a snapshot here of the most glaring problems. First, though the South African consultants had scheduled only two to three days to train the 15 enumerators – because these were primarily the same people who had conducted the initial "baseline" survey in 2010 – it soon proved, that many of these enumerators (14 out of an initial training group of 25) could not convert spoken numbers into written figures. In other words, this largely statistical data (years of education, income per month from various agricultural products, bushels of rice produced or sold, etc.) was being collected by people who, when they heard the phrase "I made three and a half million Leone last year," in Temne, for example, were as likely to write down Le 350,000 or Le 3,000,050 as they were to write Le 3,500,000. Worse still, this was only discovered because I demanded that we conduct the training over two weeks and not the originally scheduled two days. We did not discover this problem until the end of the first week, when we conducted our first test of inter-coder reliability – a standard process which the staff of the company and the consulting firm had not initially planned to conduct at all.

In another startling development, the surveys that had been collected in 2010 – and consistently described by the company as their "baseline" data – were being entered into computer databases by "data-entry clerks" with no checks on data consistency. In my first week in the office I briefly stood behind one of these clerks and watched him make two data entry errors in a matter of minutes. There was no way to tell, when scanning the Excel sheets of data, what had been entered correctly and what was simply misinformation. In addition, the company had somehow lost hundreds of these paper surveys and whole villages were omitted from the eventual database; paper surveys were simply misplaced. Indeed, on the very first day of the new data collection in 2012, the survey team found dozens of houses in one village that had been assigned identification cards – which proved that they had provided data to the 2010 baseline survey – but that did not show up in the Excel sheets; their data had been collected but never entered by the data-entry clerks. The experience does not, in any way, provide confidence in the data collected, in the data included in those badly coded spreadsheets, in the company's ability to monitor its own processes and impacts, or in the eventual reports produced.

Again, I do not want to critique quantitative methods or social surveys in general. The more significant issue is the use of the data collected by such methods which are so easily portrayed in tables, figures, and pie-charts as accurate representations of the situation on the ground – as authoritative knowledge – by people unqualified to administer them and in settings inhospitable to their successful use. To make the point quite clear by repeating one of the most shocking problems identified; the consultant hired to manage the FDI project's large M&E survey had expected to spend two days training the survey team. If I had not insisted on two weeks, they never would have conducted any tests for inter-coder reliability, would never have realized that most of the enumerators could not accurately record numerical data, and, in short, would never have recognized that the data being collected was riddled with errors and inaccuracies. The consultant admitted to me himself that he was glad I happened to be there, because he did not know how to do social research and was only hired by the company because he was already doing their GIS and mapping work.

Problems with quantitative research in transitional states

In late September 2012, just as I was finishing my six months studying the local experiences of the FDI project, I presented preliminary findings to representatives of some funding agencies and international NGOs in Freetown. After I presented my data and then answered questions for about an hour, one of the funding agency representatives said that he appreciated the quality of information that I had presented and the depth of local knowledge that I could bring to bear in my analysis, but, he continued, this would all be more powerful if I could support these findings with quantitative assessments. He asked why I had not also done surveys and seemed to be implying that this qualitative information regarding local experiences, replete with observations of the ongoing problems in the villages, would be more convincing if it could be summarized, charted, and graphed. I was shocked by the naivety of this question but then again, I had not presented the long list of issues that make quantitative studies so problematic in Sierra Leone.

I present that list now, hoping to make clear exactly why I feel we cannot rely on findings from quantitative studies in contemporary transitional states which are almost always also settings characterized by illiteracy, inequality, poverty, lack of human and state capacity, and degraded state infrastructure. In essence, while I do not want to be interpreted as attacking quantitative methodologies *per se*, it seems that the serious limitations of such approaches in transitional states are rarely acknowledged and need to be highlighted before audiences will realize the potential added value of an ethnographic approach and the data it produces. While the list of nine problems I describe below were observed in the research process of the FDI project in 2012, and are therefore specific to this project, in this place, and at this time, I do believe that the kinds of problems identified here will be echoed in other similarly precarious post-conflict situations. I also believe that they are often completely unrecognized by those convinced of the illusory authority of quantitative findings, charts, tables, and graphs.

Defining the unit of analysis

First, I want to note a number of interrelated problems undermining very core elements of quantitative research as a practice: defining the unit of analysis, sampling from a population, and the use of control cases. The first, the problem of defining the unit of analysis, is central to any quantitative research and it requires the researcher to choose the units that are being compared to each other, or, as in the case of the FDI project's M&E process, to themselves over time. The unit of analysis might be a state, a city, a business, a person, or any unit of particular interest to a researcher. In the case of the FDI project, the unit of analysis was the household, defined by the company staff as "those who share from the same pot," or those who eat together. The pot, in this case, was used as an analogy for support, and identifies anyone who eats from a pot as the dependents of she or he who owns it. This is actually a relatively accurate and culturally sensitive concept of the household in Sierra Leone and shows some level of cultural sensitivity as the company clearly recognized that a stereotypical Western notion of a nuclear family would not be applicable in this case.

However, this definition is problematic for a number of reasons. First, in any given Sierra Leonean family group there may be two or three pots, and, indeed, more than one central household building, depending on the arrangement of wives and children. Sometimes men, co-wives, and their children will all eat from one pot, sometimes they will not. Sometimes the husband will act as the head of one household while his senior wife acts as the head of her own household. Further, who eats where and from what pot will change regularly. Young children, for example, will move between parents, uncles, aunts, and grandparents; often moving between houses or switching from village to village over the years. This is not a move in the manner of a temporary holiday, but may alter the identity of the adult responsible for their support, thus changing the household composition and making it impossible to track the changes in that household over time; which is the entire purpose of the M&E program. The FDI project failed to recognize that the household in Sierra Leone is a constantly evolving entity and that returning to a particular building does not mean returning to the same household. Hence, though the M&E process tried to define the unit of analysis in a manner suitable to Sierra Leone, it is very unlikely that it recorded an accurate assessment of its effects on these households across time.

The challenges of sampling

Second, the FDI project is required by the development banks to conduct their M&E surveys, and these banks requested that the M&E surveys collect data among a representative sample of 10 percent or 15 percent of the households within the land-lease area. However, the company wanted to track the effects of the project throughout the entire land-lease area and, apparently did not understand that a random sample would have accomplished this, chose instead to include every household. In reality, either approach would have been difficult as, even in 2012 (two years after the supposed "baseline survey"), nobody was actually sure how many villages there were on the project, how many would eventually sign the land-lease agreements, or how many households existed in each village. The project's initial assessment of the environmental, health, and social impacts of the project, for example, was published in 2010 and estimated that there would be 13,617 people impacted by the project – a figure which exhibits, in its ridiculous precision, the false authority of figures – but by May of 2012, the company thought, based on the likely still quite incorrect 2010 baseline data, that this number was somewhere closer to 27,000.

In addition, as noted above, a great number of households had been included in the baseline survey but had then been lost and never entered into the database. As a result, the company simply had no way of knowing how many households or how many individuals there were within the land-lease area. Alternatively, there were a number of villages, and therefore even more households, which had been included in the 2010 baseline, as they were located within the land-lease area, but which had not yet signed the company's lease agreement. Should these be included in the population of households affected by the land-lease project? It is difficult to see how the project could accomplish either a survey of the whole population or sample 10 percent or 15 percent of the population, when they were unsure what the population was or where they were located.

Indeed, this issue of identifying the population may be moot, as the infrastructural problems in Sierra Leone, as in many contemporary transitional states, make it extremely difficult to actually conduct surveys among any sample. Even if the company could correctly identify every village and household, and could then randomly select a 10 percent or 15 percent sample, they would still be left with the challenge of traveling to each of those villages. This is the same limitation faced by the TRC, which conducted its sensitization programs and collected statements primarily in villages located along major roads and near to major towns, so as to facilitate easy access, i.e. generally failing to contact or engage with isolated villages in rural areas. Indeed, through geographical cluster sampling I randomly sampled only ten villages out of the 90 or more villages within the FDI project's land-lease area for my own interviews and getting to two of those ten (20 percent) required that I leave the *okada* in a nearby village, walk for a half hour or more into the bush, and then take off my boots, hike up my jeans, and wade through water to reach the destination. One of these villages had been previously visited by the company's survey team both in 2010 and in 2012, the other had had no visitors from the company and told me that I was the first white man to ever arrive there. In short, the problems of identifying, locating, and traveling to sampled villages in post-conflict states with no history of census taking, with mobile households and communities, and degraded or destroyed transportation infrastructure are difficult to overcome and limit the validity of survey data from such settings.

No control cases

A further significant problem that will undermine the validity of any eventual findings of this quantitative work is the company's reluctance to include control villages or, more accurately, control households, in their sample. The 2010 baseline survey had only been conducted on villages within the land-lease area and when I explained the necessity to include controls in the 2012 survey, the company representatives initially acquiesced, agreeing that they wanted good data and if controls were necessary, they should do it. But after I had taken the time to randomly sample ten villages outside the land-lease area to serve as controls, they then decided that this was not necessary. I was told that all of the villages in the region had been affected to some extent by the various mining and agriculture firms, so these villages would not be unaffected. There was no point, in their opinion, of having any controls.

Again, much as with rigorous sampling procedures, including controls is a necessity for rigorous quantitative evaluation of project impact. There is no way to know if the observed effects of the FDI project within the land-lease area, whether positive or negative, are actually the result of the project unless randomly sampled controls from outside that area are included in the study. When I made this argument, I was told that the villages within the land-lease area which had not yet seen any company activity – those which had not yet signed the agreement or in areas where the company had not yet started work for their own reasons – would serve as controls. But, of course, the purpose of the surveys is to track the effects of the project over time – over 10, 20, 50 years – and in 2012 it was very much the company's plan to eventually start work in the area of these currently isolated villages. Indeed, even in 2012, these villages were not unaffected as they had already been infected by the expectations and hope that the company had inspired. Nonetheless, the company's M&E process has so far been conducted completely without controls, though this means that any "observed" impact can never be shown to be related to the company's operations.

No experienced research staff or third party evaluation

The three problems above, which undermine very fundamental aspects of the quantitative research process, result, I believe, from the failure of the FDI project to incorporate, and the failure of the funding banks to demand that they incorporate, either any experienced social science researchers on their own staff, or to accept truly independent third party evaluators. I was told, while describing the general inadequacy of the 2010 baseline data, that another PhD, working as a consultant for the company, had supervised that process. But I saw no evidence that anyone with quantitative experience had been involved, though it is possible that that person simply had a similar experience to mine and gave up on trying to convince the company to apply standard quality controls to its own M&E process. In essence, the company itself had no incentive to support any attempts to ensure rigorous research and my efforts were in vain.

Indeed, the reasons I was given when I was eventually asked to leave the company in early June of 2012 were: (1) that they were worried because I had identified weaknesses in their M&E process; and (2) that they could not have someone like me, whom they were not paying, observing how the project operates. It became very clear that no real independent third party evaluation would be welcome. Hence, the company must be responsible for its own M&E, as per the bank's demands, but they have no reason to hire people actually qualified to do this work and certainly no interest in identifying any problems with their own practice within the land-lease area. Indeed, my graduate student, working with me at the time and serving as an intern on the M&E project, noted that the company is actually incentivized to collect bad data. If their data appeared to reflect well on them, then they could pretend that it was good data and no one would be any wiser. But if it reflected negatively on them, then they can easily turn around and blame a consultant for the quality of the data. In essence, they were very much incentivized to do just enough to appease the banks, but actually avoid collecting data accurately and certainly to avoid the involvement of any truly independent third party researchers. And it may be for this reason that they relied so heavily on consultants.

Over-reliance on consultants

The PhD who had apparently been involved in the 2010 survey had been working as a consultant. Similarly, a South African consultant had been hired to come up to the project for three weeks to supervise the process in 2012. As I described above, this was the same consulting firm that is responsible for the company's GIS services, as well as their environmental M&E process. The company seems to assume that these skills are all related and they had little incentive to verify the qualifications of such consultants for social or economic research. In turn, the consulting firm is fully incentivized to portray itself as a qualified candidate for this kind of work. Indeed, unless either party interacts eventually with a more rigorous research process or a more qualified researcher, they never will have reason to question the consultant's research abilities.

This is a worrying dynamic for a number of reasons. Clearly the consulting firm gains financially from providing a service that the company wants. As such, they are incentivized to provide information that the company wants to receive. In addition, the consulting staff live and work alongside the company employees. They live in company housing, eat, drink, and party at company events, and generally interact with and identify more with the company than with the local community. As a result, the consultants were both financially and personally tied to the company. They are not independent of the company and free to conduct research and write up findings as independent evaluators or auditors. They are not paid directly by, hand data and reports directly to, or have allegiances to the development banks or another oversight body, but to the company itself. As a result, they act more as "expert" managers brought in for relatively short periods to supervise local employees. In the case of the survey, this was a very short stay indeed. For reasons that should be very clear, none of this leads to rigorous quantitative evaluation of the project.

Lack of local human capital

A further challenge is the lack of *local human capital*, which places serious constraints on any party's ability to conduct quantitative research in rural Sierra Leone; constraints that should be obvious but seem often to be ignored. As mentioned above, the data-entry clerk I observed made two glaring errors within mere minutes, and the majority of the enumerators we were training proved unable to accurately record quantitative data. This should generate significant concern about the level of skills prevalent in impoverished transitional states relative to those necessary for rigorous social science research processes. Over the course of the past 30 years the education of two entire generations of Sierra Leoneans have suffered, first, from the retraction of the state under APC rule in the 1980s, then the violence and depravation of the war throughout the 1990s, and then from a decade of slow-moving reconstruction and state-building from 2002 to the present. It should not be a surprise that the processes of rigorous quantitative evaluation are beyond the skills of the vast majority of those who have suffered through these three decades. Again, however, these limitations are unrecognized by expatriates with no training in survey methods themselves, who are largely incentivized not to produce accurate evaluations, but to produce agreeable findings and "authoritative" tables, graphs, and reports.

In addition, such quantitative surveys demand far too much of those among whom the data is collected. The FDI project was sending a survey team into an impoverished rural area where almost nobody had received an education and was asking people about agricultural productivity from various different crops, about their children's school fees, about their income from a number of different sources, and about the various different products that are bought, sold, and owned by members of the household. These kinds of questions assume a great amount about the skills not only of those carrying out the survey, but also of those responding. It assumes that, like we in the West, these people are literate and numerate, keep track of their incoming and outgoing resources, and value their lives in a quantitative fashion. But residents of rural Sierra Leonean villages do not need to know the value of their rice, only the number of bushels and whether it is enough to feed those who need fed. Questions that value everything monetarily simply do not collect data that would accurately reflect what the survey is supposedly trying to measure: the social and economic impacts of the project. In a very real sense, therefore, quantitative methodologies rely far too heavily on skills that simply do not exist in much of northern Sierra Leone. These limitations, layered on top of the cultural issues identified below, place an ever increasing strain on the credence of the quantitative approach in this setting.

The aesthetics of secrecy

The first of these cultural issues is what has often been described as the locally prevalent "aesthetics of secrecy." Along with many other researchers (Murphy 1998; Ferme 2001; Shaw 2002), I have previously noted the local cultural preference not for transparency and the sharing of information, but for the control of knowledge for the protection of, or from, power and influence (Millar 2011a). In Sierra Leone, divulging information places an individual in a disempowered and potentially vulnerable position, and information is therefore managed very closely. This allows both big men and small men to protect themselves from the dangerous intentions of others. Within this context, information is truly powerful and it is controlled as such. For this reason, information that may be requested during quantitative assessments, such as information on income, agricultural production, and even family demographics, is quite likely to be withheld or misreported by survey respondents. While a well-trained and capable survey enumerator might easily be able to record observational data – such as the size of a house or the presence and number of livestock – more sensitive household data will be very difficult to accurately record even though it is centrally important for monitoring social and economic impact.

Indeed, as noted in Chapter 4, during my own qualitative interviews within the villages it was clear that those who were benefiting financially from the project were not forthcoming about how much they were getting. Elder males were often described by other villagers as deciding among themselves how money would be spent and shared, and as keeping the money out of sight. This is not in any way a divergence from the local norm, where sources of support and income are tightly guarded secrets and any beneficial relationship can quickly become the source of jealousy and spite that can result in dangerous witchcraft or "*pul im don sindrom*" (pull him down syndrome), wherein an individual is attacked and degraded for attempting to get ahead or improve themselves without directly sharing with their family and peers. For this reason, any information on a survey instrument that cannot be directly observed by the enumerator, instead requiring the willful disclosure of important personal information, is likely to be inaccurately reported; particularly if it involves money or other resources.

Incentives for misinformation

While information is always to be kept secret in Sierra Leone as opposed to willfully distributed, when sensitive information is provided (and particularly information about resources), it is likely to be manipulated in particular directions. Individuals will manage, to the greatest extent possible, the ongoing communication in whatever direction they believe will best advantage them in the future. This is only more likely to occur when a large, rich, and apparently powerful international organization or corporation is involved. Hence, not only are Sierra Leoneans likely to be quite reticent to divulge any information, but whatever information is provided will be strategically manipulated as each person attempts to maneuver into an advantageous position for the future and to foster personally beneficial relationships with others (see examples of this in Bolton 2012: 65–66).

For example, if I am a Sierra Leonean living within the project's land-lease area and I believe this large and obviously rich European company might be about to distribute rice based on the number of people per household (as the company itself said it would be doing with its farming program), then I would be working against myself not to include a few additional dependents in my household; a new baby here, a grown son returned from Freetown there. If I believe this company wants to raise the number of children going to school (as the company representatives regularly said they did), and perhaps will be distributing scholarships to needy families (as local people interpreted such statements to infer), then I would clearly be hurting my family's chance of gaining from that program by not (1) inflating the number of children in my household while (2) deflating my household income. In this way Sierra Leoneans have little incentive to tell the truth about any such information. Quite to the contrary, they are incentivized to report slightly manipulated but just believable data so as to adjust the situation to their advantage. Indeed, no Sierra Leonean would expect another to respond truthfully to such questions; and why should they? To do so would be to work against their own interests.

Leading questions and the social hierarchy

And, finally, there are problems, within rural Sierra Leone, with having relatively elite individuals survey marginalized people about their lives. This issue relates also to the problem of local human capital, but it is rooted in the culturally specific nature of relationships between elites and non-elites in rural Sierra Leone and the necessarily educated nature of the enumerators relative to those among whom they must collect data. As described in Chapter 5, the elites are in many ways dissociated from the lived reality of rural village life, and while the enumerators hired for the FDI project's survey were all Temne-speaking, the majority of them were elite urban dwellers educated in large towns, and, as is true throughout urban Sierra Leone, they commonly held negative opinions regarding village life and village residents. Such dynamics have negative consequences for how data will be collected.

I myself have witnessed the tendency for educated Sierra Leoneans to correct non-elites as they respond to questions and to browbeat them into changing their answers. More commonly questions that are written as non-leading questions on a survey instrument become leading questions when translated; transforming, for example, from "What is your religious affiliation?" to "You're Muslim, yes?" Indeed, in the training sessions for the FDI project's survey, in discussions about the correct way to enter the village, ask for informed consent, and conduct the interview, I was told repeatedly not to worry, "we know how to handle these people." The concern is, therefore, that even if an independent third party could overcome many of the other challenges described above, the data collected will reflect not what the respondents wanted to say, but what the survey enumerators wanted to hear. In short, in rural Sierra Leone rural respondents are reticent about providing information, and any information they do provide is likely to be strategically massaged and/or realigned by the enumerator. In such situations, how can we be confident in any quantitative findings?

A multi-methodological research agenda for peacebuilding

The purpose of outlining these nine problems with the quantitative research conducted within the land-lease area of the FDI project is simply to provide the reader with a snapshot of the kinds of challenges that any such project is likely to face in most contemporary post-conflict and transitional states. While these challenges will not be mirrored exactly in another context, it is quite likely that other contexts will provide other challenges that I have not observed in Sierra Leone. I described these problems to illustrate that my doubts regarding the validity of quantitative assessments of post-conflict peacebuilding interventions, whether they are assessments of one project's impact or cross-national studies, are not based on a general distaste for or misunderstanding of quantitative methods in general, but on my first-hand experience of how difficult it is to apply such methods in contemporary transitional settings.

Most of the problems I described above are related to characteristics shared between such settings, including a lack of qualified quantitative researchers within organizations active in peacebuilding, lack of human capital, an over-reliance on consultants, and a degraded transportation infrastructure. Primary among these problems, however, is the lack of truly independent, third party evaluation. These are the reasons I have such strong doubts about the validity of quantitative studies claiming to measure the local impact of peacebuilding interventions – and particularly those relying on secondary data where even the analyst has no idea how the data was collected. Importantly, while the presence of one or two of these problems might not be such a significant challenge, it is the accumulation of all of these challenges in one project that undermines the credibility of any data or reports that might emerge. If everything was well done except the sampling, if the only challenge to overcome was the limited numeracy of the survey team, or if the only problem was the local tendency to manipulate and massage information, then perhaps a well-trained and accomplished researcher could make use of the data. But when all of these problems are identified in one project, we have to admit that there is no way to call any of the collected data or resulting analysis authoritative. When the process of designing the research methodology and collecting the data is so riddled with problems that we cannot even tell which observations are valid and which invalid, how can we analyze the data that results? In cases of single project evaluation such as the FDI project's M&E process, we cannot assume that quantitative methods of evaluation provide a clear picture of actual local impacts.

More worryingly still, however, are the repercussions of these observations for cross-case analyses. Jerven (2013) notes in his study of development statistics throughout Africa, that he was regularly told that his concerns with data collection and validity challenges were over-stated because any observed associations that were statistically significant would only be strengthened if the data were more reliable. He was told, in essence, that some problems with data collection do not invalidate a whole project. But, he notes, this is only true if errors in the research are randomly distributed, not if they are systematically distributed. But, in cross-national comparisons of development statistics – and, I would add, peacebuilding processes – data errors are not randomly distributed (ibid.: 110). In fact, the same national characteristics that lead to bad data – weakened state infrastructure, poverty, lack of local human capacity, over-reliance on external consultants, etc. – are also associated with conflict events, result from conflict itself, and lead to the failure of peacebuilding interventions. Issues of capacity, infrastructure, culture, and transparency that hinder data collection correlate closely with variables regularly regarded as central to conflict occurrence and to the success or failure of post-conflict peacebuilding.

As a result, we can rely neither on quantitative evaluations of individual peacebuilding interventions in such contexts (because of the kinds of problems identified above) nor on comparative cross-national studies because the production of invalid quantitative data at the national level will be positively correlated with state weakness and post-conflict status in general. Hence, large-N studies that include in their analysis strong states in the Global North with high levels of human capacity, and long histories of accurate data collection as well as weak states in the Global South with all of the problems identified above, ignore the fact that strong states are also likely the source of accurate data at the national level while weak and conflict-prone states are likely sources of inaccurate or completely misleading data. Data errors in such studies will not be randomly distributed, but systematically distributed and, as such, findings from such large-N studies must be seriously questioned. Again, this is particularly true in the vast majority of such studies in which secondary data is analyzed by researchers with no idea about the processes by which that data was collected.

But I want to highlight that the core elements of the ethnographic approach could help quantitative scholars to overcome some of these limitations even if they do not themselves conduct ethnographic fieldwork, particularly in studies of single process impact, such as that of the FDI project. Seeing peacebuilding as experiential (Pillar I), for example, should prompt quantitative scholars to devise new, grounded, and more appropriate measures of local people's experiences of projects as opposed to simply inferring from the existence of the project that a particular experience occurred. If more evaluators accepted that peacebuilding must be evaluated for its experiential as well as its institutional effects, studies that equate more TRC hearings with more reconciliation, more trial years with more justice, more elections with more democracy, or more employment with more empowerment, might stop using these measures as proxies for experience and instead devise new means by which to more accurately measure local experiences. They could reach out to experienced fieldworkers, diaspora communities, or expatriates with decades of experience in country to help them devise more informed survey instruments or proxy measures for complicated social dynamics.

At the same time, ethnographic preparation (Pillar II) can serve to guide scholars in research processes. A thorough review of rigorous anthropological literature specific to the country or region in which the peacebuilding intervention occurred can both guide the construction of far more relevant and valid measures and help quantitative scholars to better interpret their findings. Being knowledgeable about patron–client dynamics and the expectations that emerge from them, or the aesthetics of secrecy prevalent throughout much of the Upper Guinea Coast, would greatly assist quantitative scholars in designing survey instruments, training, and supervising survey teams, and understanding the data they collect. Indeed, preparing in this way is just as important for quantitative evaluations of peacebuilding effects as it is for qualitative or ethnographic approaches. Surveys must be designed and survey responses analyzed and evaluated by individuals with knowledge of the local socio-cultural context or any analysis may be misinformed. Jerven too consistently argues that there must be much more effort towards qualitative assessment of quantitative work (2013: 111–15).

Similarly, both local engagement (Pillar III) and the appraisal of implicit assumptions (Pillar IV), while less directly applicable, cannot help but make quantitative evaluation more accurate. Quantitative scholars who take local engagement seriously should, for example, be more attuned to issues of representativeness and the potential demographic characteristics and issues of access that could lead to biased sampling. Further, questioning one's own implicit assumptions would allow a more reflective and potentially revelatory research, analysis and writing process. Just as with the ethnographic method, questioning one's own implicit assumptions should underpin any efforts to conduct research, even quantitative research, in settings socially and culturally distinct from that of the researcher. In these ways the four pillars of the ethnographic approach may be instructive also for quantitative researchers.

At the same time, it is quite clear that qualitative researchers can and should learn from quantitative methods if they want to make their findings more pertinent to policy-makers, funders and practitioners. More attention, for example, should be paid to the systematic selection of cases used for comparison. While comparative national-level case studies of peacebuilding projects are common (Hayner 1994; Knox and Quirk 2000; Rigby 2001; Quinn and Freeman 2003; Graybill and Lanegran 2004), this is not true of ethnographic evaluations which invariably present far more fine-grained data, but usually only of a single case. To build on this, rigorous cross-case studies should be attempted using an ethnographic approach in which the cases studied are comparable and the questions explored and the units of analysis examined are coordinated across cases. While such studies may take significant coordination and funding, the rewards would be substantial and the potential contribution to policy and practice would be extremely valuable. More fruitful still, however, would be a multi-methodological approach to peacebuilding evaluation actively combining ethnographic, qualitative case study, and quantitative approaches.

Any multi-methodological approach must take each of these approaches seriously and start from the premise that all methodologies have both weaknesses and strengths. For example, a multi-methodological approach might begin with a team consisting of both quantitative scholars and qualitative scholars, including ethnographers, who are interested in answering similar questions regarding peacebuilding processes or practices (peacekeeping missions, DDR programs, decentralization, criminal tribunals, dialogue processes, TRCs, etc.) and who have a similar commitment to the evaluation of that process. From this starting point the team discusses, based on existing literature and their own collective interests, what central questions they hope to answer (Does a criminal tribunal produce experiences of justice among a particular population? How does a peacekeeping mission interact with local communities? Does DDR help former combatants to gain employment and stability in the post-conflict setting? What are the main impacts of a good governance program at the national level?), and settles on a handful of core questions. These central questions are then taken as the foundation from which the research methodology develops. Importantly, methodology would grow from the questions, not the other way around.

The quantitative scholars on the team may immediately know how they would go about asking these questions, while the qualitative case study specialists and ethnographers too will have traditions that provide a certain collection of methodological solutions. The key, however, is for the two groups to share their approaches and work collaboratively on each other's methods. For example, qualitative scholars should participate in the design of survey methodologies, including the definition of the unit of analysis, the selection of cases, and the formulation of questions. In turn, as ethnographers clearly cannot conduct research in as many sites as quantitative scholars can collect data, quantitative scholars should be involved in the choice of the potential ethnographic sites; choosing based on decisions regarding within and between case comparisons, similarities, or unique profiles. In this way, quantitative premises can inform qualitative methods and feed back into the general evaluation, and vice versa.

As data is collected, both groups of scholars should be open to the input of the others. Quantitative scholars, for example, may need to adjust their hypotheses and measures of the particular phenomena under study in the middle of the project if fieldwork on the part of the ethnographers reveals that those measures are inappropriate. Similarly, ethnographers may have to expand their fieldwork site, include more interviews, or engage with populations previously excluded if the incoming quantitative data seems to indicate that key dynamics or important relationships were originally excluded from the research design. The two groups would have to meet regularly as the research is ongoing, perhaps quarterly, to discuss preliminary observations and findings and re-establish a shared vision and approach. Throughout this period the questions being asked and the eventual evaluation should be the primary concern, with both groups of scholars making adjustments in order to serve that larger end. In both cases, input from the other party may, and probably should, prompt additional analysis of the data.

And again, in the analysis phase of research the two approaches would have to be mutually assisting. As I have already noted, ethnographic information can be invaluable for interpreting quantitative data, whether from surveys or from larger macro level national data. As such, quantitative and qualitative scholars should participate cooperatively in the analysis of quantitative data. Similarly, while the collection of the qualitative data may largely stay in the hands of the qualitative scholars, the analysis of qualitative data too should be conducted cooperatively. In essence, what this cooperative evaluation of findings will bring to light are the different standards and norms by which research and findings are judged in the quantitative and qualitative traditions, and hopefully, a way for a multi-methodological approach to make qualitative research more valid and convincing among quantitative scholars, and vice versa. The goal throughout is not simply the analysis of one or more cases using two separate methodologies, but the creation of what might more accurately be described as a unified *inter-methodological approach*.

And, finally, for obvious reasons, quantitative and qualitative members of the team should work together on the publication of results and find a way to balance the quantitative and the qualitative in order to present a more thorough evaluation of the actual effects of peacebuilding processes. The goal is to evaluate what is actually happening on the ground, and what is actually happening can best be examined by a diversity of methodologies providing for fully triangulated findings. Just as interdisciplinarity has been described as the integration of two disciplines that leads to a more holistic approach to social problems (Klein 1990: 56), so this approach to research would be integrative as opposed to cumulative. Of course, there may be many critiques of such an approach. Qualitative scholars may abhor working with quantitative scholars, and vice versa. Particular disciplinarily focused journals or conferences may be unused to such an inter-methodological approach. Even government agencies or international organizations may not initially know how to use findings of such studies for policy formulation, and for all the rhetoric about interdisciplinary research, it will probably prove very difficult to fund such projects. But the potential benefits should far outweigh any such concerns. There is so much potential for such collaborative projects that the main problem might be simply figuring out where to start; which projects to examine first, and what questions to ask.

In conclusion, this chapter has attempted to describe in more detail the serious limitations of quantitative evaluations of peacebuilding projects in post-conflict and transitional societies. These limitations are rooted in characteristics shared by many such states; which set them apart from the bureaucratized Western world in which most people who conduct such evaluations usually reside. It then described in more detail nine specific and quite serious challenges to such quantitative evaluations as observed during my time working on the FDI project's own M&E process in 2012, including limited human capital, non-existent or degraded infrastructure, lack of qualified social science research staff, complicating cultural factors, and a dependence not on independent evaluators, but on contracted consultants working on a short-term basis and reliant on return patronage. Finally, I attempted briefly to outline a future inter-methodological research agenda that can overcome the limitations and build on the strengths of these two methodological traditions.

I recognize that there are many institutional and disciplinary constraints on any truly inter-methodological research agenda such as the one I have described here. But I also believe that the very real and profound criticisms of the peacebuilding field, enumerated in many places throughout this book, demand a greater effort at more thorough evaluation, and particularly evaluation of local experiences. Innumerable scholars are working in the various fields and methodological traditions associated with the larger international peacebuilding agenda, but scholars in different fields often fail to communicate, fail to learn the lessons of past scholarship, and, in the end, fail to move peacebuilding towards more emancipatory theory, policy, practice, and experience. Instead of working always at cross-purposes and constantly reinventing the wheel, it is time for a new research agenda – one which has the potential to provide generalizable lessons while also taking local needs and experiences seriously.

9 Conclusion

In the world today, dozens of large international organizations and thousands of national and local-level NGOs in transitional states include peacebuilding as one of their primary objectives. The field of peacebuilding has undergone increasing professionalization over the past two decades, both as an academic discipline and as an ever more important form of international intervention, and a veritable industry has arisen around the various processes and techniques of building peace. Professional cadres of peacebuilders are educated, trained, and disciplined into the world of the international peacebuilder, or what Autesserre (2014) calls "Peaceland," and participate, much as with those who inhabit the development field, in a mutually constructed world characterized by particular dynamics, rules, and norms. However, as many of the authors I have quoted in this book have highlighted, even as it has become increasingly visible and influential, this industry has also proven distressingly inept at building peace (Richmond and Franks 2009). While ever more technocratic and institutional solutions have been designed to meet the challenges of peacebuilding, many of these solutions fail to have predictable beneficial effects on the ground.

However, while the limits of contemporary peacebuilding seem clear to many scholars, standard practices continue unabated; largely unproven technocratic solutions applied in support of normative ideals that remain, for the most part, disconnected from local needs or concerns. Indeed, until very recently there has also been a serious lack of systematic evaluation of such projects. Admittedly, evaluating the effects of peacebuilding is no easy task. But it is nevertheless necessary if the effects of peacebuilding interventions are to be understood. While there have been a number of small-N comparative case studies of such processes over the past 20 years (Hayner 1994; Popkin and Roht-Arriaza 1995; Knox and Quirk 2000; Chapman and Ball 2001; Rigby 2001; Quinn and Freeman 2003), a number of scholars have lamented the lack of systematic quantitative analysis of peacebuilding and transitional justice processes (Mendeloff 2004; Brahm 2007; van der Merwe, Baxter, and Chapman. 2009: 4) and only recently have substantial large-N quantitative evaluations emerged (Gibson 2004; Flores and Nooruddin 2009; Olsen, Payne, and Reiter 2010; Wiebelhaus-Brahm 2010; Sikkink 2011). In addition, the prominent examples of evaluation guidance that are targeted at practitioners in the field are heavily reliant on checklists, tick-boxes, and short "field missions" and risk themselves becoming additional technocratic or "tool-kit" solutions to be applied as cookie-cutter approaches for evaluating cookie-cutter interventions.

While these contributions are valuable steps towards better evaluation I have argued in this book that they nonetheless fail to evaluate the *local experiences* of peacebuilding interventions among the supposed beneficiaries of such processes. This is primarily because they rarely engage with local understandings and perceptions of conflict and peace, or with local ideas of what would constitute the social goods that peacebuilding interventions claim to provide, such as experiences of justice, reconciliation, healing, empowerment, development, security, or dignity. While a handful of ethnographic works have engaged with these issues in local settings (Shaw 2007; Isaacs 2009; Millar 2010; Robins 2011; Theidon 2013), such studies seem largely to be ignored or simply unread by policy-makers and practitioners in the fields of peacebuilding, transitional justice, and post-conflict development. In response, over the preceding eight chapters I have tried to present a new ethnographic approach to evaluating the local impact of peacebuilding interventions which combines the contextual depth of ethnographic analysis with an explicit focus on evaluation of peacebuilding interventions.

This approach was presented in a four-pillar model. The first pillar is a commitment to seeing *peacebuilding as experiential*, as opposed to institutional. This pillar demands that evaluators recognize that all contemporary peacebuilding interventions claim to provide experiences of social goods, and recognize the potentially dangerous effects of failing to predictably foster those experiences in sensitive post-conflict settings. An institutional approach, on the other hand, assumes that institutions lead predictably to theorized experiences. Proponents of security sector reforms, for example, argue that such interventions will provide experiences of security and safety, while democratization proponents claim that elections will provide experiences of empowerment and legitimate government. But what happens when security sector reform gives rise to a powerful army or police force in a society where such institutions are identified with repression and fear instead of security and safety? While an institutional approach to peacebuilding focuses on the establishment of the institution and measures impact by related outputs, such as the numbers of police officers employed or police vehicles bought, numbers of military retrained or deployed, or the number of successful apprehensions or convictions, the ethnographic approach demands that we look not at the institution, but how people understand, perceive, and experience that institution. The ethnographic approach demands that we evaluate, among local "beneficiaries" themselves, how they experience those institutional impacts; positively, negatively, or not at all.

In this way, Chapter 3 illustrated the value of the ethnographic approach for understanding *how* local people experience peacebuilding interventions on the ground in transitional states. This was accomplished by describing both the expected impacts and the actual local experiences of the two large international peacebuilding projects I have evaluated in northern Sierra Leone over the past six years; the Truth and Reconciliation Commission's public hearings process in the town of Makeni, and the large bio-energy corporation operating a 40,000-hectare FDI project encompassing approximately 90 villages in the rural north of the country. This chapter illustrated the very clear differences between the impact these projects claim to have and the actual local experiences of these projects. In short, instead of providing experiences of justice, healing, and reconciliation, the TRC hearing was experienced by most non-elites in Makeni as either a waste of money or an actively provocative event, while the FDI project is currently being experienced not as providing empowerment and opportunity, but largely as a disruptive and disempowering imposition. While there are of course different experiences within these settings, the majority of experiences are not what were predicted by the theorists, policy-makers, and practitioners who promote such processes.

In Chapter 4, I progressed to the second pillar of this model, *ethnographic preparation*, which I argue is central to explaining *why* intervention is experienced as it is on the ground. Ethnographic preparation demands that evaluators take the time to conduct a thorough review of the ethnographic literature on the local setting and society in which the peacebuilding project was conducted before they attempt to evaluate its impact. As it stands today, evaluations are often conducted by peacebuilding practitioners, consultants, INGO staff, or academics with expertise in the form of peacebuilding intervention (democratization, marketization, security sector reform, TRCs, criminal tribunals, decentralization, etc.), but with little or no knowledge of the local culture or society. I argued that this approach fails to understand the local impacts of a peacebuilding intervention as all such projects are experienced within a cultural context and evaluators will require sufficient knowledge of that context to evaluate the data they themselves collect regarding local experiences.

I proceeded to illustrate the importance of this second pillar by showing the added value of ethnographic knowledge in understanding the negative experiences of the TRC and the FDI project. Asking people about their experiences can tell us much about *how* they experienced peacebuilding projects, but often not much about *why* they experienced those projects as they did. I demonstrated how local experiences of these particular projects were greatly affected by the locally dominant patron–client system and the expectations that local people developed regarding what the TRC and the FDI project would provide. As both projects claimed to be coming to "help" local people and were overwhelmingly staffed by individuals seen as "big men," both projects were interpreted, within the local cultural milieu, as patrons. However, as neither was seen to perform the culturally appropriate roles of resource provision that would have been interpreted as "help" by local clients, they were experienced negatively. I further argued that ethnographic preparation is necessary even for quantitative evaluations, as designing proxy measures or survey instruments, as well as interpreting collected data, demands a sufficient understanding of the local context, culture, and norms.

In Chapter 5, I described the third pillar of the ethnographic approach: *local engagement*. First, I argued that the "local" must be interpreted specific to each peacebuilding project and that each evaluation must be conducted among representatives of that "local" through engagement on the ground and over time. As opposed to other methods of evaluation that suggest short "field missions" or interviews primarily with those who administer peacebuilding interventions, the ethnographic approach requires that evaluators engage substantively with local "beneficiaries" and the context in which they live, spending enough time in the local setting to begin to understand the way that challenges and hardships affect local lives and the worldviews and lifeways of the beneficiaries of the peacebuilding intervention. I also argued that it is of paramount importance for evaluators to interview representative samples of the beneficiaries of any peacebuilding project as there are distinct differences between how different sub-samples of the beneficiary group will experience peacebuilding.

In my cases, as I illustrated, the experiences of local elites differed substantially from those of the majority of local people: the non-elites. Specifically, the English-speaking educated elites in Makeni and the land-owning males and traditional authorities such as the paramount chiefs in the land-lease area of the FDI project have reported far more positive experiences of the two interventions than have the non-elites in each setting. This is because they are situated in privileged positions that provide both great understanding of these peacebuilding processes and greater access to the benefits of these international interventions. As a result, their experiences of these interventions were actually more positive. However, when interviewed, these elites project that positive experience onto those they claim to represent; the non-elites whose positions provide them with none of the privileges and benefits of these projects and who therefore have far less positive experiences. I believe this will likely be the case in many contemporary transitional states. As a result, evaluations based on data collected primarily among local elites will privilege the voices of the already empowered, while accurate evaluation of local experiences demands that evaluators privilege the voices of the non-elites who are otherwise disempowered, marginalized, and often ignored.

And, finally, in Chapter 6, I introduced the final pillar of the ethnographic approach, the need for *appraisal of one's own implicit assumptions*. As described, whereas the first three pillars can be considered steps in an evaluative process – from committing to seeing peacebuilding as experiential, through ethnographic preparation, and on to local engagement – the need to critically examine one's own implicit assumptions about the world underpins the entire approach. This fourth pillar is so central because only those with a willingness to question the way they see and experience the world will be prepared to consider peacebuilding as experiential instead of institutional, and only those who recognize that justice, reconciliation, healing, empowerment, development, legitimacy, authority, dignity, security, etc. may be culturally variable social experiences will be likely to commit to ethnographic preparation and local engagement. Hence, the ethnographic approach to peacebuilding evaluation depends on the willingness of the evaluator to question their own implicit assumptions; it demands a healthy anthropological imagination or what Jayawickrama (2013) has called "cultural humility."

I illustrated the value of this fourth pillar by showing how our core conceptions of self and sociality are foundational for what I described as second-order concepts, such as justice, reconciliation, empowerment, or security. I argued that these foundational concepts of self and sociality in the West – the setting where peacebuilding interventions are designed and planned and from which the vast majority of those who administer such projects emerge – are distinct from and perhaps even inconsistent with alternative conceptions in many settings of contemporary conflict and post-conflict peacebuilding, including Sierra Leone. I therefore concluded that a willingness to critically engage with one's own implicit assumptions about the very core and foundational concepts that govern how we see the world, and how we act within it, will allow us to consider alternatives and, thus, will allow us to more accurately evaluate local experiences of peacebuilding intervention. As noted, this fourth pillar is not a step in the process, but is a necessary conceptual shift that both underpins and is also further promoted by accomplishing the previous three pillars

In Chapters 7 and 8, I progressed to a more reflective consideration of the challenges and strengths of the ethnographic approach. In Chapter 7, I described the challenges to both physical and psychological security that may make ethnographic analysis of peacebuilding in contemporary transitional states quite difficult for many, and tried to provide some guidance, based on my own experiences in Sierra Leone, for scholars who wish to adopt this methodology. I highlighted the particular risks posed by disease, crime, and accidents in contemporary transitional states often characterized by poverty, degraded state infrastructures, and a lack of social services and argued that the key to physical security is a conscious effort to *avoid* such threats. Alternatively, I argued that the researcher can gain valuable insight into the local setting by experiencing first-hand some measure of poverty, isolation, hardship, and the psychological stress that may result. Such pressures and experiences should be *managed*, not fully avoided, because, while they may create additional stress, they also provide a great amount of insight and perspective. While both physical and psychological pressures clearly present challenges for anyone wanting to follow an ethnographic approach to peacebuilding evaluation, these are not insurmountable challenges, and the rewards will usually outweigh the costs.

And, finally, having noted the challenges to the ethnographic approach in Chapter 7, in Chapter 8, I addressed far more directly my concerns with a quantitative approach to peacebuilding evaluation in transitional states by first describing two such processes I was involved with in 2008 and in 2012, and then explicating in far more detail a list of nine specific and debilitating problems identified with the FDI project's own M&E process with which I worked in 2012. These problems covered a range of issues including; problems with foundational premises of quantitative research, such as defining the unit of analysis, sampling, and including control cases; problems finding qualified staff, over-reliance on consultants, and a general lack of independent assessment; and local cultural issues such as a tendency to withhold information, local incentives to misinform survey teams, and the tendency for educated locals hired as survey enumerators to actively affect the data collected through leading questions and correcting survey respondents. I highlighted each of these particular problems, not to argue that quantitative methods are invalid or useless in general, but to highlight the very specific problems common within contemporary transitional states that pose great challenges to such an approach in those particular settings and which argue against Esser and Vanderkamp's recent and somewhat naïve faith in the validity of systematically collected data in complex transitional, post-conflict or divided societies (2013: 51–52). I concluded this chapter by briefly sketching a potential inter-methodological approach which would combine qualitative and quantitative methodologies and hopefully overcome the challenges of each while building a unique capability for peacebuilding evaluation both within and across cases.

As I expressed in the Introduction, the aim of this book was to both describe and illustrate the value of a new ethnographic approach to evaluating the impact of peacebuilding interventions. I hope that the last six chapters have provided enough evidence from my two cases in northern Sierra Leone to make clear the added value of this approach and the added value, in general, of evaluating local experiences of peacebuilding projects among those who are supposed to benefit from interventions. While the academic end of the peacebuilding field has produced a great amount of criticism of the "liberal peace" over the past 15 years, to a great extent, policies and practices of post-conflict intervention have not responded. As Mac Ginty and Richmond have recently argued, "the core of international programmes [*sic*] remains the same" (2013: 776). Further, the ongoing professionalization and standardization of practice in the field provide little of the flexibility or nuance that is necessary if peacebuilding intervention is ever to respond to local needs on the ground in transitional states. This is true also regarding currently dominant methods of evaluation, in that there are few studies that truly understand the relevance, sustainability or impact of peacebuilding interventions (Jayawickrama 2013: 28), nor clear practical guidelines for an evaluation process that could accomplish this.

An emancipatory peace, however, that can both respond to immediate post-conflict needs and build a sustainable peaceful future in any given context must be one built on the ideas and needs of those who live in that context. The only way to contribute to such a peace is to ask local people what they themselves need in the post-conflict period, and this is where the ethnographic approach can be most powerful. Further, understanding how the international community can best contribute to emancipatory peace more generally and across cases demands that the international community understand both how intervention is experienced in individual cases, and how particular mechanisms or modes of intervention are experienced across cases. It calls, in essence, for both qualitative and quantitative evaluation, both single-case and cross-case. Only an inter-methodological approach can generate the kind of information needed to guide the further development of the peacebuilding field. We have entered a bottleneck in which the liberal peace practice and its critics are no longer responding to one another and criticism is more and more seen as providing no actionable suggestions. As argued below, however, the best response is not for increasing division between the practice and analysis of peacebuilding, but for greater incorporation of the two in the field.

An ethnographic approach to peacebuilding: the intervention lifecycle

As I have noted multiple times throughout this book, a great amount of academic work published on peacebuilding involves extremely little time in the field, little to no engagement with the actual beneficiaries of such programs, and only short-term engagement with those who practice peacebuilding. Critique from academics therefore, from any discipline, is easily dismissed by policy-makers, funders, advocates, and practitioners of peacebuilding. Even as a fieldworker with extensive experience in one of the most difficult post-conflict cases of the past two decades, I have often been dismissed by practitioners (staff of both international NGOs and corporations in Sierra Leone) for being "disconnected" in my "ivory tower;" even during discussions that have occurred in "the field." Academics – I'm told in such conversations – do not understand the limitations on or the day-to-day operations of projects in the field, and so all these articles and critiques have little to say about how to "get the job done." I imagine most academics studying peacebuilding have had similar experiences. It can be very frustrating and disheartening.

But when I read much of the literature on peacebuilding – its often disconnected theorizing and overly normative institutional assumptions – I often find myself agreeing with these practitioners. Such theory often is wholly disconnected from situations in the field and it is regularly based not on evidence but on "gut" feelings, intuitions, or implicit assumptions (Blum 2011: 9). It is, therefore, often misinformed and commonly quite unhelpful as guidance for practitioners. Peacebuilding, as a field, needs something more; it needs something better. Throughout this book I have tried to describe the ethnographic approach to evaluation and illustrate its strengths (as well as noting some of its challenges). However, here in this final chapter I want to make a bigger argument. I want to propose that the ethnographic approach is not only needed in evaluation of peacebuilding interventions, but in the entire life cycle of peacebuilding interventions; from conceptualization and planning, through funding and administration and, of course, on through post-project evaluation.

An ethnographic approach to planning

First of all, we must recognize that improving the experiences local people have of peacebuilding interventions in the future – whether of democratization, marketization, transitional justice mechanisms, or any number of security sector or social service reforms – demands more than an institutional approach. The effects of such approaches have been shown time and again to be unpredictable and potentially negative. The recent explosion of the hybrid peace literature, as discussed in the Introduction, is attempting to grapple with complex post-conflict environments characterized by the operation of parallel peacebuilding processes and the inordinate amount of evidence showing that peacebuilding interventions in socially and cultural diverse settings will not lead cleanly to the experiences policy-makers, funders, and planners expect (Millar, van der Lijn, and Verkoren. 2013). Further, this literature clearly shows that overcoming this challenge demands a move away from a top-down institutional approach. What is necessary is the incorporation of an ethnographic approach to peacebuilding into the *planning phase* of intervention.

Local conditions must guide peacebuilding planning, and incorporating an ethnographic approach into this phase of intervention can provide much-needed insight into these conditions. Policy-makers and planners must direct more attention towards the local context in planning and avoid the urge to turn immediately to "tool-kit" solutions. The nature of the conflict waged, the local social, cultural, economic, and political realities, and the restrictions and limitations placed on intervention by these dynamics, must all be considered in this early phase of intervention. However, the ethnographic approach demands more than the simple conflict analyses that have often been used in the past. The same four pillars that compose the ethnographic approach to evaluation can be applied to planning. For example, seeing peacebuilding as experiential would demand that those planning an intervention process not only count the injured, assess the parties involved, or study the economic or social precursors to conflict, but realize also that it is local experiences of these events that should drive planning for peacebuilding intervention.

As I have shown elsewhere, a simple institutional analysis of the conflict in Sierra Leone leads many to consider inter-group reconciliation processes as necessary for peace because, after all, one armed group was fighting another, so surely there are now two groups that need to be reconciled. But an ethnographic analysis – asking people how they experienced violence or how they feel about the "other" after the war – would have revealed the redundancy of such processes in a context where there was little tendency to "otherize" or "demonize" those who were sucked into the use of violence during the war

(Millar 2012a, 2012b). Unfortunately the planners did not conduct such an analysis – instead commissioning a superficial analysis of "local processes" of conflict resolution (Manifesto '99 2002) – and proceeded to administer projects that have been accorded little value by local beneficiaries. In this way, seeing peacebuilding as experiential is as useful for planning as it is for evaluation.

Similarly, both ethnographic preparation and local engagement would be invaluable at this stage. Ethnographic preparation would allow planners to understand the setting into which they are about to intervene and perhaps allow them to avoid some of the problems that contemporary peacebuilding has so often produced. For example, if planners had any notion of the depth and importance of patron–client relationships in Sierra Leone, and the manner in which terms like "help" and "consider" would be interpreted as promises of resources, surely they would have been less likely to use such terms in their sensitization plans. Similarly, in the case of the FDI project, a good faith effort at local engagement as I described it in Chapter 5 might have provided much-needed insight that could have avoided some of the problems the company is now experiencing on the ground. An effort to engage with youth, with stranger families, and with women – instead of engaging almost solely with the chiefs and elder male heads of land-owning families – would have allowed the project to avoid many of the problems they are now experiencing.

And, finally, the fourth pillar of the ethnographic approach, as it demands a critical appraisal of one's own implicit assumptions, is also imperative at the planning phase of intervention. In allowing only a few voices from specific countries, organizations, and disciplines to dominate the choice of peacebuilding mechanisms, often included not for their contextual knowledge but for their technical expertise, we risk intervention driven largely by normatively guided conceptions of how peacebuilding should function, as has prevailed in the past (Brahm 2007: 23), and we both limit the number of options available and restrict the development or adaptability of the mechanisms of intervention we already use. But across the range of current and potential sites of peacebuilding interventions there are already a diverse range of actors – academic and practitioner and from various countries, backgrounds, and disciplines – working to understand the local dynamics both of the conflict and of the social, cultural, political, and economic context. In addition, local people themselves can be a source of information regarding what is needed and what is wanted during post-conflict transition. Across all cases, therefore, there is a great need to include more such voices that force planners to question their own implicit assumptions.

I believe that this is true both in the local context – planners should engage local non-elites as well as elites and privilege the voices of the marginalized as opposed to the empowered – as well as in the international context – planners should actively seek out and consult with anthropologists, international and national NGO staff, business people, volunteers, clergy, and anyone else with substantial experience in the local context. This inclusion should be multidisciplinary and avoid simply reaffirming existing biases. In short, and to make this very clear, we must include more people in the debate, and cannot, as scholars of peacebuilding, post-conflict reconstruction, or transitional justice allow ourselves to become closed off to alternate conceptions, whether from other disciplines or from local people. We must, if we hope to contribute anything even close to a peace that works for local people, question our own normativity and assumptions and be open to other ideas and other voices. While I recognize that a greater inclusion of voices will also add complexity and most likely slow the process of planning and funding peacebuilding, in order to avoid actually doing harm where we mean to help, or causing conflict where we propose to build peace, we must expand the community of voices involved in making decisions. In these various ways, incorporating the ethnographic approach into the planning phase of peacebuilding intervention can contribute, not only to better use of scarce funding, but also to the emancipatory potential of peacebuilding generally.

An ethnographic approach to administration

Similarly, I believe that the four pillars of the ethnographic approach to evaluation can be valuably applied to the administration phase of peacebuilding interventions. Just as planners and evaluators must consider peacebuilding to be experiential, so peacebuilding administrators must recognize the end product of their work to be experiences as well as institutions. If it is accepted that the ethnographic approach is a valuable way to evaluate peacebuilding intervention, then it must also be recognized that the time to do this is not only after intervention is complete but as it is ongoing. Seeing peacebuilding as experiential therefore (Pillar I), will allow administrators to maintain ongoing assessment of their processes and catch any problems as they occur, not simply to reflect back on them after the fact, when nothing can be done to improve the situation. Seeing peacebuilding as experiential would allow practitioners to more immediately identify problems with their practice and make alterations, cut out those practices that are having negative impacts, or even pull the plug on a certain intervention altogether.

In addition, recognizing the experiential nature of peacebuilding would hopefully shift the focus and efforts of practitioners away from a technocratic or institutional approach. From discussions with acquaintances in Sierra Leone, for example, I know that practitioners themselves are often aware that particular individuals or sections of society may experience an institution or a new process negatively, but this does not hinder or contradict, for them, the value of the institution. In such perspectives a Western-style judicial system, an open market, an election, or a human rights commission are considered to be inherently good; the experiences individual people have of the institution are secondary. Further, as many practitioners are technical experts with little knowledge of the local context – disciplined to consider their own institutional approach to be the correct and necessary intervention – they have little reason to consider individual experiences to be important. But over the past 15 years many scholars have noted that institutions can have just as many negative impacts as they can positive (Anderson 1999; Paris 2004), and that experiences on the ground spur individual choices regarding participation in violence and support of conflict parties (Archibald and Richards 2002; Kalyvas 2006). If the ethnographic approach was inserted into the administrative phase of peacebuilding, practitioners would be more likely to recognize the balance necessary between institutional and experiential perspectives and, indeed, the dependence of an institution's eventual impact on its ability to provide positive local experiences.

I believe the second pillar of the ethnographic approach – ethnographic preparation – would also prove invaluable to practitioners during administration of peacebuilding interventions. It is the practitioner, after all, who translates the mandates of the international community into practice on the ground and has a great amount of autonomy in how that happens. While the broad outlines of an intervention mechanism may be driven by policy-makers or funders, it is the practitioner who decides how mechanisms operate on a daily basis, which local actors are invited to participate on the ground, or how rules are applied. A greater knowledge of local culture and context would clearly provide insight that practitioners would find useful in this task. As described in Chapter 8, for example, the seven different development banks that funded the FDI project demanded that the company conduct bi-annual evaluations, but how those were conducted was up to the company and indeed they chose to go against the bank's advice by conducting the survey among the entire population instead of a 15 percent sample. As such, while the company is given guidance on how to meet general targets driven by policy – acquire signatures on all of the land-lease agreements, complete the construction of all the pivots, finish construction of an ethanol factory – how it goes about doing all of this is decided by the practitioners and many of the problems on the ground are in response to those practical decisions. Incorporating ethnographic preparation into the administrative phase of the process would, therefore, assist the company in avoiding many of these problems.

Similarly, local engagement would be invaluable in the administrative phase of most peacebuilding interventions which struggle to incorporate local voices and have a very difficult time making sure their processes are understood. In private conversations with senior officials of the SCSL, for example, I was told that the court conducted a great amount of public sensitization, communicating to local people the purpose and describing the practices of the court. These practitioners felt that the court had successfully communicated *with* the local people, and that there had been valuable and useful exchange between the parties. In Makeni, however, those I spoke with about the SCSL felt that it was a waste of money and one individual who had attended one of these sensitization meetings mocked it as a complete waste of time. He described how the court officials had come and lectured about the operation of the court and how it would provide justice, but when anyone had questions or wanted clarification, he said, they were ignored.

This kind of story reminds me of my experiences with the FDI project, where village "consultation" was simply a form of "management;" telling people what would happen and how, instead of conducting any conversation or give and take with the communities that might lead to a shared process. This also echoes Donais's observation that most liberal notions of "local ownership" are more akin to local acceptance of a "largely predetermined vision" than to anything we might consider actual local control of the process (2012: 6). In this way the ethnographic approach, if applied to the administrative phase of peacebuilding, would require a new focus on substantive local engagement and, when combined with the application of Pillars I and II, may inspire practitioners to engage more fruitfully with a more diverse cross-section of local actors and prioritize the voices of the marginalized and disempowered. In the end, this incorporation of the ethnographic approach would make peacebuilding more accountable, and more likely to result in emancipatory practice.

The ethnographic approach as continuous assessment

What is perhaps necessary, and what I very much believe would go a long way to creating a more emancipatory peace, is a process of ongoing or continuous assessment of peacebuilding interventions. As I have described, my evaluation of the TRC was conducted about four years after the commission had finished its work and presented its report. As such, that evaluation of local experiences of the TRC could not inform the operation of the process itself. While I hope the various articles I have published on the topic have informed ongoing debates about the local experiences of TCs as a class of post-conflict intervention and that they might be able to influence the administration of future TCs in other contexts, they can do little to assist the local people in Sierra Leone – even those I myself interviewed. But if the ethnographic approach was integrated into the planning and evaluation phases of peacebuilding interventions, then surely it might be possible to conduct an ongoing assessment of that process and influence the practice of peacebuilding *as it happens.*

Further, incorporating the approach into the life-cycle of a peacebuilding intervention would allow evaluators to incorporate local people and expatriates with knowledge of the local culture and language into the ongoing evaluation of peacebuilding processes. In this way the ethnographic approach could be an overarching structure for evaluation, within which local people and expatriates with pertinent local knowledge could both inform peacebuilding practice. This is what I was hoping to do with the FDI project before the company decided they could not provide a truly independent evaluator access to their processes. As the project will be ongoing over the next few decades, my evaluation of local experiences and, most importantly, the reasons behind these experiences – the why – could have then fed back into the process; allowing the company to reflect on project design and administration, its farming and engineering plans, and its general interaction and communication with local communities. In essence, the ethnographic approach would become not only an evaluation tool, but a means to improve practice. Perhaps more importantly, as such an evaluation would listen to and understand local voices, it would also provide a way for local communities to provide input and to contribute to the projects of the liberal peace. By giving local non-elites a voice and holding peacebuilding interventions in some measure accountable to the supposed beneficiaries of those interventions, incorporating the ethnographic approach into peacebuilding administration opens the door to a more emancipatory peace.

As peacebuilding has evolved over the past decade from an area of post-conflict work dominated by relatively short-term UN operations (Paris 2004), to a broad collection of actors involved in a diverse array of interventionary mechanisms and what can now be considered a peace industry in both the national (Byrne *et al.* 2008: 110; Goetschel and Hagmann 2009: 66) and the international context (Mac Ginty 2012: 289), we are seeing peacebuilding processes that extend 10, 15, or 20 years past the end of violent hostilities. In this context it has become ever more important that peacebuilding processes incorporate internal mechanisms for continuous assessment and reflective learning that can create, over time, better practice. No longer is it necessary for evaluation to be limited to the post-administrative phase. No more can lessons be learned only by comparing national-level data across cases. It is perfectly possible in such long-term peacebuilding processes to conduct longitudinal studies of the local experiences and impacts of individual mechanisms as well as the larger peacebuilding endeavor within a state. This is where the ethnographic method could be most useful, working alongside but independently from peacebuilding interventions and conducting life-cycle evaluations that can feed back into the process.

The challenge and promise of the ethnographic approach

I want to finish this book with a short reflection on the challenges that face not only attempts to incorporate an ethnographic approach into peacebuilding practice, but any efforts that seek to create accountability of the interveners to the beneficiaries. In both development and peacebuilding there has been consistent demand for local inclusion, ownership, buy-in, or participation over the past 20 years. But yet, as I and others cited in these pages have noted time and again, little of this has really been accomplished. The very structures of the peacebuilding industry and the economic incentives that drive the international system seem to work against any truly local ownership of peacebuilding processes in contemporary transitional states. Those who hold the power and the money refuse to write blank checks, for what are perhaps obvious reasons. But in their control of the process they fail even to give local people on the ground an equal voice in the peacebuilding endeavor and, in the end, often fail to facilitate the building of peace.

Indeed, it seems this situation is only getting worse, as peacebuilding becomes an industry, like international development before it, and ever increasing numbers of peace technicians and social engineers emerge from American and European graduate schools ready to democratize, marketize, and reform. In the post-9/11 and post-Arab Spring environment, where Western powers are increasingly concerned with threats from fragile and weak states and social and economic development is closely related to new ideas of "securitization," the conventional modes of peacebuilding into which young professionals are disciplined are ever more devoid of any impetus to critically reflect on the kind of peace being built (Newman 2010); or on the kind of international order to which they contribute. In essence, while I have tried to argue in these pages that peacebuilding is in great need of an ethnographic approach, the entire structure of the field – and particularly that outside the halls of academia – seems to militate against any such change. But there is reason for hope hidden in this professionalization and "disciplining" of the peacebuilding field and one place it can be found is in academia itself.

Just as various academic fields emerged after WWII to counter or refute the central premises of security studies and international relations (including conflict resolution, peace studies, restorative justice, and alternative dispute resolution), so have critical studies of peacebuilding emerged over the past 15 years to counter the liberal peace model. So far, as noted numerous times in this book, this critical approach has not been able – or is at least not considered by most policy-makers and practitioners – to offer any workable or practical solutions to the problems they identify with the liberal peace. As a result, master's programs, which are technically and practically oriented by their nature, rarely include much consideration of critical approaches. When critical peacebuilding is considered in such programs it fails to provide any practical solutions to its own critiques; it provides students with critical but not practical skills. As a result, while the conventional liberal and institutional approach to peacebuilding can offer future practitioners technical and marketable skills, critical theories do not.

This is where the ethnographic approach can begin to overcome the resistance of professionalized peacebuilding to critical, reflective, and non-conventional methods. As it provides technical skills and responds proactively to current demands in the field for evaluation, the ethnographic approach can and should be incorporated into conflict resolution, transitional justice, post-conflict reconstruction and peacebuilding programs in academia in order to provide future graduates with marketable and useful skills for work with international organizations, corporations, or governments which run counter to those provided by the conventional approaches. Just as there has been increasing interest in the importance of culture in conflict resolution (Avruch 1998), negotiation (Cohen 1997), mediation (Augsburger 1992), and peacekeeping (Rubinstein 2003) theory and practice in the past, so graduate programs can supplement their existing peacebuilding curricula with courses on the ethnographic approach that incorporate critical perspectives on contemporary theory and practice, while training their graduates to conduct valuable evaluation on an array of peacebuilding mechanisms in socially and cultural diverse settings; skills that are much in demand today within the peacebuilding industry.

Some may argue that the ethnographic approach could in this way be co-opted by international actors for their own agendas, just as has occurred with ethnographic methods in the US military's "Human Terrain Program" (González 2007). But the fact remains that those with power and wealth are intervening and will continue to intervene in transitional states and will do so whether they are sensitive to local needs and wishes or not. The UN, the EU, the US, development banks, multinational corporations, the large INGOs, smaller national NGOs, and scores of think tanks and consultant firms will continue to intervene in post-conflict and transitional states and they will hire those who graduate from any number of programs claiming to provide training and expertise in peacebuilding practice. This provides an entry point for more critical or post-liberal approaches to peacebuilding in the form of the ethnographic approach.

As described by Lederach, "to be at all germane to contemporary conflict, peacebuilding must be rooted in and responsive to the experiential and subjective realities shaping people's perspectives and needs" (1997: 24). Only when those who make the decisions about what will happen on the ground in transitional states are willing and able to include local voices and respond actively to local needs will peacebuilding have any hope of promoting or contributing to an emancipatory peace. The ethnographic approach – incorporated into planning, administration and evaluation – provides one powerful route to move towards such a peace, and the current demands for professional qualifications and knowledge of evaluation methodologies among organizations involved in peacebuilding provide an open opportunity to influence the evolution of peacebuilding practice over the coming years through post-graduate academic training. In short, criticism of the liberal peace as peacebuilding practice has gone as far as it can unless alternative modes of practice are proposed that take professionalization, international power, and the political economy of international peacebuilding as an industry seriously. Incorporating the ethnographic method to peacebuilding evaluation into graduate training, and thus, into future practice, is one way to accomplish this and to offer a practical alternative to the liberal, institutional, and technocratic practice that characterizes the field today.

Bibliography

Abdullah, Ibrahim. 1998. "Bush Path to Destruction: The Origin and Character of the Revolutionary United Front/Sierra Leone." *The Journal of Modern African Studies* 36(2):203–35.

Abraham, Arthur. 2004. "State Complicity as a Factor in Perpetuating the Sierra Leone Civil War." Pp. 104–20 in *Between Democracy and Terror: The Civil War in Sierra Leone*, edited by I. Abdullah. Dakar: Council for the Development of Social Science Research in Africa.

Abu-Nimer, Mohammed. 2001. "Education for Coexistence in Israel: Potential and Challenges." Pp. 235–54 in *Reconciliation, Justice, and Coexistence*, edited by M. Abu-Nimer. Lanham, MD: Lexington Books.

Abu-Nimer, Mohammed, Amber Hill, Thomas Oldfield, Laurie Segel-Moss, and Leah Wilkes. 2013. "Linking Program Design and Evaluation in Peacebuilding: A Challenging Task. A Meta-Review of Peacebuilding Initiatives in Active Conflict Zones in Africa." Report for the Center of Peacebuilding and Development School of International Service, American University, and Search for Common Ground. Retrieved July 26, 2013. Available at: http://dmeforpeace.org/sites/default/files/Linking%20Program%20Design%20and%20Evaluation.pdf.

Addison, Tony. 2001. *Reconstruction from War in Africa: Communities, Entrepreneurs, and States.* World Institute of Development Economics Research, Discussion Paper No. 2001/18. Retrieved June 5, 2013. Available at: www.csae.ox.ac.uk/conferences/2001-DPiA/pdfs/Addison.pdf.

Akhavan, Payam. 2009. "Are International Criminal Tribunals a Disincentive to Peace? Reconciling Judicial Romanticism with Political Realism." *Human Rights Quarterly* 31(3):624–54.

Allan, Alfred and Marietjie M. Allan. 2000. "The South African Truth and Reconciliation Commission as a Therapeutic Tool." *Behavioural Sciences and the Law* 18(4): 459–77.

Anderson, Mary B. 1999. *Do No Harm: How Aid Can Support Peace – Or War.* Boulder, CO: Lynne Rienner Publishers.

Antkowiak, Thomas, M. 2002. "Truth as Right and Remedy in International Human Rights Experience." *Michigan Journal of International Law* 23(4):977–1013.

Arbour, Louise. 2007. "Economic and Social Justice for Societies in Transition." *New York University Journal of International Law and Politics* 40:1.

Archibald, Steven and Paul Richards. 2002. "Converts to Human Rights? Popular Debate about War and Justice in Rural Central Sierra Leone." *Africa* 72(3):339–67.

Augsburger, David W. 1992. *Conflict Mediation Across Cultures: Pathways and Patterns*. Louisville, KY: Westminster/John Knox Press.

Autesserre, Severine. 2010. *The Trouble with the Congo: Local Violence and the Failure of International Peacebuilding*. Cambridge: Cambridge University Press.

——2014. *Peacebuilders: An Ethnography of International Intervention*. New York, NY: Cambridge University Press.

Averill, James R. 1985. "The Social Construction of Emotion: With Special Reference to Love." Pp. 89–110 in *The Social Construction of the Person*, edited by K.J. Gergen and K.E. Davis. New York, NY: Springer-Verlag.

Avruch, Kevin. 1998. *Culture and Conflict Resolution*. Washington, DC: United States Institute of Peace.

Azar, Fabiola and Etienne Mullet. 2002. "Willingness to Forgive: A Study of Muslim and Christian Lebanese." *Peace and Conflict: Journal of Peace Psychology* 8(1):17–30.

Azar, Fabiola, Etienne Mullet and Geneviéve Vinsonneau. 1999. "The Propensity to Forgive: Findings from Lebanon." *Journal of Peace Research* 36(2):169–81.

Ballentine, Karen. 2003. "Conclusion." Pp. 259–83 in *The Political Economy of Armed Conflict: Beyond Greed and Grievance*, edited by K. Ballentine and J. Sherman. Boulder, CO: Lynne Rienner Publishers.

Ballentine, Karen and Heiko Nitzschke. 2005. *Profiting from Peace: Managing the Resource Dimensions of Civil War*. Boulder, CO: Lynne Rienner Publishers.

Ballentine, Karen and Jake Sherman. 2003. "Introduction." Pp. 1–15 in *The Political Economy of Armed Conflict: Beyond Greed and Grievance*, edited by K. Ballentine and J. Sherman. Boulder, CO: Lynne Rienner Publishers.

Bangura, Yusuf. 1997. "Understanding the Political and Cultural Dynamics of the Sierra Leone War: A Critique of Paul Richard's *Fighting for the Forest*." *African Development* 22(3/4):117–48.

Barclay, Craig R. and Peggy A. DeCooke. 1988. "Ordinary Everyday Memories: Some of the Things of Which Selves Are Made." Pp. 91–125 in *Remembering Reconsidered: Ecological and Traditional Approaches to the Study of Memory*, edited by U. Neisser and E. Winograd. Cambridge: Cambridge University Press.

Bastida, Elena M., Tung-Sung Tseng, Corliss McKeever and Leonard Jack Jr. 2010. "Ethics and Community-Based Participatory Research: Perspectives from the Field." *Health Promotion Practice* 11(1):16–20.

Battaglia, Debbora. 1992. "The Body in the Gift: Memory and Forgetting in Sabarl Mortuary Exchange." *American Ethnologist* 19(1):3–18.

Bichsel, Christine. 2005. "In Search of Harmony: Repairing Infrastructure and Social Relations in the Ferghana Valley." *Central Asia Survey* 24(1):53–66.

——2009. *Conflict Transformation in Central Asia: Irrigation Disputes in the Ferghana Valley*. New York, NY: Routledge.

Bell, Christine and Catherine O'Rourke. 2007. "Does Feminism Need a Theory of Transitional Justice? An Introductory Essay." *International Journal of Transitional Justice* 1(1):23–44.

Bell, Daniel A. and Thaddeus Metz. 2011. "Confucianism and *Ubuntu*: Reflections on a Dialogue between Chinese and African Traditions." *Journal of Chinese Philosophy* 38(1):78–95.

Berdal, Mats and David Keen. 1997. "Violence and Economic Agendas in Civil Wars: Some Policy Implications." *Millennium: Journal of International Studies* 26(3):795–818.

Berdal, Mats and David M. Malone. 2000. "Introduction." Pp. 1–15 in *Greed and Grievance: Economic Agendas in Civil Wars*, edited by M. Berdal and D.M. Malone. Boulder, CO: Lynne Rienner Publishers.

Biggar, Nigel. 2002. "Peace and Justice: A Limited Reconciliation." *Ethical Theory and Moral Practice* 5(2):167–79.

——2003. *Burying the Past: Making Peace and Doing Justice after Civil Conflict*. Washington, DC: Georgetown University Press.

Bledsoe, Caroline. 1984. "The Political Use of Sande Ideology and Symbolism." *American Ethnologist* 11(3):455–72.

——1990. "'No Success Without Struggle': Social Mobility and Hardship for Foster Children in Sierra Leone." *Man, New Series* 25(1):70–88.

Bloomfield, David. 2006. *On Good Terms: Clarifying Reconciliation*. Berlin: Berghof Research Center for Constructive Conflict Management.

Bloomfield, David, Teresa Barnes and Luc Huyse. 2003. *Reconciliation after Violent Conflict: A Handbook*. Stockholm: International IDEA.

Blum, Andrew. 2011. *Improving Peacebuilding Evaluation: A Whole-of-Field Approach*. Special Report #280. Washington, DC: United States Institute of Peace,. Retrieved August 12, 2013. Available at: http://www.usip.org/sites/default/files/SR-Improving-Peace-Building-Evaluation.pdf.

Bøås, Morten. 2001. "Liberia and Sierra Leone-Dead Ringers? The Logic of Neopatrimonial Rule." *Third World Quarterly Journal of Emerging Areas* 22(5):697–723.

Bolton, Catherine. 2012. *I Did it to Save My Life: Love and Survival in Sierra Leone*. Berkeley, CA: University of California Press.

Boog, Ben W.M. 2003. "The Emancipatory Character of Action Research, its History and the Present State of the Art." *Journal of Community and Applied Social Psychology* 13(6):426–38.

Borras Jr., Saturnino M. and Jennifer C. Franco. 2012. "Global Land Grabbing and Trajectories of Agrarian Change: A Preliminary Analysis." *Journal of Agrarian Change* 12(1):34–59.

Bourdieu, Pierre. 1977. *Outline of a Theory of Practice*. Cambridge: Cambridge University Press.

Bourgois, Phillippe. 2012. "Confronting the Ethics of Ethnography: Lessons from Fieldwork in Latin American." Pp. 318–30 in *Ethnographic Fieldwork: An Anthropological Reader*. 2nd edn, edited by A.C.G.M. Robben and J. Sluka. Malden, MA: Wiley-Blackwell.

Boutros-Ghali, Boutros. 1992. "An Agenda for Peace: Preventive Diplomacy, Peacemaking and Peace-keeping: Report of the Secretary General." New York: United Nations. Retrieved June 3, 2013. Available at: www.unrol.org/files/A_47_277.pdf.

Boyce, James K. 2002. *Investing in Peace: Aid and Conditionality after Civil Wars*. Adelphi Paper No, 351. London: The International Institute for Strategic Studies.

Brahm, Eric. 2007. "Uncovering the Truth: Examining Truth Commission Success and Impact." *International Studies Perspective* 8(1):16–35.

Brett, Rachel and Irma Specht. 2004. *Young Soldiers: Why They Choose to Fight*. Boulder, CO: Lynne Rienner Publishers.

Brooks, Roy L. 1999. *When Sorry Isn't Enough: The Controversy Over Apologies and Reparations for Human Injustice*. New York, NY: New York University Press.

Brounéus, Karen. 2010. "The Trauma of Truth Telling: Effects of Witnessing in the Rwandan Genocide Courts on Psychological Health." *Journal of Conflict Resolution* 54(3):408–37.

Bush, Kenneth. 1998. *A Measure of Peace: Peace and Conflict Impact Assessment (PCIA) of Development Projects in Conflict Zones.* Ottawa: International Development Research Centre.

Bush, Kenneth and Colleen Duggan, eds. 2013a. "Evaluation in Violently Divided Societies." *Journal of Peacebuilding and Development* 8(2) (Special Issue).

——2013b. "Evaluation in Conflict Zones: Methodological and Ethical Challenges." *Journal of Peacebuilding and Development* 8(2):5–25.

Byrne, Sean, Chuck Thiessen, Eyob Fissuh, Cynthia Irvin and Marcie Hawranik. 2008. "Economic Assistance, Development and Peacebuilding: The Role of the IFI and EU Peace II Fund in Northern Ireland." *Civil Wars* 10(2):106–24.

Carsten, Janet. 1995. "The Politics of Forgetting: Migration, Kinship and Memory on the Periphery of the Southeast Asian State." *The Journal of the Royal Anthropological Institute* 1(2):317–35.

Castillejo Cuellar, Alejandro. 2007. "Knowledge, Experience, and South Africa's Scenarios of Forgiveness." *Radical History Review* 97:11–42.

Cater, Charles. 2003. "The Political Economy of Conflict and UN Intervention: Rethinking the Critical Cases of Africa." Pp. 19–46 in *The Political Economy of Armed Conflict: Beyond Greed and Grievance*, edited by K. Ballentine and J. Sherman. Boulder, CO: Lynne Rienner Publishers.

Catholic Relief Services. 2010. *GAIN Peacebuilding Indicators.* Baltimore, MD: PQSD Publications Team. Retrieved July 17, 2013. Available at: http://c.ymcdn.com/sites/www.allianceforpeacebuilding.org/resource/collection/9E786610-CF07-4073-9E34-A03818697B2E/GAIN.pdf.

Chabal, Patrick and Jean-Pascal Daloz. 1999. *Africa Works: Disorder as Political Instrument*. Bloomington, IN: Indiana University Press.

Chandler, David. 2006. *Empire in Denial: The Politics of State-Building*. London: Pluto Press.

——2010. *International Statebuilding: The Rise of Post-Liberal Governance.* New York, NY: Routledge.

Chapman, Audrey R. and Patrick Ball. 2001. "The Truth of Truth Commissions: Comparative Lessons from Haiti, South Africa, and Guatemala." *Human Rights Quarterly* 23(1):1–43.

Chauveau, Jean-Pierre and Paul Richards. 2008. "West African Insurgencies in Agrarian Perspective: Côte d'Ivoire and Sierra Leone Compared." *Journal of Agrarian Change* 8(4):515–52.

Chesterman, Simon. 2007. "Ownership in Theory and in Practice: Transfer of Authority in UN Statebuilding Operations." *Journal of Intervention and Statebuilding* 1 (1):3–26.

Chu, Jessica. 2010. "Gender and 'Land Grabbing' in Sub-Saharan Africa: Women's Land Rights and Customary Land Tenure." *Development* 54(1):35–39.

Clammer, John. 1984. "Approaches to Ethnographic Research." Pp. 63–85 in *Ethnographic Research: A Guide to General Conduct*, edited by R.F. Ellen. London: Academic Press.

Clark, Janine Natalya. 2011. "UN Peacekeeping in the Democratic Republic of Congo: Reflections on MONUSCO and Its Contradictory Mandate." *Journal of International Peacekeeping* 15(3–4):363–83.

Cohen, Raymond. 1997. *Negotiating Across Cultures: International Communication in an Interdependent World.* Washington, DC: United States Institute of Peace.

Coleman, Simon and Peter Collins. 2006. "Introduction: 'Being … Where?' Performing Fields on Shifting Grounds." Pp. 1–21 in *Locating the Field: Space, Place and Context in Anthropology*, edited by S. Coleman and P. Collins. Oxford: Berg Publishers.

Collier, Paul. 1999. "On the Economic Consequences of Civil War." *Oxford Economic Papers* 51(1):168–83.

——2000. "Rebellion as a Quasi-Criminal Activity." *Journal of Conflict Resolution* 44(6):839–53.

Collier, Paul and Anke Hoeffler. 1998. "On the Economic Causes of Civil War." *Oxford Economic Papers* 50(4):563–73.

Collier, Paul, Anke Hoeffler and Mans Soderbom. 2004. "On the Duration of Civil War." *Journal of Peace Research* 41(3):253–73.

Collins, Peter and Anselma Gallinat. 2010. "The Ethnographic Self as Resource: An Introduction." Pp. 1–22 in *The Ethnographic Self as Resource: Writing Memory and Experience into Ethnography*, edited by P. Collins and A. Callinat. New York, NY: Berghahn Books.

Colvin, Christopher J. 2006. "Trafficking Trauma: Intellectual Property Rights and the Political Economy of Traumatic Storytelling." *Critical Arts* 20(1):171–82.

Cotula, Lorenzo, Sonja Vermeulen, Rebeca Leonard and James Keeley. 2009. "Land Grab or Development Opportunity? Agricultural Investments and International Land Deals in Africa." London: IIEE/FAO/IFAD. Retrieved June 5, 2013. Available at: http://dlc.dlib.indiana.edu/dlc/bitstream/handle/10535/6178/land%20grab%20or%20dev%20opportunity.pdf?sequence=1.

Cubitt, Christine. 2012. *Local and Global Dynamics of Peacebuilding: Post-Conflict Peacebuilding in Sierra Leone*. London: Routledge.

Dancy, Geoff and Eric Wiebelhaus-Brahm. 2011. "Justice and the Peace: A Time-Sensitive Empirical Evaluation." Paper presented at the International Studies Association Convention, Montreal, March 1. Retrieved June 4, 2013. Available at: https://www.researchgate.net/publication/228256401_Justice_and_the_Peace_A_TimeSensitive_Empirical_Evaluation.

Das, Veena. 2007. *Life and Words: Violence and the Descent into the Ordinary*. Berkeley, CA: University of California Press.

De Certeau. M 1984. *The Practice of Everyday Life*. Berkeley, CA: University of California Press.

De la Rey, Cheryl and Ingrid Owens. 1998. "Perceptions of Psychosocial Healing and the Truth and Reconciliation Commission in South Africa." *Peace and Conflict: Journal of Peace Psychology* 4(3): 258–70.

Del Castillo, Graciana. 2011. "The Economics of Peace: Five Rules for Effective Reconstruction." Special Report. Washington, DC: United States Institute of Peace. Retrieved June 5, 2013. Available at: http://www.usip.org/files/resources/SR286_The_Economics_of_Peace.pdf.

Denskus, Tobias. 2009. "The Fragility of Peacebuilding in Nepal." *Peace Review: A Journal of Social Justice* 21(1):54–60.

——2010. "Peacebuilding Does Not Build Peace." Pp. 235–43 in *Deconstructing Development Discourse: Buzzwords and Fuzzwords*, edited by A. Cornwall and D. Eade. Oxford: Oxfam.

——2012. "Challenging the International Peacebuilding Evaluation Discourse with Qualitative Methodologies." *Evaluation and Program Planning* 35(1):148–53.

De Soto, Hermine G. and Nora Dudwick. 2000. *Fieldwork Dilemmas: Anthropologists in Postsocialist States*. Madison, WI: University of Wisconsin Press.

De Soysa, Indra. 2000. "The Resource Curse: Are Civil Wars Driven by Rapacity or Paucity?" Pp. 113–35 in *Greed and Grievance: Economic Agendas in Civil Wars*, edited by M. Berdal and D.M. Malone. Boulder, CO: Lynne Rienner Publishers.

Dimen, Muriel. 1977. *The Anthropological Imagination*. New York, NY: McGraw-Hill.

Donais, Timothy. 2009. "Empowerment or Imposition? Dilemmas of Local Ownership in Post-Conflict Peacebuilding Processes." *Peace and Change* 34(1):3–26.

——2012. *Peacebuilding and Local Ownership: Post-Conflict Consensus-Building*. New York, NY: Routledge.

Dorjahn, Vernon R. 1990. "The Marital Game, Divorce, and Divorce Frequency among the Temne of Sierra Leone." *Anthropological Quarterly* 63(4):169–82.

Doyle, Michael A. and Nicholas Sambanis. 2000. "International Peacebuilding: A Theoretical and Quantitative Analysis." *The American Political Science Review* 94(4):779–801.

Duffield, Mark. 2001. *Global Governance and the New Wars: The Merging of Security and Development*. London: Zed Books.

——2007. *Development, Security and Unending War: Governing the World of Peoples*. London: Polity Press.

Duggan, Colleen. ed. 2010. "Transitional Justice on Trial: Evaluating its Impact." (Special Issue). *International Journal of Transitional Justice* 4(3).

Easterly, William. 2006. *The White Man's Burden: Why the West's Efforts to Aid the Rest Have Done So Much Ill and So Little Good*. London: Penguin Books.

Elsass, Peter. 2001. "Individual and Collective Traumatic Memories: A Qualitative Study of Post-Traumatic Stress Disorder Symptoms in Two Latin American Localities." *Transcultural Psychiatry* 38(3):306–16.

Esser, Daniel E. and Emily E. Vanderkamp. 2013. "Comparable and Yet Context-Sensitive? Improving Evaluation in Violently Divided Societies Through Methodology." *Journal of Peacebuilding and Development* 8(2):42–56.

European Centre for Conflict Prevention. 1999. *People Building Peace: 35 Inspiring Stories from Around the World*. Utrecht: European Centre for Conflict Prevention.

Evenson, Elizabeth M. 2004. "Truth and Justice in Sierra Leone: Coordination between Commission and Court." *Columbia Law Review* 104:730–67.

Fanthorpe, Richard. 2001. "Neither Citizen nor Subject? 'Lumpen' Agency and the Legacy of Native Administration in Sierra Leone." *African Affairs* 100(400):363–86.

——2006. "On the Limits of Liberal Peace: Chiefs and Democratic Decentralization in Post-War Sierra Leone." *African Affairs* 105(418):27–49.

Fearon, James D. 2005. "Primary Commodity Exports and Civil War." *Journal of Conflict Resolution* 49(4):483–507.

Ferme, Miriam C. 2001. *The Underneath of Things: Violence, History, and the Everyday in Sierra Leone*. Berkeley CA.: University of California Press.

Ferrell, Jeff and Mark S. Hamm. 1998. *Ethnography at the Edge: Crime, Deviance and Field Research*. Dexter, MI: Northeastern University Press.

Fletcher, Laurel E. and Harvey M. Weinstein. 2002. "Violence and Social Repair: Rethinking the Contribution of Justice to Reconciliation." *Human Rights Quarterly* 24(3):573–639.

Flores, Thomas Edward and Irfan Nooruddin. 2009. "Democracy under the Gun: Understanding Postconflict Economic Recovery." *Journal of Conflict Resolution* 53(1):3–29.

Forman, Johanna Mendelson. 2002. "Achieving Socioeconomic Well-being in Postconflict Settings." *The Washington Quarterly* 25(4):125–38.

Fortna, Virginia Page. 2004. "Does Peacekeeping Keep Peace? International Intervention and the Duration of Peace after Civil War." *International Studies Quarterly* 48(2):269–92.

Foucault, Michel. 1990. *The History of Sexuality: An Introduction*, Vol. 1. New York, NY: Vintage Books.

——1995. *Discipline and Punish: The Birth of the Prison*. New York, NY: Vintage Books.

Freeman, Mark. 2006. *Truth Commissions and Procedural Fairness*. New York, NY: Cambridge University Press.

Fromm, Erich. 1974. "Psychoanalytic Characterology and its Application to Understanding of Culture." Pp. 1–12 in *Culture and Personality*, edited by S.S. Sargent and M.W. Smith. New York, NY: Cooper Square Publishers.

Fulton, Richard M. 1972. "The Political Structures and Functions of Poro in Kpelle Society." *American Anthropologist, New Series* 74(5):1218–33.

Furedi, Frank. 2004. *Therapy Culture: Cultivating Vulnerability in an Uncertain Age*. London: Routledge.

Galtung, Johan. 1969. "Violence, Peace, and Peace Research." *Journal of Peace Research* 6(3):167–91.

——2001. "After Violence, Reconstruction, Reconciliation, and Resolution: Coping with Visible and Invisible Effects of War and Violence." Pp. 3–23 in *Reconciliation, Justice, and Coexistence: Theory and Practice*, edited by M. Abu-Nimer. Lanham, MD: Lexington Books.

Gberie, Lansana. 2004. "The 25 May Coup d'Etat in Sierra Leone: A Lumpen Revolt?" Pp. 144–63 in *Between Democracy and Terror: The Civil War in Sierra Leone*, edited by I. Abdullah. Dakar: Council for the Development of Social Science Research in Africa.

——2005. *A Dirty War in West Africa: The RUF and the Destruction of Sierra Leone*. Bloomington, IN: Indiana University Press.

Gergen, Kenneth J. 1994. "Mind, Text, and Society: Self-Memory in Social Context." Pp. 78–104 in *The Remembering Self: Construction and Accuracy in the Self-Narrative*, edited by U. Neisser and R. Fivush. Cambridge: Cambridge University Press.

Gibson, James L. 2004. "Overcoming Apartheid: Can Truth Reconcile a Divided Nation?" *Politikon* 31(2):129–55.

Glaser, Barney G. and Anselm L. Strauss. 1967. *The Discovery of Grounded Theory: Strategies for Qualitative Research*. Chicago: Aldine.

Gobodo-Madikizela, Pumla and Chris van der Merwe. 2009. *Memory, Narrative and Forgiveness: Perspectives on the Unfinished Journeys of the Past*. Newcastle: Cambridge Scholars Publishing.

Goetschel, Laurent and Tobias Hagmann. 2009. "Civilian Peacebuilding: Peace by Bureaucratic Means?" *Conflict, Security and Development* 9(1):55–73.

Goffman, Erving. 1959. *The Presentation of Self in Everyday Life*. Garden City, NY: Doubleday.

González, Roberto J. 2007. "Towards Mercenary Anthropology? The New US Army Counterinsurgency Manual FM 3–24 and the Military-Anthropology Complex." *Anthropology Today* 23(3):14–19.

Graybill, Lyn and Kimberly Lanegran. 2004. "Truth, Justice, and Reconciliation in Africa: Issues and Cases." *African Studies Quarterly* 8(1):1–18.

Green, Eva G.T., Jean-Claude Deschamps and Dario Páez. 2005. "Variation of Individualism and Collectivism within and between 20 Countries: A Typological Analysis." *Journal of Cross-Cultural Psychology* 36(3):321–39.

Hartzell, Caroline, Matthew Hoddie, and Donald Rothchild. 2001. "Stabilizing the Peace after Civil War: An Investigation of Some Key Variables." *International Organization* 55(1):183–208.

Hayner, Priscilla B. 1994 "Fifteen Truth Commissions – 1974 to 1994: A Comparative Study." *Human Rights Quarterly.* 16(4):597–655.

——2002. *Unspeakable Truths: Facing the Challenge of Truth Commissions.* New York, NY: Routledge.

Hirsch, John L. 2001. *Sierra Leone: Diamonds and the Struggle for Democracy.* Boulder, CO: Lynne Rienner Publishers.

Hoffman, Danny. 2011. *The War Machines: Young Men and Violence in Sierra Leone and Liberia.* Durham, NC: Duke University Press.

Hofstede, Geert. 1980. "Motivation, Leadership, and Organization: Do American Theories Apply Abroad?" *Organizational Dynamics* 9(1):42–63.

——2001. *Culture's Consequences: Comparing Values, Behaviours, Institutions and Organizations across Nations.* 2nd edn, Thousand Oaks, CA: Sage Publications.

Holtzman, Wayne H., Rogelio Diaz-Guerrero, and Jon David Swartz. 1975. *Personality Development in Two Cultures: A Cross-Cultural Longitudinal Study of School Children in Mexico and the United States.* Austin, TX: University of Texas Press.

Honwana, Alcinda. 2006. *Child Soldiers in Africa.* Philadelphia, PA: University of Pennsylvania Press.

Humphreys, Macartan and Jeremy M. Weinstein. 2007. "Remobilization and Reintegration." *Journal of Conflict Resolution* 51(4):531–67.

——2008. "Who Fights? The Determinants of Participation in Civil War." *American Journal of Political Science* 52(2):436–55.

Ignatieff, Michael. 2003. *Empire Lite: Nation-Building in Bosnia, Kosovo, and Afghanistan.* London: Random House.

Inikori, Joseph E. 2003. "The Struggle Against the Transatlantic Slave Trade." Pp.170–98 in *Fighting the Slave Trade*, edited by S.A. Diouf. Athens, OH: Ohio University Press.

Isaacs, Anita. 2009. "Truth and the Challenge of Reconciliation in Guatemala." Pp. 116–46 in *Reconciliation(s): Transitional Justice in Postconflict Societies*, edited by J. Quinn. Montreal: McGill-Queen's University Press.

Isichei, Elizabeth Allo. 1977. *History of West African since 1800.* New York, NY: Africana Publishing Company.

Jackson, Michael. 2004. *In Sierra Leone.* Durham, NC: Duke University Press.

Jackson, Stephen. 2005. "Protecting Livelihoods in Violent Economies." Pp. 153–82 in *Profiting from Peace: Managing the Resource Dimensions of Civil War*, edited by K. Ballentine and H. Nitzschke. Boulder, CO: Lynne Rienner Publishers.

James, Wendy. 2000. "Beyond the First Encounter: Transformations of 'The Field' in Northeast Africa." Pp. 68–90 in *Anthropologists in a Wider World*, edited by P. Dresch, W. James, and D. Parkin. New York, NY: Berghahn Books.

Jarstad, Anna K. and Roberto Belloni. eds. 2012. "Hybrid Peace Governance" (Special Issue). *Global Governance* 18(1).

Jayawickrama, Janaka. 2013. "'If They Can't do Any Good, They Shouldn't Come': Northern Evaluators in Southern Realities." *Journal of Peacebuilding and Development* 8(2):26–41.

Jerven, Morten. 2013. *Poor Numbers: How We Are Misled by African Development Statistics and What to Do About it.* Ithaca, NY: Cornell University Press.

Jones, Adam. 1983. *From Slaves to Palm Kernels: A History of the Galinhas Country (West Africa), 1730–1890.* Wiesbaden: Adam Steiner.

Kadiangandu, Joachim Kadima, Melanie Gauché, Geneviève Vinsonneau and Etienne Mullet. 2007. "Conceptualizations of Forgiveness: Collectivist-Congolese Versus Individualist-French Viewpoints." *Journal of Cross-Cultural Psychology* 38 (4):432–37.

Kaldor, Mary. 1999. *New and Old Wars: Organized Violence in a Global Era.* Stanford, CA: Stanford University Press.

Kalyvas, Stathis N. 2006. *The Logic of Violence in Civil War.* New York, NY: Cambridge University Press.

Kandeh, Jimmy D. 1992. "Politicization of Ethnic Identities in Sierra Leone." *African Studies Review* 35(1):81–99.

——1999. "Ransoming the State: Elite Origins of Subaltern Terror in Sierra Leone." *Review of African Political Economy* 26(81):349–66.

——2004. "In Search of Legitimacy: The 1996 Elections." Pp. 123–43 in *Between Democracy and Terror: The Sierra Leone Civil War*, edited by I. Abdullah. Dakar: Council for the Development of Social Science Research in Africa.

Karlström, Mikael. 2003. "On the Aesthetics and Dialogics of Power in the Postcolony." *Africa* 73(1):57–76.

Kaufman, Stuart J. 2006. "Escaping the Symbolic Politics Trap: Reconciliation Initiatives and Conflict Resolution in Ethnic Wars." *Journal of Peace Research* 43(2):201–18.

Keen, David. 1998. "The Economic Functions of Violence in Civil Wars." Adelphi Paper No. 320. Oxford: Oxford University Press.

——2005. *Conflict and Collusion in Sierra Leone.* Oxford: James Currey.

——2006. *Endless War? Hidden Functions of the 'War on Terror'*. London: Pluto Press.

Kelsall, Timothy. 2005. "Truth, Lies, Ritual: Preliminary Reflections on the Truth and Reconciliation Commission." *Human Rights Quarterly* 27(2):361–91.

Kirkpatrick, John. 1985. "How Personal Differences Can Make a Difference." Pp. 225–40 in *The Social Construction of the Person*, edited by K.J. Gergen and K.E. Davis. New York: Springer-Verlag.

Klein, Julie Thompson. 1990. *Interdisciplinarity: History, Theory, and Practice.* Detroit, MI: Wayne State University Press.

Knox, Colin and Pádraic Quirk. 2000. *Peace Building in Northern Ireland, Israel and South Africa: Transition, Transformation, and Reconciliation.* New York, NY: Palgrave Macmillan.

Kovats-Bernat, J. Christopher. 2002. "Negotiating Dangerous Fields: Pragmatic Strategies for Fieldwork amid Violence and Terror." *American Anthropologist* 104(1):208–22.

Kpundeh, Sahr. 2004. "Corruption and Political Insurgency in Sierra Leone." Pp. 90–103 in *Between Democracy and Terror: The Civil War in Sierra Leone*, edited by I. Abdullah. Dakar: Council for the Development of Social Science Research in Africa.

Kritz, Niel. 2009. "Policy Implications of Empirical Research in Transitional Justice." Pp. 13–21 in *Assessing the Impact of Transitional Justice: Challenges for Empirical Research*, edited by H. van der Merwe, V. Baxter, and A.R. Chapman. Washington, DC: United States Institute of Peace.

Laffey, Mark, and Sutharharan Nadarajah. 2012. "The Hybridity of Liberal Peace: States, Diasporas, and Insecurity." *Security Dialogue* 43(5):403–20.

Landsman, Stephan. 1996. "Alternative Responses to Serious Human Rights Abuses: Of Prosecution and Truth Commission." *Law and Contemporary Problems* 59(4):81–92.

Lassiter, Luke Eric. 2005. *The Chicago Guide to Collaborative Ethnography.* Chicago: University of Chicago Press.

Lastarria-Cornhiel, Susana. 1997. “Impact of Privatization on Gender and Property Rights in Africa.” *World Development* 25(8):1317–33.

Leach, Melissa. 1994. *Rainforest Relations: Gender and Resource Use among the Mende of Gola, Sierra Leone.* Edinburgh: University of Edinburgh Press.

Lederach, John Paul. 1995. *Preparing for Peace: Conflict Transformation across Cultures.* Syracuse, NY: Syracuse University Press.

——1997. *Building Peace: Sustainable Reconciliation in Divided Societies.* Washington, DC: United States Institute of Peace.

Leebaw, Bronwyn Anne. 2003. “Legitimation or Judgement? South Africa’s Restorative Approach to Transitional Justice.” *Polity* 36(1):23–51.

Lee-Treweek, Geraldine and Stephanie Linkogle. 2000. *Dander in the Field: Risk and Ethics in Social Research.* London: Routledge.

Lentz, Carola. 1998. “The Chief, the Mine Captain and the Politician: Legitimating Power in Northern Ghana.” *Africa* 68(1):46–67.

Leung, Kwok, Pamela Tremain Koch and Lin Lu. 2002. “A Dualistic Model of Harmony and its Implications for Conflict Management in Asia.” *Asia Pacific Journal of Management* 19(2–3):201–20.

LeVine, Robert A. 1982. *Culture, Behavior, and Personality: An Introduction to the Comparative Study of Psychosocial Adaptation.* New York, NY: Aldine Publishing Company.

Li, Quan and Adam Resnick. 2003. “Reversal of Fortunes: Democratic Institutions and Foreign Direct Investment Inflows in Developing Countries.” *International Organization* 57(1):175–211.

Lindner, Evelin Gerda. 2002. “Healing the Cycles of Humiliation: How to Attend to the Emotional Aspects of ‘Unsolvable’ Conflicts and the Use of ‘Humiliation Entrepreneurship’.” *Peace and Conflict: Journal of Peace Psychology* 8(2):125–38.

Lu, Xing. 1998. “An Interface Between Individualistic and Collectivistic Orientations in Chinese Cultural Values and Social Relations.” *Howard Journal of Communications* 9(2):91–107.

Lujala Paivi, Nils Petter Gleditsch and Elisabeth Gilmore. 2005. “A Diamond Curse? Civil War and Lootable Resources.” *Journal of Conflict Resolution* 49(4):538–62.

Lund, Giuliana. 2003. “‘Healing the Nation’: Medicolonial Discourse and the State of Emergency from Apartheid to Truth and Reconciliation.” *Cultural Critique* 54:88–119.

Mac Ginty, Roger. 2010a. “Hybrid Peace: The Interaction between Top-Down and Bottom-Up Peace.” *Security Dialogue* 41(4):391–412.

——2010b. “Warlords and the Liberal Peace: State-Building in Afghanistan.” *Conflict, Security and Development* 10(4):577–98.

——2011. *International Peacebuilding and Local Resistance: Hybrid Forms of Peace.* New York, NY: Palgrave Macmillan.

——2012. “Routine Peace: Technocracy and Peacebuilding.” *Cooperation and Conflict* 47(3):287–308.

Mac Ginty, Roger and Oliver P. Richmond. 2013 “The Local Turn in Peace Building: A Critical Agenda for Peace.” *Third World Quarterly* 34(5):763–83.

Mac Ginty, Roger and Gurchathen Sanghera. eds. 2012. “Hybridity in Peacebuilding and Development,” (Special Issue). *Journal of Peacebuilding and Development* 7(2).

MacKenzie, Megan H. 2012. *Female Soldiers in Sierra Leone: Sex, Security, and Post-Conflict Development.* New York, NY: New York University Press.

Madden, Raymond. 2010. *Being Ethnographic: A Guide to the Theory and Practice of Ethnography.* London: Sage Publications.

Madison, Soyini D. 2012. *Critical Anthropology: Method, Ethics, and Performance.* Thousand Oaks, CA: Sage Publications.

Mani, Rama. 2002. *Beyond Retribution: Seeking Justice in the Shadows of War.* Cambridge: Polity Press.

Manifesto '99. 2002. *Traditional Methods of Conflict Management/Resolution of Possible Complementary Value to the Proposed Sierra Leone Truth and Reconciliation Commission.* Study report submitted to the Office of the United Nations High Commissioner for Human Rights in support of the preparatory phase of the Truth and Reconciliation Commission for Sierra Leone. Freetown: Sierra Leone.

Mansley, Mark. 2005. "Private Financial Actors and Corporate Responsibility in Conflict Zones." Pp. 207–33 in *Profiting from Peace: Managing the Resource Dimensions of Civil War,* edited by K. Ballentine and H. Nitzschke. Boulder, CO: Lynne Rienner Publishers.

Marten, Kimberly Zisk. 2004. *Enforcing the Peace: Learning from the Imperial Past.* New York, NY: Columbia University Press.

Marx, Christoph. 2002. "Ubu and Ubuntu: On the Dialectics of Apartheid and Nation Building." *Politikon: South African Journal of Political Studies* 29 (1):49–69.

Maslow, Abraham H. 1954. *Motivation and Personality.* New York, NY: Harper.

Mbembe, Achille. 1992a. "Provisional Notes on the Postcolony." *Africa* 62(1):3–37.

——1992b. "The Banality of Power and the Aesthetics of Vulgarity in the Postcolony." *Public Culture* 4(2):1–30.

McAdams, Dan P. 1989 "The Development of Narrative Identity." Pp. 160–74 in *Personality Psychology: Recent Trends and Emerging Directions,* edited by D. Buss and N. Cantor. New York, NY: Springer-Verlag.

Mendeloff, David. 2004. "Truth-Seeking, Truth-Telling, and Postconflict Peacebuilding: Curb the Enthusiasm?" *International Studies Review* 6(3):355–80.

Menkel-Meadow, Carrie. 2007. "Restorative Justice: What Is It and Does It Work?" *Annual Review of Law and Social Science* 3:10.1–10.27.

Millar, Gearoid. 2010. "Assessing Local Experiences of Truth-Telling in Sierra Leone: Getting to 'Why' through a Qualitative Case Study Analysis." *International Journal of Transitional Justice* 4(9):477–96.

——2011a. "Local Evaluations of Justice through Truth Telling in Sierra Leone: Postwar Needs and Transitional Justice." *Human Rights Review* 12(4):515–35.

——2011b. "Between Western Theory and Local Practice: Cultural Impediments to Truth-Telling in Sierra Leone." *Conflict Resolution Quarterly* 29(2):177–99.

——2012a. "'Ah Lef ma Case fo God': Religious Belief and Personal Autonomy in Sierra Leone's Postwar Reconciliation." *Peace and Conflict: Journal of Peace Psychology* 18(2):131–43.

——2012b. "'Our Brothers Who Went to the Bush': Post-Identity Conflict and the Experience of Reconciliation in Sierra Leone." *Journal of Peace Research* 49 (5):717–29.

——2013. "Expectations and Experiences of Peacebuilding in Sierra Leone: Parallel Peacebuilding Processes and Compound Friction." *International Peacekeeping* 20 (2):193–207.

——2014. "Performative Memory and Re-Victimization: Truth-Telling and Provocation in Sierra Leone." *Memory Studies.*

Millar, Gearoid, Jair van der Lijn, and Willemijn Verkoren. eds. 2013. "Peacebuilding Plans and Local Reconfigurations: Frictions between Imported Processes and Indigenous Practices," (Special Issue). *International Peacekeeping* 20(2).

Miller, Peggy J. 1994. "Narrative Practices: Their Role in Socialization and Self-Construction." Pp. 158–79 in *The Remembering Self: Construction and Accuracy in the Self-Narrative*, edited by U. Neisser and R. Fivush. Cambridge: Cambridge University Press.

Minikon, Patricia B. and Susan Shepler. 2009. "Documenting Human Rights Abuses Among the Diaspora: Lessons Learned from the Liberian Truth and Reconciliation Commission." Pp. 141–58 in *Negotiating Sovereignty and Human Rights: Actors and Issues in Contemporary Human Rights Politics*, edited by N. Shawki and M. Cox. Surrey: Ashgate Publishing.

Minow, Martha. 1998. *Between Vengeance and Forgiveness: Facing History After Genocides and Mass Violence*. Boston: Beacon Press.

Moghaddam, Fathali M. 2008. "The Psychological Citizen and the Two Concepts of Social Contract: A Preliminary Analysis." *Political Psychology* 29(6):881–901.

Montville, Joseph V. 2001. "Justice and the Burdens of History." Pp. 129–44 in *Reconciliation, Justice, and Coexistence: Theory and Practice*, edited by M. Abu-Nimer. Lanham, MD: Lexington Books.

Muana, Patrick. 1997. "The Kamajoi Militia: Civil War, Internal Displacement and the Politics of Counter-Insurgency." *African Development* 22(3/4):77–100.

Mukashema, Immaculée and Etienne Mullet. 2010. "Reconciliation Sentiment Among Victims of Genocide in Rwanda: Conceptualizations, and Relationships with Mental Health." *Social Indicators Research* 99(1):25–39.

Murphy, Jeffrie G. 1988. "Forgiveness and Resentment." Pp. 17–34 in *Forgiveness and Mercy*, edited by J.G. Murphy and J. Hampton. New York, NY: Cambridge University Press.

Murphy, William P. 1990. "Creating the Appearance of Consensus in Mende Political Discourse." *American Anthropologist* 92(2):24–41.

——1998. "The Sublime Dance of Mende Politics: An African Aesthetic of Charismatic Power." *American Ethnologist* 25(4):563–82.

Murray, Jennifer. 2002. "Who Will Police the Peace-builders? The Failure to Establish Accountability for the Participation of United Nations Civilian Police in the Trafficking of Women in Post-Conflict Bosnia and Herzegovina." *Columbia Human Rights Law Review* 34:475–527.

Nadery, Ahmad Nader. 2007. "Peace or Justice? Transitional Justice in Afghanistan." *International Journal of Transitional Justice* 1(1):173–79.

Naqvi, Yasmin. 2006. "The Right to Truth in International Law: Fact or Fiction?" *International Review of the Red Cross* 88(886):242–73.

Neimeyer, Greg J. and April E. Metzler. 1994. "Personal Identity and Autobiographical Recall." Pp. 105–35 in *The Remembering Self: Construction and Accuracy in the Self-Narrative*, edited by U. Neisser and R. Fivush. Cambridge: Cambridge University Press.

Newman, Edward. 2010. "Peacebuilding as Security in 'Failing' and Conflict-Prone States." *Journal of Intervention and Statebuilding* 4(3):305–22.

Nitzschke, Heiko and Kaysie Studdard. 2005. "The Legacies of War Economies: Challenges and Options for Peacemaking and Peacebuilding." *International Peacekeeping* 12(2):222–39.

Nordstrom, Carolyn and Antonius C.G.M. Robben. 1995. *Fieldwork Under Fire: Contemporary Studies of Violence and Survival*. Berkeley, CA: University of California Press.

Nozick, Robert. 1974. *Anarchy, State, and Utopia*. Basic Books.

Nyerges, A. Endre. 1992. "The Ecology of Wealth-in-People: Agriculture, Settlement, and Society in the Perpetual Frontier." *American Anthropologist* 94(4):860–81.

OECD. 2012. *Evaluating Peacebuilding Activities in Settings of Conflict and Fragility: Improving Learning for Results*. DAC Guidelines and Reference Series. OECD Publishing. Retrieved July 26, 2013. Available at: http://www.oecd-ilibrary.org/docserver/download/4312151e.pdf?expires=1374853635andid=idandaccname=guestandchecksum = 7FC1EAA22FB76A389530735D30B5A799.

Olivier de Sardan, Jean-Pierre. 2005. *Anthropology and Development: Understanding Contemporary Social Change*. London: Zed Books.

Olsen, Tricia D., Payne, Leigh A. and Andrew Reiter. 2010. *Transitional Justice in Balance: Comparing Processes, Weighing Efficacy*. Washington, DC: United States Institute of Peace.

Opotow, Susan. 2001. "Reconciliation in Times of Impunity: Challenges for Social Justice." *Social Justice Research* 14(2):149–70.

Orentlicher, Diane. 1991. "Settling Accounts: The Duty to Prosecute Human Rights Violations of a Prior Regime." *The Yale Law Journal* 100(8):2537–615.

——1994. "Addressing Gross Human Rights Abuses: Punishment and Victim Compensation." *Studies in Transnational Legal Policy* 26:425–75.

Orta, Andrew. 2002. "Burying the Past: Locality, Lived History, and Death in an Aymara Ritual of Remembrance." *Cultural Anthropology* 17(4):471–511.

Osiel, Mark J. 1995. "Ever Again: Legal Remembrance of Administrative Massacre." *University of Pennsylvania Law Review* 144(2):463–704.

Ossorio, Peter G. 1985. "An Overview of Descriptive Psychology." Pp. 19–40 in *The Social Construction of the Person*, edited by K.J. Gergen and K.E. Davis. New York, NY: Springer-Verlag.

Paffenholz, Thania, Mahammed Abu-Nimer and Erin McCandless. eds. 2005. "Peacebuilding and Development: Integrated Approaches to Evaluation," (Special Issue). *International Journal of Peacebuilding and Development* 2(2).

Paffenholz, Thania and Luc Reychler. 2007. *Aid for Peace: A Guide to Planning and Evaluation for Conflict Zones*. Baden-Baden: Nomos.

Paffenholz, Thania and Christoph Spurk. 2006. "Civil Society, Civil Engagement, and Peacebuilding." Social Development Papers: Conflict, Development and Reconstruction, paper No. 36. Washington, DC: The World Bank. Retrieved June 5, 2013. Available at: http://siteresources.worldbank.org/INTCPR/Resources/WP36_web.pdf.

Paris, Roland. 2002. "International Peacebuilding and the 'Mission Civilisatrice'." *Review of International Studies* 28(4):637–56.

——2004. *At War's End: Building Peace after Civil War*. Cambridge: Cambridge University Press.

Parman, Susan. 1998. *Europe in the Anthropological Imagination*. Upper Saddle River, NJ: Prentice Hall.

Pedler, Frederick. 1979. *Main Currents in West African History 1940–1978*. London: The Macmillan Press.

Peters, Krijn and Paul Richards. 1998. "'Why We Fight': Voices of Youth Combatants in Sierra Leone." *Africa* 68(2):183–210.

——2007. "Understanding Recent African Wars." *Africa* 77(3):442–54.

Pham, Peter J. 2007. "Making Sense of a Senseless War." *Human Rights and Human Welfare* 7:35–51.

Popkin, Margaret. 2000. *Peace Without Justice: Obstacles to Building the Rule of Law in El Salvador.* University Park, PA: The University of Pennsylvania.

Popkin, Margaret and Nehal Bhuta. 1999. "Latin American Amnesties in Comparative Perspective: Can the Past Be Buried?" *Ethics and International Affairs* 13(1):99–122.

Popkin, Margaret and Naomi Roht-Arriaza. 1995 "Truth as Justice: Investigatory Commissions in Latin America." *Law and Social Inquiry* 20(1):79–116.

Porter, Arthur T. 1963. *Creoledom: A Study of the Development of Freetown Society.* London: Oxford University Press.

Pouligny, Béatrice. 2005. "Civil Society and Post-Conflict Peacebuilding: Ambiguities of International Programmes Aimed at Building 'New' Societies." *Security Dialogue* 36(4):495–510.

Pugh, Michael. 2005. "The Political Economy of Peacebuilding: A Critical Theory Perspective." *International Journal of Peace Studies* 10(2):23–42.

——2010. "Accountability and Credibility: Assessing Host Population Perceptions and Expectations." Pp. 56–65 in *Beyond the New Horizon: Proceedings from the UN Peacekeeping Future Challenges Seminar,* edited by C. de Coning, A. Stensland, and T. Tardy. Oslo: Norwegian Institute of International Affairs.

——2011. "Local Agency and Political Economies of Peacebuilding." *Studies in Ethnicity and Nationalism* 11(2):308–20.

Pugh, Michael, Neil Cooper and Jonathan Goodhand. 2004. *War Economies in a Regional Context: Challenges of Transformation.* Boulder, CO: Lynne Rienner Publishers.

Pupavac, Vanessa. 2004. "International Therapeutic Peace and Justice in Bosnia." *Social & Legal Studies* 13(3):377–401.

Quinn, Joanna. 2009. *Reconciliation(s): Transitional Justice in Postconflict Societies.* Montreal: McGill-Queen's University Press.

Quinn, Joanna and Mark Freeman. 2003. "Lessons Learned: Practical Lessons Gleaned from Inside the Truth Commissions of Guatemala and South Africa." *Human Rights Quarterly* 25(4):1117–49.

Rawls, John. 1971. *A Theory of Justice.* Cambridge, MA: Harvard University Press.

Reno, William. 1997. "War, Markets, and the Reconfiguration of West Africa's Weak States." *Comparative Politics* 19(4):493–510.

——2002. "The Politics of Insurgency in Collapsing States." *Development and Change* 33(5):837–58.

Retzinger, Suzanne and Thomas Scheff. 2000. "Emotion, Alienation, and Narratives: Resolving Intractable Conflict." *Mediation Quarterly* 18(1):71–85.

Richards, Paul. 1996. *Fighting for the Rain Forest: War, Youth and Resources in Sierra Leone.* Portsmouth, NH: Heinemann.

Richmond, Oliver P. 2006. "Patterns of Peace." *Global Society* 20(4):367–94.

——2009a. "Becoming Liberal, Unbecoming Liberalism: Liberal-Local Hybridity via the Everyday as a Response to the Paradoxes of Liberal Peacebuilding." *Journal of Intervention and Statebuilding* 3(3):324–44.

——2009b. "The Romanticisation of the Local: Welfare, Culture and Peacebuilding." *The International Spectator: Italian Journal of International Affairs* 44(1):149–69.

——2010. "Resistance and the Post-liberal Peace." *Millennium: Journal of International Studies* 38(3):665–92.

——2011. "Critical Agency, Resistance and a Post-Colonial Civil Society." *Cooperation and Conflict* 46(4):419–40.

——2012. "Beyond Local Ownership in the Architecture of International Peacebuilding." *Ethnopolitics* 11(4):354–75.

Richmond, Oliver P. and Jason Franks (2009) *Liberal Peace Transitions: Between Statebuilding and Peacebuilding*. Edinburgh: Edinburgh University Press.

Rigby, Andrew. 2001. *Justice and Reconciliation: After the Violence*. Boulder, CO: Lynne Rienner Publishers.

Robben, Antonius C.G.M. and Jeffrey A. Sluka. 2012. *Ethnographic Fieldwork: An Anthropological Reader*, 2nd edn, Malden, MA: Blackwell Publishing.

Robins, Simon. 2011. "Towards Victim-Centred Transitional Justice: Understanding the Needs of Families of the Disappeared in Postconflict Nepal." *International Journal of Transitional Justice* 5(1):75–98.

——2012. "Transitional Justice as an Elite Discourse: Human Rights Practice Where the Global Meets the Local in Post-Conflict Nepal." *Critical Asian Studies* 44(1):3–30.

Rodney, Walter. 1967. "A Reconsideration of the Mane Invasions of Sierra Leone." *The Journal of African History* 8(2):219–46.

Roht-Arriaza, Naomi. 2006. "The New Landscape of Transitional Justice." Pp. 1–16 in *Transitional Justice in the Twenty-First Century: Beyond Truth versus Justice*, edited by N. Roht-Arriaza and J. Mariezcurrena. Cambridge: Cambridge University Press.

Roseman, Sharon R. 1996. "'How We Built the Road': The Politics of Memory in Rural Galicia." *American Ethnologist* 23(4):836–60.

Ross, Fiona. 2002. *Bearing Witness: Women and the Truth and Reconciliation Commission in South Africa*. London: Pluto Press.

Ross, Michael L. 2003. "Oil, Drugs, and Diamonds: The Varying Roles of Natural Resources in Civil War." Pp. 47–70 in *The Political Economy of Armed Conflict: Beyond Greed and Grievance*, edited by K. Ballentine and J. Sherman. Boulder, CO: Lynne Rienner Publishers.

——2004. "How Do Natural Resources Influence Civil War? Evidence from Thirteen Cases." *International Organization* 58(1):35–67.

Rothstein, Robert L. 1999. "Fragile Peace and Its Aftermath." Pp. 223–48 in *After the Peace: Resistance and Reconciliation*, edited by R.L. Rothstein. Boulder, CO: Lynne Rienner Publishers.

Rubinstein, Robert A. 2003. "Cross-Cultural Considerations in Complex Peace Operations." *Negotiation Journal* 19(1):29–49.

Sarsby, Jacquie. 1984. "The Fieldwork Experience." Pp. 87–132 in *Ethnographic Research: A Guide to General Conduct*, edited by R.F. Ellen. London: Academic Press.

Saunders, Lucinda. 2000. "Rich and Rare Are the Gems They Wear: Holding De Beers Accountable for Trading Conflict Diamonds." *Fordham International Law Journal* 24(4):1402–76.

Schabas, William A. 2004. "A Synergistic Relationship: The Sierra Leonean Truth and Reconciliation Commission and the Special Court for Sierra Leone." *Criminal Law Forum* 15(12):3–54.

Schatzberg, Michael G. 1993. "Power, Legitimacy, and Democratization in Africa." *Africa, Journal of the International African Institute* 63(4):445–61.

Seigel, Jerrold. 2005. *The Idea of the Self: Thought and Experience in Western Europe since the Seventeenth Century*. Cambridge: Cambridge University Press.

Sending, Ole Jocob. 2009. "Why Peacebuilders Fail to Secure Ownership and Be Sensitive to Context." *NUPI Working Paper 755*. Oslo: Norwegian Institute for International Affairs.

Sesay, Joseph. 2009. "Comprehensive African Development (CAADP) Process: Case-Study of Sierra Leone." Paper presented at the Joint Conference of African Ministers of Agriculture, Land and Livestock, Addis Ababa, Ethiopia, April 23. Retrieved June 5, 2013. Available at: http://www.caadp.net/pdf/Sierra%20Leone%20Minister%20Statement.pdf.

Shaw, Rosalind 1996. "The Politician and the Diviner: Divination and the Consumption of Power in Sierra Leone." *Journal of Religion in Africa* 26(1):30–55.

——2002. *Memories of the Slave Trade: Ritual and Historical Imagination in Sierra Leone*. Chicago: University of Chicago Press.

——2005. "Rethinking Truth and Reconciliation Commissions: Lessons from Sierra Leone." Washington, DC: United States Institute of Peace Special Report #130. Retrieved, June 5, 2013. Available at: http://www.usip.org/files/resources/sr130.pdf.

——2007. "Memory Frictions: Localizing the Truth and Reconciliation Commission in Sierra Leone." *International Journal of Transitional Justice* 1(2):183–207.

——2010. "Linking Justice with Reintegration? Ex-Combatants and the Sierra Leone Experiment." Pp. 111–32 in *Localizing Transitional Justice: Interventions and Priorities after Mass Violence*, edited by R. Shaw, L. Waldorf, and P. Hazan. Stanford, CA: Stanford University Press.

Shaw, Rosalind, Lars Waldorf and Pierre Hazan. 2010. *Localizing Transitional Justice: Interventions and Priorities after Mass Violence*. Stanford, CA: Stanford University Press.

Shweder, Richard A. 1991. *Thinking through Cultures: Expeditions in Cultural Psychology*. Cambridge, MA: Harvard University Press.

Siddle, D.J. 1968. "War-Towns in Sierra Leone: A Study in Social Change." *Africa: Journal of the International African Institute* 38(1):47–56.

Sikkink, Kathryn. 2011. *The Justice Cascade: How Human Rights Prosecutions Are Changing World Politics*. New York, NY: W.W. Norton and Company.

Sikkink, Kathryn and Carrie Booth Walling. 2007. "The Impact of Human Rights Trials in Latin America." *Journal of Peace Research* 44(4):427–45.

Singer, Jefferson A. and Peter Salovey. 1993. *The Remembered Self: Emotion and Memory in Personality*. New York: NY: The Free Press.

Skaar, Elin. 2012. "Reconciliation in a Transitional Justice Perspective." *Transitional Justice Review* 1(1):54–103.

Sluka, Jeffrey A. 1990. "Participant Observation in Violent Social Contexts." *Human Organization* 49(2):114–26.

——2012a. "Introduction to Part V." Pp. 244–55 in *Ethnographic Fieldwork: An Anthropological Reader*. 2nd edn, edited by A.C.G.M. Robben and J. Sluka. Malden, MA: Wiley-Blackwell.

——2012b. "Reflections on Managing Danger in Fieldwork: Dangerous Anthropology in Belfast." Pp. 283–95 in *Ethnographic Fieldwork: An Anthropological Reader*, 2nd edn, edited by A.C.G.M. Robben and J. Sluka. Malden, MA: Wiley-Blackwell.

Sooka, Yasmin. 2006. "Dealing with the Past and Transitional Justice: Building Peace through Accountability." *International Review of the Red Cross* 88(862):311–25.

Sriram, Chandra Lekha and Suren Pillay. 2009. *Peace Versus Justice? The Dilemma of Transitional Justice*. Scottsville, South Africa: University of KwaZulu-Natal Press.

Sriram, Chandra Lekha, John C. King, Julie A. Mertus, Olga Martin-Ortega and Johanna Herman. 2009. *Surviving Field Research: Working in Violent and Difficult Situations*. New York, NY: Routledge.

Steinberg, Jonny. 2011. "A Truth Commission Goes Abroad: Liberian Transitional Justice in New York." *African Affairs* 110(438):35–53.

Talentino, Andrew K. 2007. "Perceptions of Peacebuilding: The Dynamic of Imposer and Imposed Upon." *International Studies Perspectives* 8(2):152–71.

Taylor, Anne Christine. 1993. "Remembering to Forget: Identity, Mourning and Memory among the Jivaro." *Man, New Series* 28(4):653–78.

Teethling, Theo. 2011. "From MONUC to MONUSCO and Beyond: Prospects for Reconstruction, State-Building and Security Governance in the DRC." *South African Journal of International Affairs* 18(1):23–41.

Teitel, Ruti G. 2000. *Transitional Justice*. Oxford: Oxford University Press.

——2005. "The Alien Tort and the Global Rule of Law." *International Social Science Journal* 57(185):551–60.

The Economist. 2011. "The Surge in Land Deals: When Others Are Grabbing Land." *The Economist*, May 5. Retrieved September 30, 2013. Available at: http://www.economist.com/node/18648855.

Theidon, Kimberly. 2006. "Justice in Transition: The Micropolitics of Reconciliation in Postwar Peru." *The Journal of Conflict Resolution* 50(3):433–57.

——2007. "Transitional Subjects: The Disarmament, Demobilization and Reintegration of Former Combatants in Colombia." *International Journal of Transitional Justice* 1(1):66–90.

——2013. *Intimate Enemies: Violence and Reconciliation in Peru*. Philadelphia, PA: University of Pennsylvania Press.

Themnér, Lotta and Peter Wallensteen. 2011. "Armed Conflict, 1946–2010." *Journal of Peace Research* 48(4):525–36.

Transparency International. 2012. "Corruptions Perception Index 2012." Retrieved June 6, 2013. Available at: http://www.transparency.org/cpi2012/in_detail.

Treisman, Daniel. 2000. "The Causes of Corruption: A Cross National Study." *Journal of Public Economics* 76(3):399–457.

Truth and Reconciliation Commission for Sierra Leone. 2004. *Witness to Truth: Report of the Sierra Leone Truth and Reconciliation Commission*. Accra: Graphic Packaging Limited. Retrieved, June 6, 2013. Available at: http://www.sierraleonetrc.org/index.php/view-the-final-report/download-table-of-contents.

Tsikata, Dzodzi. 2009. "Gender, Land and Labour Relations and Livelihoods in Sub-Saharan Africa in the Era of Economic Liberalisation: Towards a Research Agenda." *Feminist Africa* 12:1–30.

Tsing, Anna Lowenhaupt. 2005. *Friction: An Ethnography of Global Connection*. Princeton, NJ: Princeton University Press.

Tutu, Desmond. 1999. *No Future Without Forgiveness*. New York, NY: Doubleday.

United Nations. 2012. *Planning Toolkit*. New York, NY: United Nations. Retrieved June 3, 2013. Available at: www.un.org/en/peacekeeping/publications/Planning%20Toolkit_Web%20Version.pdf.

United Nations Development Program. 2013. *Human Development Report 2013 – The Rise of the South: Human Progress in a Diverse World*. New York, NY: United Nations. Retrieved June 6, 2013. Available at: http://hdr.undp.org/en/media/HDR_2013_EN_ complete.pdf.

United Nations Economic Commission for Africa. 2009. "Economic Report on Africa 2009: Developing African Agriculture Through Regional Value Chains." Addis Ababa: United Nations Economic Commission for Africa. Retrieved June 5, 2013. Available at: http://uneca.africa-devnet.org/files/ERA2009_ENG_Full.pdf.

Uvin, Peter. 2009. *Life After Violence: A People's Story of Burundi*. New York, NY: Zed Books.

Van der Merwe, Hugo, Victoria Baxter and Audrey R. Chapman. 2009. "Introduction." Pp. 1–11 in *Assessing the Impact of Transitional Justice: Challenges for Empirical Research*, edited by H. van der Merwe, V. Baxter, and A.R. Chapman. Washington, DC: United States Institute of Peace.

Wagar, Brandon M. and Dov Cohen. 2003. "Culture, Memory, and the Self: An Analysis of the Personal and Collective Self in Long-Term Memory." *Journal of Experimental Social Psychology* 39(5):468–75.

Wallerstein, Immanuel. 1974. *The Modern World-System: Capitalist Agriculture and the Origins of the European World Economy in the Sixteenth Century*. New York, NY: Academic Press.

Wang, Qi and Martin A. Conway. 2004. "The Stories We Keep: Autobiographical Memory in American and Chinese Middle-Aged Adults." *Journal of Personality* 72(5):911–38.

Wantchekon, Leonard. 2003. "Clientelism and Voting Behavior: Evidence from a Field Experiment in Benin." *World Politics* 55(3):399–422.

Webster, James Bertin and A. Adu Boahen. 1970. *History of West Africa: The Revolutionary Years – 1815 to Independence*. New York, NY: Praeger Publishers.

Wiebelhaus-Brahm, Eric. 2010. *Truth Commissions and Transitional Societies: The Impact on Human Rights and Democracy*. New York, NY: Routledge.

Williams, Paul. 2001. "Fighting for Freetown: British Military Intervention in Sierra Leone." *Contemporary Security Policy* 22(3):140–68.

Williams, Phil and John T. Picarelli. 2005. "Combating Organized Crime in Armed Conflict." Pp. 123–52 in *Profiting from Peace: Managing the Resource Dimensions of Civil War*, edited by K. Ballentine and H. Nitzschke. Boulder, CO: Lynne Rienner Publishers.

Williams, Terry, Eloise Dunlap, Bruce D. Johnson and Ansley Hamid. 1992. "Personal Safety in Dangerous Places." *Journal of Contemporary Ethnography* 21(3):343–74.

Wilson, Richard A. 2001. *The Politics of Truth and Reconciliation in South Africa: Legitimizing the Post-Apartheid State*. Cambridge: Cambridge University Press.

Winer, Jonathan M. 2005. "Tracking Conflict Commodities and Financing." Pp. 69–93 in *Profiting from Peace: Managing the Resource Dimensions of Civil War*, edited by K. Ballentine and H. Nitzschke. Boulder, CO: Lynne Rienner Publishers.

Woodhouse, Phillip and Ana S. Ganho. 2011. "Is Water the Hidden Agenda of Agricultural Land Acquisition in Sub-Saharan Africa?" Paper presented at the International Conference on Global Land Grabbing, University of Sussex, April 6–8. Retrieved June 5, 2013. Available at: http://www.iss.nl/fileadmin/ASSETS/iss/Docu! ments/Conference_papers/LDPI/12_P_Woodhouse_and_A_S_Ganho.pdf.

World Bank. 2009. *Awakening Africa's Sleeping Giant: Prospects for Commercial Agriculture in the Guinea Savannah Zone and Beyond*. Directions in Development: Agriculture and Rural Development Series. Washington, DC: The World Bank. Retrieved June 5, 2013. Available at: http://siteresources.worldbank.org/INTARD/Resources/sleeping_giant.pdf.

Zandvliet, Luc. 2005. "Assessing Company Behavior in Conflict Environments: A Field Perspective." Pp. 185–206 in *Profiting from Peace: Managing the Resource Dimensions of Civil War*, edited by K. Ballentine and H. Nitzschke. Boulder, CO: Lynne Rienner Publishers.

Zartman, William I. 2005. "Need, Creed, and Greed in Intrastate Conflict." Pp. 256–84 in *Rethinking the Economics of War: The Intersection of Need, Creed, and Greed*, edited by C.J. Arnson and I.W. Zartman. Philadelphia, PA: Woodrow Wilson International Center for Scholars.

Zeidy, Mohamed M. 2005. "The Ugandan Government Triggers the First Test of the Complementarity Principle: An Assessment of the First State's Party Referral to the ICC." *International Criminal Law Review* 5(1):83–119.

Zoomers, Annelies. 2010. "Globalisation and the Foreignisation of Space: Seven Processes Driving the Current Global Land Grab." *Journal of Peasant Studies* 37(2):429–47.

Index

20124868R00116

Printed in Great Britain
by Amazon